X 65

Real Estate Investment for the '80s

How to Build Financial Security in the Face of Inflation

Douglas M. Temple

Contemporary Books, Inc.
Chicago

Library of Congress Cataloging in Publication Data
Temple, Douglas M
   Real estate investment for the '80s.

   Includes index.
    1. Real estate investment.   I. Title.
HD1382.5.T45   332.63'24   80-68596
ISBN 0-8092-7024-2
ISBN 0-8092-7023-4 (pbk.)

To my wife
HAZEL

Published by Contemporary Books, Inc.
180 North Michigan Avenue, Chicago, Illinois
Manufactured in the United States of America
Library of Congress Catalog Card Number: 80-68596
International Standard Book Number: 0-8092-7024-2 (cloth)
                             0-8092-7023-4 (paper)

Beaverbooks, Ltd.
150 Lesmill Road
Don Mills, Ontario M3B 2T5
Canada

Preface   *iv*

Preface

A major opportunity available to most people in our society is that of building financial security through saving and investing for the future. The greatest threat in recent years to achieving this, however, comes from the double-digit inflation that mushroomed in the '70s and ushered in the '80s. How can you beat it? You must put money to work today so that it grows to an amount large enough to provide adequately for your long-range future plans, including retirement. Your investment cash must grow faster than the erosion by inflation.

Thus, when you look around at investment alternatives, it becomes apparent that you must harness inflation to work *for* you rather than helplessly and hopelessly fight *against* it. And that brings you to real estate. It is one of the few assets that has benefited from inflation. All you need to do is look at the price of real estate today to see that property values have grown faster than the inflation rate. A wise investment in property, which has always been a positive step, now more than ever clearly offers a way for you to achieve rewards even from the inflationary spiral. The path to financial security in the '80s is very definitely through sound real estate investment.

No matter what your investment objective is—income or capital appreciation—there is a real estate investment opportunity available to the amateur individual investor. Nor is it too late. There are countless buying and investing opportunities; your task and challenge is to find the one best suited to your needs. And that's how this book can serve you. It provides a step-by-step guide to evaluation and how to make an investment in all types of property—a single-family home, condominium apartment, residential and business income property, even vacant land. Through reproducing and using the fill-in forms and tables of the Appendix, you will have everything you need to determine which property to buy or how to make a mortgage loan.

How has inflation created such benefits for real estate investors in the '80s? What will happen if our double-digit inflation winds down? Will we have a bust? Decidedly, we won't. Because of inflation the cost to build or develop new properties has skyrocketed, and mortgage money has dried up. All this has kept a lid on supply. Meanwhile the number of people who need housing is increasing; this in turn increases the demand for more facilities for business and industry. Once inflationary costs moderate and the supply of mortgage money returns (and these events surely will occur), we should see the biggest real estate boom ever. But you must act now if you are going to participate in the forthcoming bonanza.

As you explore the world of real estate investment, keep the following characteristics in mind: This is a long-term investment vehicle, not a get-rich-quick scheme. It takes some time for extraordinary values to develop; the major source of gain from real estate ownership is capital appreciation. In general you should not count on being able to liquidate your investment overnight; it may take even a few months to sell at the best price. Most property will sell quickly at a bargain price; so if you are prepared to sacrifice, you'll quickly be able to get out if you have to.

But do you need a lot of cash? No, because it is customary to use borrowed funds to add to your own, and you can use the property as collateral. When it's difficult to get a loan from a financial institution, you'll find that sellers are prepared to finance the deal. The more cash you have, of course, the larger investment you can make and thus increase your returns.

Uncle Sam helps, too. And if you use borrowed funds you can structure the investment to provide tax sheltering, even if the property is your home. Then for income property, through the magic of depreciation, you can convert current income to long-term capital gain and save more taxes. But there's even more! Income from rental property, for example, is not *earned* income as are wages, so will not offset Social Security retirement payments. That could mean that you could stop working sooner if you own income property. Finally, realize that the first $100,000 capital gains from the sale of property you've used as your principal residence, once you've reached fifty-five, is exempt from all federal income tax. How can you afford *not* to own real estate? Build your portfolio of properties now and live it up later.

All you need to know (even if you weren't afraid to ask), about evaluating and investing in any form of real estate lies before you. Go!

1

Why Real Estate Is Such a Good Investment

No matter what your investment objectives are, it is likely that an investment in real estate will enable you to achieve them. Real estate truly is an all-purpose vehicle. Here we'll look at the factors that affect this type of investment and discover why superior returns are possible.

INVESTMENT GOALS

What do you want to achieve through putting your funds to work? Once you've carefully considered this question and settled on a clear-cut objective, you will then be able seriously to consider what to do about investing in real estate. You may quickly see yourself in one of the following situations and when you do, your goal will be clear.

A. You are now employed, have enough income to cover expenses, have some money set aside, and probably can save more each month. You are concerned that you may be missing chances to save on income taxes and you certainly are anxious to find a way to build, over the longer term, your financial security for retirement. Your goal, therefore, is to invest for tax sheltering combined with long-term capital appreciation. Real estate can be used to achieve this goal.

1

B. You are approaching retirement or are already retired. Your cash is in savings certificates and stocks and bonds. Your problem is that the income from all these, plus your pension, will not give you the standard of living you'd like to have. Your goal, therefore, is to find a secure investment vehicle that will give you maximum current income. Real estate can be used to achieve this goal.

C. You do not need additional income at present nor are you able to make the most of tax shelter benefits because your tax rate is not high enough. Your major interest is in investing for long-term capital appreciation. Real estate can be used to achieve this goal.

It is important to match the real estate investment with your goal. While it is quite correct to say that real estate investing can be used no matter what your goal, not every piece of real estate will serve every objective. Further, there is the matter of time. Although you can invest in real estate to maximize current income and begin receiving income immediately after you've made the investment, you should not expect to be able to liquidate in a hurry and always get your money back in full. Generally speaking, if you have to sell the property shortly after buying it, the sales expense will probably be greater than any short-term appreciation. On the other hand, because real estate typically grows in value over the longer term, by having a long-range investment objective, you should have no difficulty in achieving that goal. There's no guarantee, of course. It is possible to lose money on real estate either in the long or short term. We'll examine the factors that affect value to see what to watch for to minimize the risk of loss and maximize the opportunity for substantial longer term gain.

There are those who seek huge overnight gains. Except for some very special speculative situations, that is not a realistic expectation for a real estate investment. Instead, let's think in terms of your wanting to be an active member of *The Get*

Rich Slowly But Surely Club. There are no flamboyant claims here for vast riches, no wild swings in values to catch—just good, solid, relatively secure places to put your money to work to produce better returns than from alternatives. Welcome to the Club!

TYPES OF REAL ESTATE

One reason real estate is such a satisfactory investment vehicle is the variety available. Later we'll match types with investment objectives but meanwhile, let's explore the many different places we can put our money.

Except for nomads, everyone should seriously consider owning his or her own home. Yes, when you buy a house you are making an investment. The vast majority of homeowners occupy single-family detached homes. In recent years, however, the condominium has become a very popular substitute for the vine-covered cottage or even the large city mansion. Or you may, instead, invest in a co-op apartment and thus also be a homeowner. You can own your own mobile home which will rest on either a rented plot or one which you own. And then there are second homes; these too should be viewed as investment.

The term *income property* is applied to real estate from which rents are received. Usually it refers to apartments, all the way from a duplex to the very large complex; it also applies to single-family homes that are rented out. It applies to commercial and industrial properties where the occupant pays the owner for the use of it. Even vacant land, when rented for use either to grow crops or to park cars or store things, is income property.

Building construction and land development may also be viewed as a form of real estate investment. When you own land, perhaps subdivide it and contract to have buildings erected on it, all with a view to generating income or to make a profit on the sale, you are involved in real estate investment. The business of building contracting is closely akin to all of this but will not be considered here as a form of real estate investing.

Finally, you can invest in raw land which just sits there and grows in value, you hope.

The term *real estate* technically refers to land. When a structure is built, it automatically becomes a part of the land. In buying or selling real estate it is the title to or interest in the land that is transferred and any improvements go along with it. Buildings are known as *improvements*.

HOW TO INVEST IN REAL ESTATE

Up until now perhaps you've been thinking that the only way to invest in real estate is to buy some property. Clearly that is the primary way to put your money to work. When you purchase you obtain an *ownership equity* in real property. No matter the type of real estate, someone owns it. But how about all those mortgages you've heard about? Can an investor like yourself get a part of that action? Yes, indeed. There's an almost limitless demand for borrowed money by those who want to buy real estate; almost all such transactions use borrowed funds. Those who lend money on the security of real property are also making an investment, and so can you.

But now, if you buy some income property, do you have to deal with the tenants, collect the rents, take care of repairs and so on? Only if you choose. When you actively handle the business affairs and manage your real estate, we call that a *participative* investment. But how about having someone else do all this kind of work so that your role will simply be that of putting up the cash? That would be a *non-participative* investment. When you associate yourself with others in a group through a real estate syndicate or limited partnership you have nothing to do but put up the money; the general partner does everything else. All partners share in the profits, if any. An alternative to the limited partnership is the real estate investment trust, a REIT, pronounced "reet."

Here you put up your funds by purchasing shares of beneficial interest; these are equivalent to shares of stock. Except for voting at the annual meeting of the trust shareholders, you have nothing to do with the operation. The day-to-day business is conducted by an advisory company and a property management service firm. As a shareholder you share in the profits, if realized.

A syndicate or REIT can be established to own and operate income property, to lend money on real estate, to hold raw land, or to develop land and construct buildings for sale or income. In other words, groups of investors can do all the things any individual investor can do. Instead of doing it yourself, you can be a passive or nonparticipative investor by being part of a limited partnership or owning shares in a REIT.

So you can be active or passive and you can own real estate or lend money to others who want to own it. When it comes time to put your money to work you must make some choices.

How to Get Your Money Back

Prior to investing your cash you must decide whether you want the money back by some particular time or whether it is to be employed indefinitely. In either case, however, consideration must be given to how the investment can be liquidated. Some day you may want the money for some other purpose: to spend it, to pay off obligations, or to put it to work in some other, and presumably better, opportunity.

You should expect to incur expense to make an investment in real estate and to have costs associated with liquidating it. While it is true that for many purchase opportunities you may be able to deal directly with a seller without using a real estate broker, there may be some disadvantages to doing so. The price to be paid in the form of a real estate commission, for example, may well be worth it for the services rendered. In nonparticipative investing you may also have costs to buy and sell. But then, this is also the case for most alternative forms of investing. You simply must allow for costs, if any, when making your analysis.

Once you decide to sell your ownership interest you will have to set a sales price, terms, and conditions. After that you have to find a buyer. Even if you bought the property for all cash, don't make the mistake of assuming you can demand, and get, all cash from a buyer. You may find that some part of your investment (called *equity*) will have to remain in the property and the buyer will pay it to you in periodic payments. It's not unusual to discover at the time you want to liquidate that prospective buyers are unable to obtain adequate financing. This possibility leads some investors to limit the size of their cash investment in any single property if they expect to be involved in extensive trading, buying, and selling.

If you are a lender on real estate you will be bound by the repayment terms of the mortgage. As long as the borrower makes the loan payments on time the lender cannot demand full repayment in advance. Once you've made the loan you should expect to wait the full term to be fully repaid. Ordinarily a real estate mortgage loan payment consists of two parts: payment of interest and partial repayment of principal. You, therefore, will be receiving part of the loan principal (your investment) back each time a payment is received. If you want the funds to continue to work you will need to figure out ahead of time how to reinvest the cash. If the borrower does offer to pay off the debt early you also will be faced with a reinvestment decision.

If you are a limited partner in a syndicate it is unlikely you can liquidate your investment before the partnership itself is liquidated. As a rule, most partnerships are formed to have a life of several years although there's no prohibition to a short-time period. Except in unusual cases, the timing of the liquidation of a partnership is not determined in advance and will depend on market conditions and the will of the partners. Prior to joining the partnership you must be able to judge when it is possible for liquidation to occur and therefore when you might get your money (and profits) back. It is not unknown for a partnership to have a provision for buying out partners who wish to sell, but rarely is there any obligation for this to be done; limited partners should presume that once the investment is made the funds cannot be recovered through the sale of the partnership interest.

How about REIT shares? Many REITs are listed on stock exchanges or traded in the over-the-counter (OTC) market. In such a case a REIT shareholder is free to sell shares at a current market price. Changes in share prices are due to performance of the properties or mortgages owned by the trust, stock market activity and the general perceptions of investors. Fluctuations independently, therefore, of the underlying value can and do take place. Where the shares of a REIT which you are considering are not traded publicly, you may have difficulty finding an investor to buy you out, and that is an important consideration in making the investment decision.

After all that, why would you invest in real estate? What's so good about an investment you may not be able to liquidate when you want to or at a price you consider fair? What's so good about investing in real estate? To find out, let's examine now the sources of potential return and profit.

SOURCES OF POTENTIAL GAIN

In making any investment, you expect to receive back not only the amount invested but also a profit. When you have an ownership interest in property, the security for the investment is the property. As long as you can sell your interest for at least your cost, you can get your money back. If you have made a loan on property and the borrower is making periodic payments of interest and principal, you will be getting part of your investment back with each payment. At any point, the unpaid loan balance will equal the amount you have at risk. The interest represents your gain. Once you have set the interest rate and loan terms, your gain depends only on collecting all the payments. In turn, you have no way to increase your gain and it is limited by the terms agreed on when the loan was made. The ownership of property, however, offers three very important potential sources of gain over and above the amount invested.

Current Income and Tax Shelter Benefit

If you have an interest in property that generates an income, your current return will be the difference between rental income and the cash operating expenses. Your net income after income taxes will be calculated by subtracting from the net cash flow the amount of income tax payable. In some cases instead of reducing your cash return it will be increased as a result of the income tax computation. If your tax-deductible expenses, including noncash items such as depreciation, are large enough to produce a loss for tax purposes, your total tax bill will be reduced. The amount of this reduction, called a *tax shelter benefit*, will serve to increase your after-tax cash return from the property. Of course, you can find that your cash expenditures exceed revenue even over and above a tax shelter benefit so that you can wind up in the hole on a current basis. All of this will be discussed in greater detail in subsequent chapters. Meanwhile you should keep in mind that an investment in income property usually produces a highly satisfactory after-tax cash income each year. That will be the first gain to be measured against the amount invested.

Equity Build

If you use borrowed funds along with your cash down payment to buy property, you may have what is termed *equity build* as an important source of gain. As you make the payments on the loan, the outstanding balance will go down. If you hold the property long enough, you'll own it free and clear. But you don't have to hold the property until the loan is paid off. Whenever you liquidate the investment and pay off the loan from the sales proceeds, you'll discover that you'll get back, tax-free, the total amount by which the mortgage has been reduced. This is the equity build. If you own income property, the tenants are in effect buying the building for you. Through a mortgage on your home, you have a form of forced savings and can look forward to getting back what you've paid on the loan. But a word of caution. All this will be true only if at the time of sale you do not get less than what you paid for the property. In an inflationary period, of course, it is highly unusual to sell at a loss.

It might appear at this point that you should always use borrowed funds when investing in real estate. Perhaps, but there is also a risk here. Whether rents are in fact enough to cover expenses or your job remains steady and secure are all beside the point when it comes to your obligation to pay off the loan. That must be done whether or not the property is losing money or you have lost your income. The lender is not sharing the ownership risk, nor are you sharing the profits with the lender. How to calculate the benefits from using borrowed funds and the amount of prospective equity build will be covered later.

Capital Appreciation

Finally, as implied in the secret to successful investing—buy low and sell high—the major potential resource of gain is that from capital appreciation. This potential exists if you have an ownership interest in property, are a limited partner in a syndicate, or own shares in a REIT. A mortgage lender, however, as a rule has no opportunity for capital appreciation. The exception to this may be found when the holder of a mortgage could sell the debt at a gain because the value of money has increased. This exception will be fully explored in Chapter 10.

It usually takes at least a few years for the value of property to increase in value to the point where it can be sold at a gain over cost. In some areas where there has been an acute shortage of single-family homes, prices have been bid up and some sellers have reaped substantial profits in a very short time. Every investor should be on the lookout for such opportunities, of course, if they fit his or her strategy, but they are the exception rather than the rule. The majority of properties do, in fact, increase in value steadily over time so the investor should be patient. There are a number of factors that directly affect the rate of value growth and these must be taken into account in selecting property as well as in making the decision to sell.

So we see that those who invest in real estate may be able to achieve gains by way of current income, through sheltering other income from income tax, through equity build and, finally, through appreciation in value to be realized when the investment is liquidated. These are the reasons real estate can be such a good investment.

FACTORS AFFECTING INVESTMENT RESULTS

The price to be paid for goods or services is largely the result of the interaction of supply and demand. If either of these change, price will usually change. Prices increase when there is an increase in demand or a reduction in supply, or when both occur at the same time. Conversely, if demand drops off or supply increases, prices often (but not always) drop. The investor who chooses to buy an interest in real estate must be concerned about the future prospects of both demand for and supply of the type of property he or she is considering.

Supply

For most types of real estate in many areas of the country there is a shortage on the supply side. This is particularly so for housing, both detached homes and apartments. There is no mystery here. Because of a combination of increasing costs due to inflation and the result of no-growth policies in many communities, the total amount of new housing construction in recent years has been even less than the number of units disappearing through normal deterioration, let alone adequate enough to respond to the growing demand. Contrary to the views of most tenants, rents are not high enough; they do not cover the cost of newly constructed units so the supply of rental units is virtually nonexistent in many places. Changes in the supply of mortgage money and increased interest rates have served to reduce the number of potential buyers which in turn has discouraged builders and thus aggravated the supply situation. Obviously, the price of existing property is rising and this will continue as long as the shortage exists.

Demand

But what about demand? If people can't borrow money, or the cost is so high they can't pay, is there really an effective demand for housing? The pressure produced by the current and future family formation rates suggests that the potential demand is staggering! All that is holding back a veritable gold rush of buyers is a solution to the mortgage financing problem. This is not to overlook the impact of the very high (in historical terms) cost to build. But those families with two incomes, and the prospect for wages and salaries to increase, will be eager and able buyers once mortgage funds are available and interest rates moderate. Both the government and private industry are working on these problems and solutions may not be far away. Meantime, the upward pressure on sales prices continue as a result of the existence of the underlying demand.

But what about other types of real estate? Even in periods when economic activity slows there is always a sustained demand for commercial and industrial property. There are always opportunities to rent property to well-managed and profitable businesses that will pay the rent. When business activity responds to favorable economic conditions, there will be a scramble for new locations and for upgrading current operations, thus stimulating demand for real estate. Conversely, periods of economic contraction may produce a slackening of demand that affects particularly marginal properties.

It must be obvious there are many opportunities to lend money when the traditional money markets are charging very high rates. Even though interest rates will peak and ultimately drop, these are not abrupt changes in the mortgage markets and lenders have opportunities to lock in attractive yields when demand for loans is strong. High rates are associated, of course, with higher risk. Private lenders must act prudently while taking advantage of lending opportunities.

And all indications are that the current strong demand for both housing and mortgage money will continue in the future. The investor should seek the opportunity which will offer maximum current results as well as possess the characteristics that will best maximize the chance for long-term capital appreciation. Because of the absolutely essential need for any and all forms of property, there will always be someone ready and able to buy; that's vital for owners who wish to sell. Secure in the knowledge that everything today points to a continuing demand for real estate, the investor can concentrate on locating the investment property best suited to his or her objectives.

Inflation

No one seriously suggests that the high rate of inflation that marked the start of the '80s in the United States will disappear overnight. We must accept the notion that, even if the rate is reduced over the near term, we still must live with steadily increasing prices. For the real estate investor this has substantial significance. Of all the possible inflation-hedge investments, real estate offers probably the greatest protection. One of the primary reasons for the increase in the price of all forms of real estate has been inflationary costs. The cost to create new property has increased dramatically because of the inflationary increases in the cost of labor and materials. Higher prices for new property are inescapable. This in turn permits owners of existing property, in competition with new property, to raise prices. Increased demand in the face of limited supply, which by itself will produce increased prices, is the other major force behind increasing real estate values.

If you forecast that inflation will continue—whether at 15 percent a year or 10 percent or even 7 percent—there can be no argument that future prices of real estate will be higher than they are now. True, in selected cases, perhaps because of an owner's distress or temporary inability to get financing, some properties will be sold at a loss to the seller. You don't have to be such a seller and, in fact, it is these situations that offer the skilled investor the greatest opportunity: Find the distressed, below-market-priced properties and buy! Then, when it comes time to liquidate, inflation will have boosted the price and created your profit. The risk that you may be a distressed seller is there, of course, but through proper planning it can be avoided. Never invest in real estate under conditions where it is likely that you will have to sell at a time not of your choosing. Keep in mind the long-term nature of this type of investing. When conditions are not quite right, hold off and wait until they improve. They will. And this is particularly so because of inflation.

There's no reasonable chance that we'll have a widespread, oversupply of housing, absent a plague or other catastrophe that wipes out a significant part of the population. If that happens you'll likely be a part of the wipeout so don't worry about your investments. And as the price of all goods and services continues to rise, so will real estate. So what does this really mean? Isn't the major challenge in investing to find a place to protect and conserve your assets *against* the ravages of inflation? Well, consider this. If you put your money in something that increases in value because of inflation, when you liquidate, you'll receive more dollars than you invested. Although you can argue that those dollars will buy less than they did before, the fact is you'll at least have kept pace with inflation. Note that if this increase is no more than the rate of inflation you have been standing still. Maybe you'd settle for even that. Look at one of your alternatives: leaving your cash in a savings account.

Each year your so-called safe and secure savings account is worth less than it was at the beginning in terms of purchasing power. The interest earnings, after income tax, will provide small comfort when you compute what your real loss is as the result of inflation. So, even if your real estate investment simply kept pace with the rate of inflation, would you not be far ahead by comparison with this alternative? You can't afford to let your funds wither away in a savings account. But with real estate you can even beat inflation if you are willing to do a little studying, some research, and are prepared to make decisions. What you need to know is spelled out in this book. Don't let inflation beat you—make it work for you. That's what real estate investors do. Inflation has always been one of their best friends!

Leverage

How a real estate transaction is financed can greatly affect investment returns. Two identical properties may sell for quite different total prices because of the difference in how the purchase can be financed. If the mortgage loan cost is too high relative to the earning ability of your property you may have an operating loss. Through refinancing and modification of loan terms, losses may be changed to gains. But the even more important aspect of real estate financing is the simple fact that you can combine your funds with borrowed amounts to a total that makes much greater profits possible. Your limited resources, when employed on their own, may be quite inadequate to produce any return. When your cash can be the down payment, your profit potential is great.

The term *leverage* is applied when the investor can use his or her risk capital (cash) for part of the purchase price and can borrow the balance. This means that the borrowing is secured by a mortgage or trust deed which provides the lender with a security interest in the property purchased. It is possible, of course, to use other owned property as security and commit the loan proceeds elsewhere. If it were not possible to use leverage, there would be very little investment in real estate. Hence, it must be apparent how important is the ability to borrow money on real property. Few investors have all the risk capital they need or want for investment activities. The vast majority have relatively few dollars and probably not enough to buy outright property of any size. But as long as you have at least enough for the down payment and costs, you can use real estate to build your financial security. Not only does borrowing permit you to buy, it also makes it possible to generate above-average investment profits. Let's look at why this is so.

Gains through the use of leverage may be realized from one or both of the following circumstances: current earnings from the investment at a rate in excess of the interest rate paid on the loan and from the disproportionate increase in your equity when the total value of the property increases and is realized on the sales. Here are some examples.

1. Assume you owned a property free and clear that was returning 15 percent of the funds invested. If you could borrow funds at, say, 12 percent to replace the cash tied up in the property, you would have a gross profit of 3 percent over and above the cost of the borrowed money. (It's not quite as simple as this when you consider income taxes but we'll ignore those complexities for now and consider them in detail later.) You then could use the cash for another investment and more earnings. But why could you borrow at a rate lower than what the property is earning? It is a matter of risk.

The mortgage lender, because of the security interest in the property, is content with the lower yield, knowing that if there is a default, the property could be used to pay off the debt. With lower risk, the interest return can be lower. You, on the other hand, face the risk of loss along with the obligation to pay off the loan regardless. You have the prospect of greater risk, hence you should have a greater potential return. When using borrowed funds, however, you must do everything possible to ensure that the yield exceeds the cost of the borrowing.

2. Now let's look at the equity situation. When you make a down payment of 20 percent and borrow 80 percent we say that your equity in the property is 20 percent. Let's assume you buy an apartment for $200,000 and put up $40,000 in cash. (Ignore the settlement costs for now.) The balance of $160,000 is raised through a mortgage on the property. Let's assume further that after a few years you can sell the apartment for $250,000, after expenses. The increased price will be due to a combination of inflation and how you kept rents up to market level. It's assumed that the buyer refinances so you will be cashed out. At the time of the sale your mortgage loan balance may be down to say $150,000. After the sale is completed you'll walk away with $100,000 in cash. After deducting your original investment of $40,000 you will have $60,000 cash more than when you started. Even if during the time you owned and operated the property you only broke even, you surely would agree this return is noteworthy. Some would say fantastic! No one who is knowledgeable about real estate would say it was unusual or unrealistic. Why would you ever invest in property without using leverage?

Here's a summary of this example:

Purchase		Sale	
Original cost	$200,000	Sale price net	$250,000
Mortgage	160,000	Pay off mortgage	150,000
Cash invested	$ 40,000	Cash proceeds	$100,000
		Less investment	40,000
		Cash gain	$ 60,000

Don't overlook your obligation to share your good fortune. There will be a tax collector or two. Even after making those payments, however, you will probably be far ahead of where you'd be if you had done something else with your $40,000 cash.

Perhaps you'll agree that leverage may well be the secret to investment success through real estate. Whether it is a secret is arguable—lots of people know about it—but there can be no doubt as to how vital it is. In the final analysis, however, the most crucial matter here is finding the right real estate investment for you. That must be done through careful analysis and forecasting of just how you could use leverage for a specific situation.

An important final observation: note from the example above how you could be tempted to offer to pay more, in total price, for the apartment because of the prospective gain through using borrowed funds instead of paying all cash. Whether you could scrape up $200,000 instead of the $40,000 is not unimportant, of course. But this is, in fact, what really happens. Those who use borrowed funds either may be willing or may have to pay a higher total price in order to get the property when bidding against other buyers. On the other hand, what about the all-cash buyer? Can't he or she strike a bargain? In many cases, but not all, the answer is yes. Not all sellers want to cash out because of the tax bite and prefer to carry back some or all of the financing themselves. But when you have enough cash you will want to make the most of any opportunity to get the purchase price down. Then, to maximize your gain when you sell, you may want to carry the loan in order to get the maximum sale price. This will mean, of course, that your cash will remain tied up in the property, but perhaps at that time it is mortgage interest income you want anyway.

In the end, you will want to compute your gain in terms of a rate of return on the cash at risk. Let's see, before we leave leveraging for now, what this would show. In this example we are ignoring income tax so yields are on a before-tax basis.

Using Leverage	*All Cash*
Yield: $\dfrac{\$100,000}{\$\ 40,000} \times 100\% = 250\%$	$\dfrac{\$250,000}{\$200,000} \times 100\% = 125\%$

These are gross yields and not expressed as an annual rate of return.

Surprised? All along you thought it was sinful to borrow

money. Perhaps it's more sinful to fail to maximize investment returns.

Income Taxation

As it is no secret that people who invest in real estate can make substantial profits, it's reasonable to assume that the income tax officials, state and federal, know about it and stand ready to take a share. Yes, indeed, gains from this activity are taxed, but let's see whether that is serious. You may resent all taxes on income and consider it all a serious matter. Others are resigned to the fact we have to pay income taxes and spend their time and energies minimizing the amounts they pay.

If you own your own home you can deduct mortgage interest expense and property taxes when computing taxable income. Gain from the sale of your home may be rolled over into the value of a replacement home thus postponing the payment of tax. In addition, under current rules, $100,000 of accumulated gains from the sale of your principal residences can be exempt from tax once-in-a-lifetime at your option, once you have reached fifty-five years of age.

Those who invest in rental housing benefit particularly from two conflicting goals our legislators have: on the one hand the government wants to maximize tax revenues in order to pay for all the services it renders (or fails to render), but it is also committed to ensuring that everyone has a decent place to live. (They don't seem to have met that objective either.) As a result, to offset the impact of regular income tax rates on rental income, Congress and most states have made special rules to provide investment incentives for those who would build or own apartments and other forms of housing. This has been accomplished through allowing extra amounts of depreciation to be charged against income, resulting in lower income taxes.

But there's more for investors in all types of real property. Through the magic of depreciation, whether the special allowances are for housing or otherwise, current income can be converted to long-term capital gain. Taxable income from an investment is first computed by subtracting from gross revenues all expenses as defined by the Internal Revenue Service as deductible. In general everything you pay out in operating expenses can be subtracted. Then there is the best possible kind of expense: one that does not require paying out cash yet can be deducted. That's depreciation. So when this is done, while you may have cash left over from rents after expenses, for tax purposes you may be able to declare a deficit. Obviously there must be a catch to all this. Well, sort of. When it comes time to sell the property, to compute your taxable gain you must deduct from your original cost the sum of all the depreciation you've been charging against income during the time you've owned the property. This will serve to increase the gain and hence the amount on which you will be taxed. But, if you've held the property long enough, only part of this gain will be taxed.

Under current federal income tax rules, gain from the sale of a capital asset such as real estate, after it has been held for at least one year, is taxed on the basis of only 40 percent. States have similar but not necessarily the same rules. Note that through depreciation you reduce current taxable income and by holding the property long enough you pay taxes on only 40 percent of what otherwise would have been current income.

Before leaving capital gain taxation we need to examine another popular way to obtain preferential tax treatment: the installment sale plan. Depending on how a sale is financed, you as the seller could find that your capital gain tax liability was greater than the cash you got from the deal. If you sell on the basis of cash down not to exceed 29 percent of the price, then you can declare only a proportion of the capital gain as taxable in the year of the sale. If the buyer continues to pay off the balance in installments, your taxable gain continues to be only the proportion received. If your tax rate is declining you then ultimately pay less taxes than otherwise. So, chalk up another tax advantage for real estate investment.

But there's even more. Earlier we referred to sheltering other income from taxation. Let's take a closer look now at how that is accomplished.

Each year when you add up the income from your investment—such as an apartment, store, office building, or house you've rented out—and subtracted all the expenses, including mortgage interest and depreciation, it's possible you'll come up with a deficit. That is, for tax purposes, tax deductible expenses exceed rental income so your taxable income from the investment is negative. On paper you are losing money. By now you know better and you're even wondering if it's ever possible to lose on real estate. It is indeed but it doesn't have to happen to you. For this discussion it is assumed you have income from other sources such as employment and, perhaps, other investments; and apart from your real estate venture you are faced with paying income taxes. Now comes the interesting part. You can *deduct* the amount of your negative taxable income from that other income. Yes, the so-called loss is an offset. The net result is to reduce the total amount of income tax you have to pay that year. When you apply your combined state and federal rates to the amount of the negative taxable income (the loss on the investment) the result gives you what is termed your *tax shelter benefit*. This is real and is cash in hand. By whatever amount you have reduced your total tax bill you have a gain and the money is in your possession. This is not a tax refund, it is a tax savings. Some people make money by losing it.

All told there are many ways to minimize income taxes on gains from real estate investing, all legal and intended to be used. You will always want to consider the tax implications for each step you might take.

Problem Areas

With so many favorable aspects there simply must be some negatives, and there are. If you pick the wrong property you can find:

1. Expenses exceed the rent you can charge so you have a real operating loss.
2. You picked the wrong tenants. They don't pay the rent, you have trouble evicting them and/or they abuse the property.
3. The neighborhood declines for reasons quite beyond your control. Either you failed to notice the symptoms when you bought or failed to sell soon enough.
4. The demand for your kind of property, at the time you want to sell, is not strong and you are unable to get as high a price as you thought you should.
5. Mortgage financing is hard to come by and/or is very costly, thus restricting a prospective buyer's ability to pay your asking price or even buy at any price.
6. The community enacts rent controls so that you are stymied, cannot increase rents to protect your investment nor find a buyer.

You didn't really think there was a free lunch, did you? Yes, there are risks and reasons why your investment in real estate may not turn out as well as expected. Fortunately, through careful analysis and some hard work, most—if not all—of these can be avoided. The hard fact that many people have made substantial profits from investing in real estate attests to the possibility you can too, and that it is not an unusual or unlikely result.

No matter how good the purchase price and terms are, unless you can maximize gains on the sale, you may not achieve your investment goals. No matter how good the purchase price was, unless you manage properly your income-generating property, you will not maximize your goals. If you are a non-participative investor, the REIT advisory company or the general partner for the syndicate must avoid these problems and maximize the returns, if you are to gain all the possible benefits. These are caveats and conditions; they don't have to be hard to live with, however. It's not an impossible dream.

WHAT ABOUT A CRASH?

Some who don't really understand real estate investing cry that bad times are just around the corner, that you should put your cash in gold, gather up some dried food and K-rations, and head for the hills. Before you go, hear this.

No one can forecast accurately what the future will bring. Those whose forecasts turn out right have simply been lucky; don't bet on a repeat performance. There are, however, some fairly reasonable observations to be made. Just what economic and social conditions would have to exist for any significant number of investments in real estate to result in disaster for investors?

1. Widespread unemployment? What do unemployed people do? Some draw insurance benefits and *pay* their rent. Many have some savings and, most important, have ingenuity and ability to find ways to come up with the rent money. There is some self-reliance still around! Consider that even with great unemployment by far the majority of people will continue to be employed and, as occurred in some cases in the 1930s when people took pay cuts, there will still be enough money around to pay the rent. And because everyone has to have a place to live, even after the doubling up of families happens, there will still be people who need, and have the ability to pay for, housing.

2. Business activity falls off? Certainly with substantial unemployment there will be a reduction in business activity. If you own commercial property your business tenants may not be prosperous and you may lose out on some excess rents related to business volume or profits. The vast majority of businesses, however, survive recessions and pay at least the basic rent. Yes, you could lose a tenant and not be able to find another, but surely you took that risk into account when you chose this type of property. Don't forget, even in boom times, some firms go broke.

3. Falling real estate prices? Won't the bubble burst? How long can home prices, for example, continue to go up 10 percent a month? Obviously these have been isolated, yet real, situations. There's no question but that prices for all types of properties have been increasing at rates greater than the inflation rate. Surely a prudent person would not be surprised if this changed. What constitutes a disaster? Would it be one if you could achieve only a 15 percent annual gain in value? Is it tough if it takes five years to double your money? Is it really a tragedy if you had to reduce your sales price by several thousands when the price represented an unreasonable markup in the first place? These are things that go on in an inflationary era. Unusually huge gains are mistaken for norms and when they are harder to come by, Chicken Little tells us the sky is falling.

Try not to ever forget, it always stops raining. Even though prices rise steadily, they will stop. In turn, falling prices also stop. Ride it up when you can; bail out before the cycle changes if you can identify that condition. If you are caught in a downdraft, remember, conditions will change once again. Investing in real estate is not an overnight proposition. Look to the longer term; look beyond the current crop of doomsayers. They're probably investing the proceeds from their book royalties in real estate.

CLOSING THOUGHTS

It is well established that you can make money and build your financial security through investing in real estate. Real estate is a *good* investment. As with other human activities, you have to learn how to do what you want. In the following chapters we will discuss how to identify opportunities, evaluate them, and make investments. You're on your own after that to learn how to count all the money you'll have.

2

Gathering Cash to Invest

*The more cash you can use as risk capital the great-
er will be your choice and the more favorable will
be your potential return.*

RISK CAPITAL

It is important to distinguish between the total purchase
price of property and the amount of cash or risk capital
needed to buy it. Because of the widespread use of leverage
in real estate investing we will assume you plan to combine
your cash with borrowed funds. Here we'll look at a variety of
ways in which you can gather up as much risk capital as possible. Later we'll consider sources for mortgage funds and
how to get them.

As a general rule, the larger the property, the greater will
be your investment return, proportionately. Alternatively,
the more cash you have to commit, the more property you can
buy, thus diversifying your risk. All told, then, to invest in
real estate you want to have as much cash as possible. This
does not rule out, however, starting with a small amount.
Mighty oaks grow from small acorns. So, where can you get
your acorns?

SOURCES

The most obvious place to look for your risk capital is your savings account. Perhaps you've been accumulating funds just for this purpose and the time is now approaching to put them to work. If you're reluctant, however, actually to withdraw the money you do have a choice: use the account as security for a loan. If the yield from the investment is satisfactory you may find it to be a quite rational step to borrow; the cost may be no more than 1½ percent over the interest rate being earned on the account. You then may feel better about having kept the money in the account and can plan to pay off the loan, perhaps from other income. Meanwhile you'll have cash to use for your investment project.

How about your checking account balance? Many people enjoy the comfort of a sizeable balance and never worry about overdrawing. Take another look. Do you have a larger balance than you really need? There are other ways to take care of overdrafts; many banks have plans through which you simply pay a fee if you exhaust your balance. The cost of maintaining an excess balance is what you might be earning with the excess in a real estate investment.

Home Equity

For many homeowners, the largest single source of cash to invest in more real estate is the equity in their home. But how do you get your hands on it? Realize that your equity is the difference between the market value of the property and the unpaid mortgage balances. Many banks and savings institutions, mortgage loan companies, and private investors will lend money on this equity and if you do own a home, you should explore this source of risk capital.

The maximum prospective loan here will usually be 80 percent of the market value less the outstanding loan balances. For example:

Your home would sell for	$ 175,000
Current loan balance	35,000
Your equity	$ 140,000
Potential home equity loan	$ 112,000

But if you do get cash this way don't you have to pay it back? Yes indeed you do. It will be important to determine the interest rate, length of term, and what the monthly payments will be. This is where you need to have a well-oiled family budget in operation. In many cases the family might well afford much higher monthly payments for housing. Here we're talking about the sum of the existing mortgage payment and the new payment for the home equity loan. If the old loan was obtained a long time ago when interest rates were modest by today's standards and the amount was relatively small, the monthly payment would now be very easy to handle. Wages and salaries have increased and there may even be more wage earners in the family today. Yes, it can be quite practical to raise cash in this way and not have trouble paying it back independently of the investment.

This raises another alternative. Why not just refinance the present loan on your home and not bother with a second mortgage? To reach a satisfactory conclusion you need to do your homework. Perhaps the existing home loan carries such a low interest rate you are quite reluctant to give it up. Refinancing means paying off the old loan. On the other hand, a new loan might well be granted for a longer term so that even with current interest rates, the actual monthly payment would not be much, if any, larger than the sum of the old loan and the payment for the second. Whether you refinance or get a home-equity loan you will have loan expenses for title insurance and perhaps loan fees; these costs must not be overlooked in your planning.

Remember that mortgage interest expense, whether for your home or for an investment, is tax deductible. As a consequence, depending on your income tax rate, you may find that on an after-tax basis, the increased cost for a higher rate on refinancing or a second loan is not all that bad.

You must put together the figures for each of your alternatives if you are going to borrow risk capital. Given that the monthly payments can be handled without undue strain from sources other than the investment, whether you will be ahead to borrow on your equity will depend on what you can earn over time with the cash, related to its cost. How to measure investment yields will be discussed fully later.

Life Insurance

Your life insurance protection will be either *term* coverage, without a cash surrender value, or a form of *whole* life with a savings feature. By examining your policies or speaking with your life insurance agent, you quickly can determine whether you have an opportunity to raise cash through borrowing on your life insurance. The cash surrender value will be displayed prominently in the policy if you have the whole life type. Look for the provision relating to a *policy loan*. In this type of life insurance a part of each premium is set aside to accumulate; policy loans are made against the security of this cash value. The rate of interest to be charged will also be stated. If you bought the contract a long time ago, you'll be amazed at how little it will cost to borrow on it.

The cash surrender value stated in the policy is the amount you can get if you cancel it. If your need for life insurance protection is met in other ways, you may wish simply to turn in the contract and take the proceeds and add them to your risk capital. In the vast majority of cases, however, it is quite unwise to cancel life insurance so the more prudent thing to do here is borrow against the cash value and keep the insurance in force. You will not have to make periodic repayments of principal, only the interest. As surplus funds become available in the future you can pay off the loan. Meanwhile the loan proceeds can be at work in real estate. Note that in the event of the death of the person covered by the policy, any outstanding loan balance will be paid off from the death benefit and the balance paid to the beneficiaries.

Pension Resources

If you are approaching or have reached retirement and will have retirement funds available in a lump sum, you can seriously consider using them for a real estate investment. Usually the plan is for the pension accumulation to provide a monthly income to replace discontinued earnings. Whether a particular real estate investment will provide the required monthly income must be calculated carefully. Obviously, you would want to maximize current income and pay little attention to the long-term capital appreciation potential to the extent, at least, it was unimportant. In general, the greater the prospects for capital appreciation, the smaller will be the current payout. The importance of matching an investment opportunity to your investment objectives cannot be overemphasized.

If you have been accumulating funds in a Keogh or IRA tax-deferred pension account and are approaching age fifty-nine and a half, be aware you may be able to withdraw the balance. You will have to pay income taxes on the money but you might find it worthwhile to do so. Again you will need to compare the prospective investment return against the alternative of leaving the cash where it is.

Other Assets

As your life-style changes you may find you no longer need some of your assets. These could include an extra automobile, excess furniture, vacation property, and so on. The time to liquidate your investment in antiques, art, coins, or stamp collection may now be at hand. An important consideration is the timing of the sale and the strategy for making it. These assets are not always readily saleable for the maximum return because there isn't an efficient marketplace in all cases. If you hurry and make a sale without checking around, you will probably receive less than you could otherwise. In any case, this can be an important source of cash. By putting it to work in real estate you could improve your return.

Perhaps you've been accumulating an investment in stocks and bonds. By checking the status of each holding carefully, you can see where you stand and when might be a good time to liquidate. Long gone is the time when you could safely buy stocks, put them away, and forget them, secure in the feeling they would grow in value. Through an evaluation of your securities you may find you should make some sales. You know where you want to put the proceeds!

Temporary Investment

If you have diverse holdings and plan systematically to liquidate them, it may take a while before you have gathered up all the cash. What do you do with proceeds as they come in and before you put them to work in real estate?

In recent years as interest rates have increased steadily into the stratosphere, money market funds have offered maximum returns for at least the short term. Some government securities and short-term savings certificates also carry favorable rates. You might use one of these vehicles as a repository for your cash until it's needed. Note that you must make sure you can get the money when it's needed and without paying a penalty for an early withdrawal. It is in that regard the money market funds have great appeal. Of course, rates are volatile and no one should expect very high rates to last forever. You could deposit funds temporarily in a savings account but the passbook account pays the lowest rate in town. For higher yields you have to commit the money to a specific term and that could interfere with your investment plans.

AMOUNT OF CASH REQUIRED

Your risk capital is needed for two basic purposes: the

down payment or full cash price, and for the settlement or closing costs. Until you set your sights on a specific property you won't know how much is needed, but that shouldn't hold you back. Get busy and raise all the money you can.

Once you know roughly how much cash you can use for the project, you will be able to estimate the price range and maximum price it will be reasonable to consider. If you are going to use leverage, the total price of the property should range between four and five times the cash you have for a down payment. For example, let's assume that you can get together $55,000. (Don't let that scare you; that does not imply a minimum amount needed to invest in real estate.) If you allow about $5,000 for the costs, you then would have about $50,000 for equity. If you can borrow 80 percent of the purchase price, you could swing a $250,000 deal. If through some imaginative and creative financing you can borrow, say, 90 percent, then you could consider twice that amount— $500,000. On the other hand, if when you go to the mortgage market and find conditions unfavorable, you might be limited to a loan of 75 percent, or even less. This will reduce the size you can handle. To obtain the maximum purchase price, multiply your down payment cash according to the following table.

Loan Percentage	Multiply by
90%	10
80%	5
75%	4
66%	3

From this you can see that for the largest possible deal you need to borrow 90 percent and, as a consequence, your cash payment will do the most. Whether it is profitable is quite another matter. It should be clear that you should make every effort to scare up as much money as possible in order to maximize your opportunities. Note that this money will be committed to the project and will not, except under most unusual circumstances, be available before the investment is liquidated. That is why it is not wise to borrow money for a down payment unless repayments can be made from sources other than the property.

In the scramble for cash once you've determined that you can liquidate an asset, you may wish to delay actually doing so until you are ready to go. That would not be wise, of course, if a delay could mean a reduced realization. Whenever possible, liquidate to raise cash simultaneously with being able to put the money to work.

Let's assume now that, notwithstanding your valiant efforts to convert assets into cash, the net result is obviously inadequate at least for any of the investment opportunities you've explored. What do you do now, forget it? Not at all. Just find a few other people who are in the same position and join together.

GROUP INVESTING

Although the following material relates more directly to the subject for the next chapter, it's important here and now for those who find themselves with more enthusiasm than cash for investing in real estate to be aware of how very modest sums of money can be employed.

There are a number of reasons why those who invest in real estate prefer to do it with others. Here we're considering group investing because of a shortage of enough cash to handle an investment by yourself. Some would prefer a passive role with no day-to-day activity, regardless of the amount of funds available, so they seek to put their money with others. All this can be accomplished through a real estate syndicate or an investment in shares of a real estate investment trust. Partnership interests are often available for as little as $3,000; REIT shares can be bought through stockbrokers for as few dollars as one is willing to handle. A minimum transaction is usually a few hundred dollars. But is there any other alternative? Yes, form your own group.

Let's assume you find you have several thousands of dollars but are reluctant to try to swing an investment on your own. After checking around you discover perhaps that some friends or relatives are in the same boat: not enough cash to do it on their own but a strong desire to invest in real estate. Now's the time to consider forming a partnership or even a corporation. Legal fees and other expenses do not have to run more than a few hundred dollars to accomplish this. True, your group will have to organize and make decisions as to who is going to run the investment activity and do the work. Once those matters are settled you can get on with the challenge of finding opportunities and making investment decisions. Don't overlook the possibility that a real estate broker, investment advisor, or building contractor might be available to join your group. Because this would not be a public partnership or corporation, few regulatory matters have to be considered and it does not have to be difficult for a few people to get together for the purposes stated.

CLOSING THOUGHTS

Use your ingenuity to find ways to maximize the amount of hard cash you can come up with to commit to your project. Never use money that may be needed for emergencies. This is a long-term investment. Before actually liquidating an asset to get money for investment, wait until you are satisfied that the potential return justifies that action. And make certain that you have your investment objectives clearly in mind and that the property offers at least a reasonable opportunity to achieve your goals. To be able to do all this, you will need to learn everything that is spelled out in the following chapters.

3
Identifying Investment Opportunities

Real estate can be called the cafeteria of the investment world. You can indeed serve yourself, look carefully at the property before deciding, and choose from many very attractive alternatives. Cafeteria indeed!

WAYS TO INVEST

Once you've reached well-defined conclusions as to your investment objectives, the next step is to explore all the real estate opportunities you can find. Your first problem, if you are new to the field, is learning enough about how these investments operate so that you can select a few and concentrate on those most likely to meet your needs. That is the purpose of this chapter—to introduce the basics of real estate investment and show you how to find usual, and even some unusual, ways to put your money to work.

HOUSING

With more than 70 million housing units in the United States, you shouldn't find it difficult to locate one or more to buy. Prudent investors, however, are interested only in certain properties: those that will serve as safe, secure places for invested funds to grow and, for some, provide an income.

Your Own Home

For a home today you can choose from single-family detached houses, condominiums or townhouse units and co-op apartments. In each case you have ownership rights, privileges, and obligations. But why should you look upon these as an investment? Simply because of the experience homeowners have had in the past. The market value for most homes has increased at a rate far in excess of inflation. Isn't that what you want your investment to do? But is it too late to catch this boom? No, but there certainly are some factors to consider.

If you now rent your living accommodation, you can compare your present costs with those you'd have if you were to buy. Costs are all-important, of course. If you buy comparable housing, your costs may even drop slightly, as explained below. If you buy property that gives you more than you now have as a tenant, don't be misled by the change in costs; if you have more, you should expect to pay more. When you buy a home to live in, your choice should be dictated by your family requirements, likes, dislikes, employment, and financial resources. You may not choose the same property if, instead, you bought strictly as an investment. The property you select because of its unique characteristics relative to your needs may not turn out later to be so attractive to subsequent buyers. For now, that is unimportant. To maximize your standard of living you should choose the property you buy to live in first for how suitable it is as a living accommodation and only secondarily as an investment. Regardless, an investment it is.

How do you measure an income return from property you own and live in? In some cases, the total cost for housing—including a return on the funds invested—may be less than what you'd pay in rent for an equivalent house. If you itemize your deductible expenses for income tax purposes, the amount by which the total exceeds the standard deduction becomes the basis for a saving in tax liability and hence can be considered an investment return. Property taxes and mortgage interest expense are two important items here. On the other hand, if you find that because of maintenance costs and repairs you have increased what it costs for housing, don't despair. Think of this as an increase in your investment and be content with the idea that you likely are going to recover it all when you sell the property. Meanwhile you have in addition all the intangible values of owning your home.

Yes, you might conclude you waited too long to buy a home. Current prices when compared to even the recent past appear to be totally unreasonable. Don't think you'll gain much by waiting any longer. Except for some emergency situation, sellers will be asking even more in the future. What about the high cost of mortgage financing? Does it make any sense to tie into a 12 percent or even higher rate? To answer this question, consider two important matters: the potential for lower rates in the future and the treatment of mortgage interest for income taxes.

Visit mortgage lenders such as your bank and savings institution to learn about alternatives to the fixed rate mortgage loan. We'll consider these in more detail shortly but now, while you may be wondering about getting a loan to buy a house, let's allay some concern. It is quite possible to borrow money today on a basis that will give you the benefit of an interest rate reduction if and when it occurs. You can even get a loan that calls for lower payments at the beginning with higher amounts later on which presumably will match your increased income in the future.

By the time you consider the reduction in income taxes you might have because of what you pay out in mortgage interest, you may take a different view on what mortgage financing is really costing. High interest rates taken by themselves may be misleading. Don't reject out of hand the idea of buying your own home. Check it out carefully and you may be pleasantly surprised.

Now let's look at the prospects for liquidating the investment in your home and the potential returns to be realized when it occurs. Of course, if your employment or other factors dictate that you must move frequently, it is unlikely you would be wise to own your home. The costs to buy and sell would probably more than eat up short-term increases in value. Given that you do wait a few years before selling, what can you expect?

If you used borrowed funds to make the purchase and have been paying down the mortgage, you should expect to recover most, if not all, of the equity build. If you sell the property for not less than what you paid for it, and the purchaser cashes you out, you'll have in hand not only the amount by which you reduced the mortgage but also your down payment. But that's not all. Using the past as an indicator for the future, you should have every right to expect to sell the property for more than you paid for it and thus you'll achieve some capital appreciation. Single-family homes and even condominium units, in recent years, have been the source of unbelievable investment returns for many people. Whether this will continue cannot be assured, however. It clearly is not unrealistic to judge that all the factors that have brought about such great increases in property values in recent years are still applicable —reduced supply, higher and higher costs for new construction, and increasing numbers of people who have the ability to buy because of two incomes. The liquidation of inflated home equities has also been an important factor. The only significant "fly in the ointment" is the fluctuation in the supply of mortgage funds. We'll look at this important matter in more detail shortly.

But what is your position if you sell your home and reap all these rewards? Many, of course, move up. That is, they use the sales proceeds to buy another home with more accommodation and features. Certainly the property you buy will have been increasing along with the one you sell, so are you really ahead? For many, being able to just stay even is considered an accomplishment. But note where the possible advantage lies. When it comes time to sell and buy again you will likely have increased your cash equity, especially through the return of your mortgage reduction; if you have improved the property you should, in effect, get cash for that increase in value too. If you buy a new home, you'll be able to get a longer term mortgage with probably a minimum down payment, so the cash from the sale will go further. If the seller of a used home is willing to carry the financing, you may find you can do more with your cash than with a conventional lender.

If there are capital gains, aren't they considered profits and subject to income taxes? Only if you don't put the sales proceeds into another property for use as your principal residence. When you buy another home for at least the price of the one you're selling, you pay no tax on the gain at that time; the gain is rolled over into the new property. When you make a last sale, at age fifty-five or over, you can even exempt $100,000 of the accumulated gains from any income tax.

With all these goodies how can you afford NOT to own your own home? Choose it first, however, to meet your housing needs. It will almost surely also serve admirably as an investment. And if this is such a good idea, why not buy homes strictly for investment once you've got yours?

Rental Homes

When you invest you must be concerned about the potential resale value of the property as well as how safe your funds will be. If you buy a house to rent out, you must be careful to select property that will, in fact, appeal to tenants and at rents high enough to cover your costs and provide a fair return. Never select rental property, however, according to your own dislikes and preferences—you are not going to be the tenant. Fortunately, not everyone has the same ideas as to what is desirable. The property must provide satisfactory housing for someone who has the ability to pay the rent but it does not have to meet your personal requirements. If the property you are considering has a history of successful renting, you may be able to dismiss that concern. You do have to estimate what changes may take place during the time you'll own it, however. Careful examination of the neighborhood and plans, if any, for major changes in the community is required. Not all changes are for the worse, of course. So, you must reach a conclusion when examining prospective investments whether the property can be rented and whether it will have maintained its value by the time you want to sell.

The major disadvantage of owning single-family home rental property, from the investor's point of view, is the likelihood that the rent that can be charged will not be enough to cover all costs and provide a fair return on the cash invested prior to resale. The majority of those who buy this type of property as an investment do so in anticipation of capital appreciation, not as a way to produce current income. Here's an example to illustrate how you can judge a particular opportunity.

Assume the property can be bought for $75,000 and rented for $500 a month. The relationship between sales price and rents varies somewhat throughout the country but you will likely find that the annual rent will generally be about 8 percent of the sales price of the house. Assume here that you borrow 80 percent of the cost at 12 percent interest for thirty years. (These terms are quite liberal; you may not be able to do so well depending on the local current situation.) Here's a possible income statement for a typical year:

ANNUAL CASH IN AND OUT

Gross Rental Income		$6,000
Less: Mortgage Payments	$7,409	
Property Taxes	800	
Insurance	250	
Repairs	300	8,759
Operating Deficit		$2,759

As we'll see later, there's more to this situation than presented here; the cash deficit may at least be partially offset by tax shelter benefits accruing from the operating loss. Meanwhile, it can be seen that when the rental income is less than the total cash expenditures, the investor may have to come up with extra cash each year. In such a case you would have to consider that you simply were increasing your investment each time you made up the shortage. There can be no doubt that this would *not* provide a source of current income.

But let's consider an alternative. Assume you have owned your home for a long time, wish to move to an apartment, and wonder whether you should sell or keep it and rent it out. Should you convert your home to income property? How do you determine whether you'd be better off to sell, take the cash, and put it to work elsewhere? We'll assume that the property is free and clear—you've paid off the mortgage by now.

First, what rent can you get? You look around the neighborhood to find comparable property occupied by tenants and learn what rent is being charged. Through research you should be able to judge the market rent for your home. In the process you should also try to find out what it would bring in a sale. It can be very useful to discuss values with real estate brokers who operate in the area. You might learn in this exercise that some of your neighbors are not charging enough rent, and that may preclude you from getting what your property is worth. Some owners in this situation will charge only enough rent to give them whatever supplemental income they need, regardless of what the house might really be worth; this is especially the case when the owner does not have a mortgage payment to meet. Further, as we get older we have trouble relating to current prices. If you bought your home say for $12,000 a long time ago and someone today says you should now rent it out for $750 a month, you'd probably think that was outrageous and not even consider asking that much. It's not likely a prospective tenant will tell you the rent is too low. As long as owners of other property think this way, you will be affected adversely.

Back now to the previous example where the property has a value of $75,000 and you could rent it for $500 a month. Assuming you owned it free of any debt, what might your cash operating statement look like?

ANNUAL CASH IN AND OUT

Gross Rental Income		$6,000
Less: Property Taxes	$800	
Insurance	250	
Repairs	300	1,350
Cash Operating Gain		$4,650

How's that for current income? The old homestead might produce almost $400 month, a dandy supplement to your pension. But is it an adequate return? What are your alternatives? What could you earn with the cash that's tied up in the property?

Assume you could sell the property for a net cash realization after sales and fix-up expenses of $68,000. If you put that cash in a savings certificate account at as little as 8 percent (to be conservative), your annual interest income would be $5,440. In view of this, is it really such a bargain to use your home as rental income property?

Before reaching a satisfactory conclusion, you would need to consider some important additional factors. Can you obtain further capital appreciation by holding it? What about income taxes? If you sell and don't use the once-in-a-lifetime $100,000 exemption, you would not have the full $68,000 cash to invest. Further, you would have income tax to pay on the net rental income, after depreciation; it's important to compare after-tax investment returns. Remember, the interest income from the savings account is taxable at your full current income rate. What we have learned here shows how important it is to analyze all the choices before deciding. First appearances may be deceiving.

Mobile Homes

Can a mobile home be an investment, you ask? Yes, it's

quite practical to employ your investment funds here. If you haven't looked at mobile homes (don't call them "trailers") lately you're due for a surprise. Visit a modern mobile home park and see what's happening.

There are two basic ways in which real estate is handled in a mobile home park. The owner of the park may rent the ground to the mobile home owner; these are called "pads." The rent for the pad may run from $50 up to several hundred dollars a month. Alternatively, in some parks you can buy the lot. In that case you will be subject to property taxes and, in addition, a fee charged by the park operator to cover maintenance of the roads and facilities.

Mobile homes are typically owner-occupied but there are opportunities for income property investors. If you already own a mobile home, you probably can rent it out quite readily; the demand is strong everywhere. You may want to consider buying a mobile unit for use as income property. Since once a unit is installed on the pad it no longer is mobile, ownership can be transferred in the same manner as other property, but without relocation. The reasons this could be a satisfactory investment have changed in recent years. Today, financing of a mobile home is much more like a regular home loan. This means that loans are for longer terms and lower interest rates than they were in the past. Although purchase prices will likely startle you, they are less than for single-family, detached homes of comparable accommodation, and it does not take a large sum to obtain an equity. In some situations the value of mobile homes has actually appreciated, whereas in days gone by that rarely, if ever, happened. Some parks are considered to be highly desirable and the demand by those who wish to get in serves to increase the value of units installed.

Just as for other types of income property, here you can deduct depreciation, mortgage interest expense, repairs and maintenance, insurance, and other costs when computing taxable income. There is, of course, still the matter of obtaining enough rental income to cover your expenditures. Investment opportunities do exist and you owe it to yourself to check them out.

Second Homes

Before leaving the subject of individual unit housing we need to examine an important development in the recent past. Many recreation and vacation areas have been created to provide second homes for those who can afford it. Many projects have been promoted on the idea that the buyer could treat the property as an investment by renting it out during times when it was not used by the owner. In some cases this has proven to be quite successful but there are some pitfalls. Before jumping in to purchase a mountain cabin or vacation condominium, consider carefully the following matters if you are counting on the potential investment return to make it feasible.

The key matter here is finding people to rent your second home. This may work quite well if the property is part of a development where there is a rental office staffed to maximize rental activity. Attempting to drum up tenants on your own, far from the property, will be a trying experience. Remember that the rental service will cost, so you cannot count on having the full gross rent to provide you return. Yes, for income tax purposes you may be able to deduct depreciation, but only if you generate enough rental income to qualify. Casual rentals combined with your personal use of the property will severely limit the amount of depreciation you can charge against income. The IRS tightened up its rules for this in recent years. You can, of course, fully deduct mortgage interest expense without regard to rental income. But to maximize the tax benefits, you would need to hold the property for rental all year round, qualifying it as regular rental income property rather than a part-time second home.

What about capital appreciation and equity build? Yes, there is a potential gain here, assuming the development remains viable and there is in fact, when you need it, adequate demand for the property. Certainly in some areas the increase in value of this type of property has been phenomenal and some investors have done very well. Judging the future market is vital and there's great risk that these types of property will not appreciate as expected. Note that it is most unlikely that second home recreational property would provide current income for an investor.

Summary

There are indeed investment opportunities for you in housing. You probably ought to give first consideration to owning the place you live in; investment results from it will probably surprise you. After that you should explore, as part of your investment research, opportunities described above. But don't forget what you do in a cafeteria—keep going and look at some more dishes before making your final choice.

COMMERCIAL INCOME PROPERTY

In this section we'll look at a variety of income properties grouped together as *commercial* because, by definition, owners are running a business—the business of renting property. Further, for some of the types considered here, the investment return is a function of the success or failure of the commercial activity conducted on the property.

Residential Income Property

For nonprofessional investors, residential income property is by far the most popular of all types of real estate available. In this class we include multiple units from duplexes or flats all the way to large-scale apartment complexes containing hundreds of units. This type of property is attractive primarily because it is not hard to see how you could do it yourself. If you own and manage the property you can, to a large extent, control the income and expenses. That is to say, getting tenants just may be a matter of properly promoting and advertising the property and screening applicants carefully. You must be forceful in collecting rents to avoid delinquencies. You may be able to handle repairs yourself and thus keep expenses to a minimum. You should be able to control when the investment is to be liquidated and obtain the maximum returns. Whether you can in fact get a buyer at your price remains to be seen, of course.

Everywhere there is the cry that apartments are hard to find and rents are too high. As an owner you should have a steady stream of rental applicants; whether the rents you can charge will be high enough to cover increasing operating costs is another matter. In some areas the biggest threat to this type of investment is that posed by rent controls already in place or proposed. You may have to face up to that problem, among others. But you don't have to be involved face to face with the public and thus can avoid some of the aspects of landlording. You can employ a property manager or contract with a property management service. As a rule, however, only large properties will produce a return large enough to justify that expense.

In reviewing investment opportunities you will find that as the number of rental units increases, the potential for investment return will often increase, proportionately. A duplex, for example, will be better than two single-family dwellings; ten units will be better than fourplexes, and so on. The basic reason lies in the greater utilization of land so that its cost is spread over a larger base, thus improving the rate of return. There should be, as well, a reduction in the cost of management per unit, and perhaps even maintenance and supplies. For all these reasons, you will want to look for the largest number of units your cash will allow you to buy.

The prospective sources of return from this type of property include cash flow (the difference between cash income and cash expenses), tax shelter benefits depending on how the property is financed, equity build if borrowed funds are used, and long-term capital appreciation. The value of residential income property is directly related to its income-generating ability. As we'll see in more detail later, the price reflects the income level so the amount of capital appreciation is very much affected by how well the owner maximizes rents and minimizes operating expenses, relative to similar properties.

The shortage of apartments, extreme in some areas, and the increasing cost of new construction both serve to make rent increases inevitable. As rental income increases, provided operating expenses are controlled, the market value of the property will increase. For the past twenty-five years the market value of apartment properties has increased at rates in excess of inflation.

In view of all this you may wish seriously to consider putting your cash to work in residential income property. You certainly can structure a deal to receive tax shelter benefits and probably achieve superior capital appreciation relative to alternatives. If you buy for all cash you can have highly satisfactory current income as well as capital gain. There's no guarantee, of course, that you will reach these goals just because you own this type of property. You can lose the advantage gained by shrewd purchase negotiations by failing to manage the property. Your timing of the resale may not maximize long-term gain; market conditions are very much subject to change. Rent controls could jeopardize your investment. All things considered, however, if the characteristics appeal to you, there should be no difficulty finding enough opportunities from which to choose. There's a steady supply of landlords who want to cash in their chips and give someone else a turn. Through careful analysis you'll be able to find just the right apartment property to buy.

Conversions

By now you know that a fundamental feature of income property is that its value is directly related to its income-generating capacity. This can be demonstrated easily by considering a typical conversion. Many people have converted a large single-family, older home into two rental units, for example. By doubling the number of units, you are not likely to double the rental income but you certainly should be able to increase the net income and the return even considering the investment on the conversion. Some people have done exceedingly well with this process. Look for this opportunity in the older sections of town which previously had been an area of large family homes. For a conversion to be practical the area must be zoned for multiple occupancy. Key concerns beyond zoning include the extent of the remodeling needed to create separate units and the cost involved. You must estimate carefully what rents you could reasonably get for the finished apartments and confirm there really is a demand in that location. The more work you do yourself, the better the economic gains will likely be. If you are able to live in the property while the conversion is taking place, so much the better, as you will be saving on living expenses. Some marriages could not be saved, however, under these conditions, and that is a hazard to be measured for some.

Many investors have built substantial estates through the remodeling and conversion process followed by exchanging and trading up. Some have started with a single-family home and a few dollars and used their talents and resources ultimately to control properties worth millions. Others have done it—so can you.

But there's a new type of conversion opportunity today for apartment owners: the condominium conversion. Assume you own an apartment complex but believe it's time to liquidate. After determining the market value and what you think you could sell it for, you still would like to get more. Or, perhaps there's a threat of rent control and that is limiting what you can realize if you sell. Well, what do you do? Should you be satisfied with the current market price? Well, you may not have to be.

You probably think that all things are the sum of their parts. If you slice up an apple, how could you possibly have more than the whole? How could you possibly increase the amount by slicing it? By converting your apartment to condominium units, that's how. To further understand what this is all about, let's learn more about condominiums.

Condominium is a form of ownership interest in property invented by the Romans; there's nothing new about condominiums. When you buy a condominium you acquire joint ownership of adjacent property together with individual ownership of the unit. You take title typically to the airspace located between the walls of a structure and own jointly with other unit owners, the exterior walls, hallways and other common areas, and the land. (There are variations on this arrangement including the townhouse, for example, where you own the land and interior individually and the balance of the structure jointly.) Condominium ownership is commonly found as, but not limited to, residential income property. Office buildings, commercial and industrial properties and, in fact, virtually any kind of real estate can be subject to this type of joint ownership. Concentrating on housing, however, let's see why condominium ownership has become so popular in recent years.

You can finance and buy and sell condo units as easily as a single-family detached home and all the tax advantages of the single-family dwelling apply. But what is otherwise appealing? When you own that vine-covered cottage, you have to trim the vine, mow the lawn, remove the snow, repair the roof, paint the outside, and so on. In a condominium apartment property, all those things are taken care of through the condo homeowners' association. Of course, you pay for the cost through payments to the association and you may even serve on the board of directors and be involved in making decisions concerning the property. Because you will be assessed property taxes on your unit, and may have mortgage interest expense, you retain the income tax advantages they give you. Many condo buyers are former single-family homeowners who want the independence a condo gives along with most of the advantages of home ownership. It is also clear why apartment tenants may be interested in buying a condo. And that's why we're interested in the condo conversion process.

The owner of an apartment property has three choices: sell the property, keep it and continue to manage it, or liquidate the investment by converting it to condo units and selling them off. As a rule, the total realization from selling all the units will far exceed the amount otherwise to be obtained through an outright sale as rental property, even allowing for the cost of conversion. In areas where there are limits on increasing rents, owners are very much attracted to the idea of converting to condominium ownership. In fact, where there has been a lot of conversion activity, you may find some ordinances restricting it. When exploring investment opportunities with an eye to this type of conversion, check carefully to be certain you won't encounter any legal roadblocks.

What else is involved in a prospective conversion? There may be serious construction problems. What must be done in order to make each apartment unit completely independent for heating and other utilities? In some areas it has been customary to use centralized facilities and it can be costly to refit each unit. Some structural changes may be required by building codes imposed since the structure was built. You will need to employ professional services to have a subdivision map prepared for presentation to local authorities for approval of your plans. You will likely be far ahead if you can locate contractors, engineers, and attorneys who have learned condo conversion expertise on someone else's property, and use them for your project. The ultimate gain can be so attractive that you will decide it is worth all the effort, turmoil, and the challenge. The sum of the parts can far exceed the value of the whole.

Business Income Property

The vast majority of small and medium size retail and service businesses operate from rented premises. When you drive around a business district, realize that real estate investors own much of what you see; it's not only in shopping centers where the operators are tenants. Does this suggest an opportunity for you? Well, what are the angles? First, many investors would prefer doing business with business people. There's an assumption that those who run a business will always pay their rent because they want to keep the location. Be careful. Many who run businesses have had lots of practice stiff-arming suppliers and creditors, and a landlord doesn't intimidate them one bit. Yes, a business is just as subject to eviction as an apartment dweller but it's not necessarily easy to accomplish. Overall, however, most businesses are successful and the landlord does receive rents when due.

The second favorable feature of this type of income property has to do with operating expenses. When your apartment expenses go up you may not be able automatically to raise rents. This problem is avoided when you rent to a business on a *net* basis. In many cases business tenants pay the property operating expenses such as utilities, property taxes, and even maintenance so the payment to the property owner is termed "net." Alternatively, the lease agreement may have an escalator clause requiring an increased rental payment if property taxes or other expenses increase.

But what is the risk here? Now we come to the third feature: rents geared to sales or profits. If you own an apartment and a tenant becomes unemployed, you may suffer through lost rent. Most apartment tenants, however, do find ways to pay rent rather than having to move out. With a business it may be somewhat different. If the business fails the tenant will close up and leave and the landlord will likely be out some rent. But what if the business is highly successful? Under these conditions the tenant could pay more rent but certainly won't volunteer it. Because the property owner in effect is sharing the business risk, there should be a way for him or her to share in success when it occurs. This is customarily accomplished through a lease provision in which the rent is a combination of a minimum or base amount plus extra rent geared to the success of the business; this is often measured through sales volume. How this is done varies widely from one kind of business to another. For example, a hardware store might pay a rent override of say 2 percent of sales over a stipulated minimum volume. This arrangement is referred to as a *percentage lease.*

If you were a business property landlord and your tenants were on percentage leases, you would be motivated to do what you could to attract business to the property. The more business your tenants do the greater will be your rental income. If they are successful, you will be, too. Would you like to be one of these landlords? There's an infinite variety of opportunities to own property used in business. There are small, medium, and huge properties to be owned and operated by investors. Some firms choose to build premises to suit their special needs but do not want to continue to own the property. By the sale and leaseback method, the tenant gets property precisely geared to its operation and the investor probably has an above average tenant. Major chain stores, for example, use this method to keep funds invested in the business instead of real estate. The lease under these conditions can be used as security by an investor to obtain financing; lenders typically look with favor on sale and leaseback situations. The investor must look to ultimate liquidation through resale. One reason the tenant in this situation wants to be a tenant is to avoid being stuck with property no longer suitable for the business. This, then, is the investor's risk and needs to be guarded against. Rent payments should be structured so that there is enough income to pay off the mortgage and the down payment before the tenant can exercise an option to leave.

An investor may combine forces with a building contractor to finance construction of new rental property. Perhaps the contractor owns the land and has waited for the right time to develop it. You might just be the person to take advantage of the opportunity to own a new building. In addition to special tax advantages through maximum accelerated depreciation available to first users, you may also have the benefits of reduced maintenance and repairs often associated with new construction. You should line up your tenants before committing yourself, however, to avoid being stuck with nonrevenue-producing property.

Some of the innovations taking place in business have created many opportunities for real estate investors. Think of the number of franchised outlets built throughout the country in just the past few years. In most cases the locations are owned by private investors rented to the franchisee; often they are on a percentage lease basis. If you've had a hankering to get involved in any one of a host of popular businesses but didn't have quite the courage or time to be directly engaged in running one of them, the next best thing might be to participate through owning the real estate they need. It could turn out to be even better!

Owning commercially-used property can produce satisfactory current income, depending on the financing. There may also be equity build and a potential for capital appreciation. The greatest risk factor is that faced by your business tenant. If the business is successful you will be too, provided you use the appropriate lease provisions. Otherwise, you clearly could be a loser.

THE GOOD EARTH

Have you ever experienced the satisfaction that flows from owning a piece of the earth? This is part of the American heritage, of course, and is founded at least in part by the experience of our forefathers in homesteading and striving to own their plots of land. Owning ground can be a sound investment, too.

Vacant Lots

You can make money buying and selling plots of ground. On a larger scale you can take acreage, subdivide it, and sell the lots. Current conditions in most areas make this activity much less desirable than in days gone by. In many places we now have strong no-growth movements and ordinances and zoning controls so strict that it's a miracle there's any subdividing and building taking place at all. These actions, of course, put a premium on vacant lots, especially in communities where the demand is very strong for new construction. Perhaps maximum opportunities for profit can be found in areas where there has been a virtual stoppage in new building because of the controls—if you can assume that at some point in the future they will be lifted. Here you probably can buy property at bargain prices from those who can't wait and will sacrifice. By holding vacant lots until conditions change, you may well achieve far above average capital appreciation. Don't overlook the cost of carrying your investment, however. Not only must you count the opportunity cost of the cash invested but also the property taxes to be paid during the holding period. By opportunity cost we mean the loss of what you might have earned if the money had been employed elsewhere. As a minimum this would be interest earned in a savings account.

To find this type of investment opportunity, explore both residential and commercial areas for vacant lots, especially those between buildings. For these it is unlikely there would be a need to incur costs to provide water and sewer service other than to a structure itself. You probably should avoid lots for which substantial funds must be invested to improve the property before it can be built on. You'll need to check on building and zoning regulations and their impact on your project before you commit your money. After you locate one or more vacant lots you must track down the owner. This can be done through the local tax assessor's office. Watch also for ads in the real estate section and check with real estate brokers; your banker may know of someone who wants to sell a lot. Sometimes you'll find the trust department of a bank a fruitful source of property for sale. No doubt about it, you can make some money buying and selling vacant lots.

Predevelopment Land

Many people dream of owning some land outside of town and waking up one day to an offer to sell it to a developer for many times its original cost. Yes, it can happen. For you to have this experience, you need to do a better-than-average job of guessing where and when the next wave of development will come.

If you examine how your community has grown, you'll find that each extension of the developed areas involved conversion of raw land into streets and lots. As a rule, the owner of the acreage was able to sell the land at a profit because of the potential profit to be gained by the conversion. In some cases the landowner did the subdividing and in others the development was carried out by development organizations. Ideas as to where there might be some predevelopment land may be found in ads and articles in such newspapers as the *Wall Street Journal*, and from discussions with local planning commission staff members, real estate brokers, and the Chamber of Commerce. If you keep alert to what's going on in your community, it may not be difficult at all to uncover an opportunity to invest in land with a strong potential for future development.

As a rule, this type of property will require relatively large amounts of cash; regular bank financing is not usually available. There is the risk that development restrictions may be imposed and that could make a big difference to you. Don't forget to include in your analysis the property taxes to be met while you are waiting. To offset these costs you may be able to use the land for agricultural purposes or business storage such as for idle equipment. There's a large potential gain for those who control land needed for development.

Recreational Land

Some of the more spectacular land frauds committed in recent years have involved the sale, often sight unseen, of recreational land. Perhaps you've seen the advertising; let's hope you weren't taken in by it. This is not to say there aren't some perfectly respectable and legitimate offerings but, regrettably, many have not been and the public has been cheated.

The usual pitch is that by getting in on the ground floor you can own a plot of ground in one of the world's greatest recreational areas, use the property when you want for your own recreation, then sell it later for huge profits because the demand will be so great. In most cases, if you inspected such offerings carefully, your common sense would tell you that such claims for future gains are implausible. The easiest way to avoid this fraud is to look at the property, ask enough questions, evaluate the answers, and thus reach a sound conclusion. This, of course, will not absolutely guarantee success but it will eliminate much of the risk. The pity is that so many people do, in fact, part with their money for land they've never seen.

An important element here is the developer's track record and reputation. The federal government requires, through the Department of Housing and Urban Development (HUD), that developers present facts in a *Property Report*, which must be written to meet the regulations prescribed by the Interstate Land Sales Act. You should explore beyond such a report and investigate the project and the developer further by talking to those who already own property in the area, those who have done business with the developer, and with local banks and public authorities. There's no excuse for making an investment decision without all the pertinent information in hand for a wise choice.

It is quite unlikely this type of land could be used to generate current income; its major investing characteristic is its potential for long-term capital appreciation. Your hedge ought to be a plan to use it yourself while waiting for it to appreciate rather than having it just sit there, unused. Then, if no appreciation occurs, at least you've had the return from such activities as skiing, swimming, or fishing.

GROUP INVESTING

We touched on group investing briefly in the preceding

chapter. We come back to it now to round out the discussion of all of the choices you have in the real estate cafeteria. Before reaching your final conclusion about where you want to put your money to work, you should consider the pros and cons of investing in either a REIT or a syndicate. When you invest with others, you are relieved of any operating responsibility both with respect to selecting properties and day-to-day management. You will have some say in any decision to sell, but only with respect to liquidation, not individual properties. You may well be attracted to this when you think of all the things you'd have to do as an active landlord and investor. But what about investment returns? Is it really better to pay someone else to do all these things? Are the prospective results likely to be that much better? Well, maybe.

When the REIT's advisory company is skilled and successful, the operating results will justify the cost. If the general partner in a syndicate is experienced and handles affairs properly, the limited partners will likely come out ahead. All of this says, of course, that there's no more guarantee of success as a member of a group than when you are free to suffer for the mistakes you make yourself. For investors new to real estate there may be some initial advantage to participating in a group; they have an opportunity to see how real estate investing operates without the apprehension associated with making operating decisions. But how do you minimize your risk? By doing your homework and developing pertinent information before you part with your money.

REITs

In order to match appropriately your investment objectives with a potential group investment, you must consider the characteristics of the operation. There are three types of REITs: construction and development lenders, mortgage lenders, and equity. The majority of trusts can easily be classified as one of these; there are some that operate in more than one category.

If you want to maximize current income, you will invest in a trust that concentrates on lending money. Those that lend for construction and development have the potential for large returns but also present the greatest risk. Investors seeking primarily capital appreciation may do very well by investing in an equity REIT. Here there can be some current return, usually on a tax-free return of capital basis during the holding period. If the properties are sold later at a gain, the REIT shareholder will receive a cash distribution and thus achieve capital appreciation. A REIT cannot provide, however, tax shelter benefits because operating losses cannot be passed through. Shortly, we'll explore how such losses are available to limited partners in a syndicate.

How do you locate an opportunity to invest in a REIT? The usual source is your stockbroker. The vast majority of currently operating REITs were established in the 1970s and the shares of beneficial interest were sold to the public by stockbrokers and investment dealers. Today there are some new offerings but the activity is much less than it was in the past. At present there are a few hundred REITs in operation, the vast majority of which are publicly traded. You can find REITs listed on both the New York and American Stock Exchanges and in the over-the-counter market. Using customary sources such as Standard and Poor's *Stock Guide,* which can be found in your public library, and information from brokers, you can trace the performance of most REITs and judge any particular opportunity against standards you have set. An additional source of very useful and highly current data on REIT performance is *Realty Trust Review,* published by Audit Investment Research, Inc., 230 Park Avenue, New York, N.Y. 10017.

You may have heard nasty things about REITs and were warned against this type of investment. Yes, in the mid and late '70s a number of REITs did founder, and investors who bailed out did so at a loss. The problem area was that of construction and development lending. These REITs, using borrowed funds to maximize leverage, discovered that their interest costs were going into the stratosphere and their borrowers were going broke, leaving unfinished projects. On the other hand, REITs that owned income property, such as apartments and shopping centers, not only survived the interest rate crunch but gained substantially when they were able to liquidate some of the properties at large gains over cost. It appears most probable that equity trusts will continue to have this experience as the market value of income property continues to rise. Many equity trusts operate nationwide and are able to sell when an area appears to have peaked and put the money to work in some other geographic section in which expansion is taking place. Note that a REIT investment offers the opportunity for diversification both of types of property and location. We can conclude that not all REITs are the same nor is a past record necessarily indicative of the future. Some mortgage REITs became equity REITs through foreclosures and now provide shareholders with highly satisfactory returns. You can easily determine the record and situation today for any REIT you are considering.

A basic characteristic of all REITs is the legal requirement for a trust to distribute not less than 95 percent of its taxable income each year to shareholders to avoid the REIT being taxed itself. Many investors look with favor on this investment vehicle because, unlike the situation for conventional equities where corporations are taxed on earnings before dividends, the REIT escapes double taxation. When you check out share prices by looking through stock exchange listings, you'll find that it doesn't take a lot of money to buy the usual, round lot of 100 shares; many sell for less than $25 a share. It's likely, therefore, that you could participate simply by going to a stockbroker.

If your REIT shares pay a cash dividend (not all do), you will treat it as income and pay the appropriate income tax; such dividends, incidentally, do not count toward the dividend exclusion for individual taxpayers. The distribution may be monthly or quarterly. In some cases it will be designated as a return of capital and hence will not be treated as income subject to tax at the time of receipt. When you receive this type of dividend you can look upon it as tax free and as such the return on your investment may be viewed as handsome indeed. There may be some tax to pay ultimately, however. Here's an example of what is meant by the expression "return of capital." It comes about because the trust distributes more than its taxable income. It can do this because it can charge depreciation against income yet not actually pay it as a cash expense.

EXAMPLE: Assume you buy 100 shares at $15 each. During the time you hold them, you receive $300 in dividends declared to be return of capital. Then you sell the shares more than a year later for $18 each.

Your original cost basis	$ 1,500
Less return of capital	300
Revised cost basis	$ 1,200
Sales proceeds	$ 1,800
Less cost, revised	1,200
Long-term capital gain	$ 600

The income tax payable on long-term capital gain is much less than on current income, so you have a reduced tax liability. Watch for REITs that have this feature in their operating results.

Some investors feel that the most important feature of using REIT shares as a way to invest in real estate is the ability to liquidate the investment simply by placing a telephone call to a stockbroker. Recall that when you own real estate by yourself you may have quite a wait to find the right buyer; we describe the ownership of real estate as a very illiquid investment. Further, the owner of property would have to go to some real effort to learn at any given time just what the property is worth. When you invest in publicly traded REIT shares all you have to do is look at the newspaper to see the current market price. Most REITs offer a dividend reinvestment program making it very easy to automatically put your cash distributions to work in more shares.

In general, a REIT can and will do everything associated with investing in real estate that you could do if you made the investment yourself, assuming you had enough cash and managed it. But, are there any disadvantages? Perhaps. If you are seeking the thrill, excitement, and satisfaction possible through actively seeking and finding properties, analyzing them, negotiating with sellers, arranging financing, dealing with tenants, keeping track of repairs and, finally, determining the best strategy for liquidating the investment, then *don't* put your money in a REIT. Otherwise you may want others to do all these for you and simply send you the profits. But there's a further alternative, the limited partnership, often called a syndicate.

Syndicates

To participate in a syndicate you put up your money in exchange for a limited partnership interest. A general partner handles all the day-to-day operating details. Basically, once the investment is made, you will be able to get it back only when the partnership is dissolved. In some rare instances you may have a chance to sell your interest to another partner but it is best to consider, before investing, that this will be a nonliquid asset. That's not necessarily bad, of course. As long as you don't anticipate the need for cash and are anxious to have your funds hard at work without needing to reinvest them periodically, the nonliquid aspect is of value.

Because a partnership is not taxed on its results, each partner reports on his or her own tax return, a share of the syndicate's profits or losses. If there are profits, they may not necessarily be distributed in cash, so a partner may have to pay taxes without getting any money from the partnership to do so. Of course, the expectation would be that ultimately the retained profits would be disbursed, but that might be a long time after you've had to pay your tax bill. On the other hand, many partnerships are deliberately constructed to produce operating losses, primarily through the use of depreciation expense, and these losses pass through to the limited partner-investors. For this reason, the higher your personal income tax rate, the more value will be a tax shelter benefit accruing from such operating losses. This operates, of course, in exactly the way you, as the individual owner of property, would generate tax shelter benefits.

EXAMPLE: Assume you paid $5,000 for a partnership interest in a syndicate formed to purchase and operate apartment properties. After a year's operation, the partnership tax return shows your share of the operating loss to be $3,000. Assume further that because of your other income from employment and investments, your marginal income tax rate for state and federal combined is 50 percent; without considering this investment, your income tax liability totals $15,000.

TAX SHELTER BENEFIT COMPUTATION

Total income tax liability	$15,000
Partnership loss $ 3,000	
Tax benefit @ 50%	1,500
Total income taxes payable	$13,500

Note that when you combine your share of the partnership return with your own tax return, you will actually be reducing your taxable income by the amount of the operating loss. This is why we say that you are "sheltering other income" from taxes. The result will be the same as in the above example.

How do you reflect a tax shelter benefit when measuring your investment yield or return? You treat the amount of the tax shelter benefit, $1,500 in our example, as though it were cash received. Here, your first year after-tax yield would be:

$$\frac{\$\ 1,500}{\$\ 5,000} \times 100\% = 30\%$$

Because you have to pay $1,500 less in taxes, the benefit is equivalent to cash.

From this example you should not jump to the erroneous conclusion that all syndicates typically produce such tax shelter benefits. In days gone by, there were opportunities to generate substantial amounts of tax sheltering; but changes in tax regulations have eliminated most, but not all. Still, tax sheltering can, in fact, be done through ownership of income property and the objective of minimizing income taxes can be achieved either on your own or as a limited partner.

Where can you learn about joining a syndicate? Because of the relative inability to transfer partnership interests, the practical way to invest is to make a contact with those forming a new partnership. Some stock brokerage firms handle the sale of interests, especially for syndicates intending to operate nationwide. Locally you might find a building contractor or developer who will serve as the general partner and who is seeking limited partners to put up the cash. You probably can discover these opportunities by talking with your banker and with real estate brokers. It does not have to take a large investment to become a limited partner. If your cash is not enough to swing the purchase of property by yourself, why not consider becoming a limited partner and thus learn more about real estate and make some money at the same time?

Summary

Once you've decided you want to achieve your investment objectives through real estate, you do need to determine whether you have enough cash to handle an investment on your own. You also must decide whether you want to have the challenges of selecting, financing, managing, and selling property yourself. If you don't have enough cash, or if you don't want to be a participative investor, you should then consider investing in a real estate investment trust or a limited partnership. If you are seeking maximum tax sheltering, look for a syndicate that has been formed to generate tax shelter benefits. (Not all syndicates do.) If you wish to maximize current income, a mortgage lender REIT will probably provide what you need. If you want capital appreciation but need to be able to liquidate quickly, invest in an equity REIT that is publicly traded; if there is no need for quick liquidation, then consider either a syndicate or a private REIT with the appropriate objective.

When you invest with a group, you have no operating responsibilities. Surely everyone should have at least one experience being an income property landlord, however. If you haven't had yours yet, try that first. Later you may wish to be a nonparticipative investor and know what you are missing.

CLOSING THOUGHTS

Even if you are quite undecided as to whether to put your investment dollars into real estate, you owe it to yourself to explore the alternatives. The purpose of this chapter is to introduce you to the wide range of ways available. You should check each of them out to find which has the most appeal. Gather facts, organize them in a notebook or file folders, and summarize what you learn to make easy comparisons. Shortly, we'll treat how and where you can get information and how to analyze and measure each specific opportunity to determine those that are better than others. The systematic approach to all this can pay off handsomely and you can have some fun doing it as well.

And a last admonition: Carefully determine your investment objectives and the total amount of cash you can commit to the venture. These two guides are absolutely essential if you are to reach rational decisions and have any chance of employing your dollars to reach your objective.

4
Gathering Information

Now that you are enthusiastic about investing in some form of real estate, you probably are eager to take the next step. Start looking around for possible deals and gather enough information so you can make an investment decision through analysis and comparison. Here we learn where to look and what to record. Later we'll see how to put it all to use.

EXPLORATION AND FACT-FINDING

Unless you are already firmly convinced as to which form of real estate investment is for you, keep an open mind and explore several specific opportunities before narrowing the search. Surely, however, some of the ideas covered in the preceding chapter have stimulated special interest and as you look for particular examples, you can test that interest. As you make use of each of the sources described here you'll need to keep in mind the limitations imposed by the amount of funds you have for the purpose as well as whether you face other limitations, such as location or whether you wish to avoid being an active landlord. In the ultimate decision-making process you will need accurate data for a number of different opportunities so that a comparison can be made. This means you will want to know beforehand just what data are needed. For the sake of efficiency you will also want to record the information in a convenient form. To accomplish these objectives, the fact sheets illustrated here were devised. Note that a set of blank forms is presented in the Appendix; these can be readily photocopied in quantity for use in your search.

SOURCES

Whether you are looking for a home, condominium, co-op, apartment house, office building, vacant lots or land, or a commercial property, you'll need to find people who have suitable property for sale. How do property owners let prospective buyers know they want to sell? They advertise in newspapers, list property with real estate brokers, or they ask bankers and other lenders to spread the word.

Newspapers and Magazines

The primary source of data concerning property for sale is the newspaper published in the community where the property is located. If you don't already live there, you can easily pick up the phone and arrange to obtain newspapers that will have advertising of use to you. More than one investor has been inspired by newspapers picked up while on vacation. Whenever you travel, make it a point to learn something about local real estate. Don't expect to obtain everything you want to know, however, simply by studying classified newspaper advertising. At best you should hope to uncover something that meets your overall criteria; you will then have to take the next step and contact advertisers for more detailed information. In some cases the advertiser will be the owner-seller; in others, a real estate broker is soliciting inquiries. Remember that total price and location are likely to be the main points to consider before expending effort to get all the information needed.

A number of specialty magazines such as *The New Yorker*, *Forbes*, *The Hollywood Reporter*, and *New York*, to mention only a few, publish real estate ads. Once you start your search, you will likely be surprised at the number and variety of sources available. Keep your scissors handy to clip out ads that have promise. Make contact and build your research file.

After reviewing these sources you may decide to do what some investors do: place an ad yourself. In this way you may be able to get in touch with an owner who doesn't want the world to know that his or her property is for sale but who is anxious to deal directly with prospective buyers. At any time there are probably twice as many properties for sale than those listed with agents or advertised. Keep your eyes open and you can see how other investors solicit contacts by sellers.

Real Estate Dealers

Countrywide, probably more than half of all real estate transactions are handled by licensed real estate brokers. The remainder are negotiated by owner-sellers and buyers between themselves. You do have a choice; you do *not* have to use a real estate agent. But let's discuss the pros and cons of doing this by yourself and then perhaps you can better judge which choice to make.

In virtually every state a person must be licensed to transact a real estate business. In general, however, this does not apply to the property owner; he or she is free to buy and sell for his or her own account. It is only when you are to represent someone as his or her agent to solicit purchasers that a license is required. To get a license you must meet educational and experience requirements and pass a written examination; requirements are usually more onerous for a broker's license than for a salesman's license. In most cases a person will serve first as a salesman before seeking to be a broker. In addition to licensing real estate dealers in order to protect the public, some states have a recovery fund available to meet claims from persons who can establish that they were injured through the fraud of a licensee.

As with every line of endeavor, some persons are more qualified and competent than others; the holding of a license by itself cannot be taken as a guarantee of either competency or integrity. Further, there are areas of specialization in real estate. The vast majority of those licensed are involved in handling single-family homes; very few are qualified through experience and expertise in investment real estate. Those who specialize usually make their qualifications known through advertising, such as in the *Yellow Pages* of the phone book and in their newspaper advertising. Each state has a trade association which is affiliated with the NATIONAL ASSOCIATION OF REALTORS®, (NAR). Members in good standing are permitted to display themselves as REALTORS®. This is a registered service mark owned by NAR and may be used only with the organization's permission. Members of NAR subscribe to a code of ethics and are subject to the rules and regulations of the local association as well. It is not difficult to tell whether a particular real estate practitioner is a REALTOR®—he or she will display it clearly. Realize, however, that by no means is everyone engaged in real estate entitled to call himself a REALTOR®.

One of the arms of the REALTORS'® group, the REALTORS' NATIONAL MARKETING INSTITUTE®, provides advanced educational programs for REALTORS® which lead to the attainment of a professional designation, *Certified Commercial Investment Member* (CCIM). Prospective real estate investors may wish to tap the prospective expertise of a holder of this designation. Such a person has studied all the subjects involved in making successful investments and will likely be quite helpful. It's important, however, to point out that there are obviously many very competent real estate practitioners who do not have professional designations; they should not be considered deficient solely because they don't.

Why use a real estate agent and pay a substantial charge for the services? First, what is the likely charge? Typically, a real estate broker receives a commission in the range of 4 to 7 percent of the sales price of improved property; it may be as much as 10 percent on vacant land. It is not easy to say who actually pays this commission. In the majority of transactions the real estate commission is deducted from the sales proceeds of completed transactions so the seller clearly feels he or she is paying it. On the other hand, it can be argued that the selling price was made higher than it would otherwise have been in order to cover the sales expense. From that point of view, the buyer is convinced that he or she is paying it. When buyers and sellers deal directly with each other they both expect to save the sales commission.

Inasmuch as all real estate sales are at negotiated prices, who is to say who has saved or paid what? Note carefully that real estate commission rates are *not* fixed and buyers and sellers are free to negotiate the payment for services rendered. Today you will see evidence of the competition between practitioners in advertising that states commissions are less than those charged by others. Well, so much for the fact that if you use a broker you will have to pay for the services. Incidentally, the owner of property who lists it with a broker ordinarily is committed to paying a commission if the broker produces a willing buyer at the terms stated, even if the deal is not made. The obligation to pay is stated in the listing agreement and should be reviewed carefully before a person signs it. But let's look now at what a real estate dealer might do for you in your search for an investment property.

You should view a broker as a source for property; this is the primary function of a real estate dealer. He or she brings buyers and sellers together. Many owners feel unable, or are unwilling, to handle the sale themselves and wish to have an agent represent them. For that reason a prospective buyer would have no way of knowing of properties for sale except through the listing broker. A live-wire practitioner makes it his or her business to know what properties are selling for and can provide current market information to clients. This can be extremely important to both buyers and sellers.

Many brokers participate in the *Multiple Listing Service* through which a large percentage of listed properties is publicized. Truly, a member of the MLS has access to a large number of properties. The information about each is disseminated in a form that makes it easy and efficient for a prospective buyer to locate real estate with sought-after characteristics. Some would say that such access is worth far more than the cost incurred by paying a commission on the sale. Note, however, that although the MLS typically includes commercial and other types of investment properties, the bulk of the listings are single-family homes. Further, medium- to large-scale apartments, office buildings, and industrial properties are not generally serviced by the MLS. The *Wall Street Journal* carries substantial amounts of advertising of this type of property and, through it, the names of real estate firms specializing in it can be determined.

What else does a broker do to earn the commission? One of the most important aspects of a deal is the financing. Here the broker has a real opportunity to provide the service needed for buyer and seller to conclude a transaction. If you are active in making real estate investments, you will have developed your own contacts with lenders. If not, you may have only limited ability to obtain financing. In that case, a qualified real estate broker will be invaluable. Once again the commission may be a small price to pay for being able to obtain a mortgage loan in a tight money market, for example. Note that you do not pay beyond the commission for financing to be arranged unless the loan is made through a mortgage loan broker.

When it comes to the price for the property, the broker may have some unique qualifications. He or she can advise what the market value is so that you can judge an offering. When it comes to negotiating with a seller, the broker may be able to do a better job than you could yourself. Not only can he or she play the role of an intermediary, providing an opportunity to negotiate, but when experienced, the broker ought to be better at it. Notice how, as a rule, we find it easier to speak in behalf of someone else rather than for ourselves. (Remember John Alden.) That's why there are agents in many types of business. But you may ask: "Doesn't the broker represent the seller, so how can he or she represent me?" It's true that often the buyer is dealing with the listing broker who, right enough, was engaged by the seller. Through custom and practice, however, and motivated by the desire to complete the deal, the broker readily can represent both parties and protect everyone's interests. There's no prohibition to your engaging a broker to find a property and negotiate a deal solely in your behalf; you then will be responsible for paying for those services and the seller will likely pay for his or her representative as well.

As we will see later when exploring how a real estate transaction is handled, there are other matters to be considered beyond finding the seller, negotiating the price, and arranging the loan. Many buyers and sellers feel more comfortable when these are handled by someone who, at least allegedly, knows how. As you develop experience and confidence, you may decide to take care of the details yourself. If you decide to work on your own, there is nothing to stop you from doing so. Whether you should use the services of professionals such as appraisers and attorneys will be considered shortly.

If you have a fairly clear idea of the type of real estate investment property you're looking for and you decide to use a real estate dealer, choose one who specializes in what you want. Ideally you should also be able to obtain recommendations from others who have had experience with the brokers from whom you can choose. It's in order also to seek help in locating a qualified broker through discussion with lending officers.

Financial Institutions

Lending officers at banks and savings institutions are good people to know. You may want to borrow some of their money. Here, however, we're interested in them as prospective sources of property to buy. Lending officers have been known to make a mistake in granting a loan so that, after a default, the lender has a foreclosed property on its hands. You might be able to pick up a bargain by keeping in touch with them. You can also learn of foreclosure sales through legal advertising in newspapers. Property being sold to liquidate an estate may also be advertised in this way by a bank's trust department.

Tax Sales

Astute investors have been known to pick up worthwhile property at the city or county tax collector's annual sale of property forfeited to the state for nonpayment of property taxes. Contact the tax collector's office to get on the mailing list. These leads, however, need to be checked carefully. If the property was really worth something, the owner would not likely have failed to pay the taxes. Sometimes, of course, there's been a death and no one is around to keep track of the property. Vacant lots are the most likely type of property to become available this way.

Stockbrokers

No, it's not commonplace yet to buy real estate as well as stocks and bonds from a stockbroker, but the world is changing. Some brokerage houses are, in fact, acquiring real estate firms and so-called "one-stop" investing appears to be a possibility for the future. Meanwhile, if you wish to be a nonparticipative investor, your stockbroker can fix you up with REIT shares or partnership interests. Before making your final decision you probably ought to get information from this source and make some comparisons.

FACT SHEETS

Part of the secret to successful investing is the use of a systematic way to gather information so that when it comes time to make a choice you have accurate and sufficient data. This will lead to better than average results. You need to know, of course, what questions to ask when talking with a seller or broker. Then you need an efficient system to record what you find out. In this section, we have both. The Fact Sheets have been devised to show what information is required and to provide a place to write it down. Once you've gathered facts on each of several potential investments, you can analyze the data and make a good choice.

The process outlined here is to be used regardless of the type of property you are pursuing. It is needed whether you're exploring the purchase of your home or checking out vacant land to subdivide—and all ideas in between. Your goal is to complete a set of fact sheets for each property. In the following pages you will have a discussion of the use of the forms in general together with illustrations of completed forms for a particular property. When you need a set to use, recall that blank forms are illustrated in the Appendix.

The Property

Everything you need to know about the property itself is set forth on the first page. When you visit the location and fill out this sheet, make certain you put down items that will help you remember what you've seen. After you've checked out a number of places, you'll find that some of them blur together in your memory; notations here will help you avoid that.

For investment features, put down both positive and negative items. In the case of rental apartments, consider those features that would appeal, such as landscaping, transportation, nearness to shopping, and so on. If parking is a problem, or if there's limited storage space, write it down. How about schools, parks, and other features of importance to children? The location of property, whether a house, apartment, or commercial property, is quite important. The more desirable the location is, the higher the price should be. The investor should always keep in mind that some day the property, if bought, will be put on the market again. Will it appeal to future buyers? Property you can buy at a bargain price because of its lousy location will have to be sold at a bargain price— the chances for above average returns will be limited indeed. Watch out for bargains.

You can expect to pay top dollar for property that is without physical deficiencies. Some investors prefer to bargain hard for properties that need repair; these are often called "fixer-uppers." If you are handy with a hammer, saw, and paintbrush and can find a suitable property, you probably can make much more than wages for your efforts. Be careful, however, not to underestimate the extent and cost of the repairs needed. Those who lack experience in judging construction should consider using an inspection service. Minimally, you may have to have a pest control or termite inspection report prepared. Beyond that there are inspection service firms that will examine a structure and report on its structural problems, whether there may be a drainage or earth movement risk, and so on. You would do well to have the plumbing and heating systems checked out by a qualified specialist. If you are athletically inclined and know what to look for, you may want to check out the roof. The critical items for most structures are listed here. You need to determine the current or future repair and replacement expenses. These are important matters when it comes time to judge the offering price and to consider whether or not you might have some unpleasant future surprises if you are the owner.

How do you determine the age of property? Probably the best way is to inquire at the local building department to find out the date the building permit was issued. Failing that, you may need to check around, including asking the neighbors if they remember when the building was built. In some cases you can find a date on the underside of the toilet tank lid; it will show when it was manufactured. If this is the original equipment, the date will give you a good approximation. In one way or another, you should determine the age of the building for calculating past depreciation.

If equipment or furnishings are included in the proposed sale, make a list of the items and estimate their current market value. Later, if a purchase is made, these will be stated in a bill of sale; for now, determine their possible value. Such information may also be helpful if there is ever a dispute as to what is to be included in the deal. Sellers have been known

PROPERTY ANALYSIS FACT SHEET

Date _1-15-19XX_

Property address _220 ANBUS CRESCENT, ANYTOWN_

Owner or contact _JOE SELLER_ Phone _123-4567_

Description/use _8 - 2 BR UNITS UNFURNISHED RENTALS IN ONE BUILDING_

Investment features _BASE SHELTERING, LOW MAINTENANCE, MODERATE RENT LEVEL, TENANTS PAY ALL BUT WATER AND GARBAGE._

Location/neighborhood factors _GOOD PUBLIC TRANSPORTATION, STORES NEARBY_

Physical condition overall _AVERAGE_ Age _10_

Foundation/cellars _LOOKS OK_

Heating system _SEPARATE IN EACH APARTMENT_

Plumbing/water supply _OK_

Sewer/septic tank _PUBLIC SEWER_

Exterior paint _OK FOR NOW_

Interior paint/maintenance _2 UNITS NEED DECORATING_

Roof _LOOKS OKAY, SHOULD BE CHECKED_

Garaging/storage _GARAGES AT REAR FOR EACH UNIT - RENT EXTRA_

Laundry _4 WASHERS AND DRYERS IN SERVICE ROOM_

Furnishings/equipment _STOVE AND REFRIGERATOR IN EACH UNIT - SOME MAY HAVE TO BE REPLACED SOON_

Lot Lines/easements _APPEAR WELL DEFINED_

Special title aspects _NONE KNOWN_

Need appraisal? _NO_ Need pest control report? _NO_

Special features (remodeling, rehabilitation, subdividing) _NONE_

Comments _SELLER HAS DEAL ON OTHER PROPERTY, NEEDS TO CASH OUT THIS PROPERTY._

to have short memories of statements made in the excitement of offering property to a potential buyer. Again, for rental property, be certain you evaluate whether furnishings and equipment may have to be replaced at an early date; that could require a significant additional investment and something to be anticipated.

One of the potential hazards of owning property is the prospect of a dispute with a neighbor over the property line. Where there is a strong likelihood of this—and you should look for it when inspecting the property before the sale—you should consider obtaining a survey. By making this a condition of the purchase, most, if not all, of these difficulties can be avoided; you can determine in advance just what you are getting in the deal. Similar problems may exist with the title. Although these can be resolved through the use of title insurance, be alert for such problems when first exploring the property. If the seller remarks, for example, that he has inherited the property, that could tip off the possibility of an unclear title. You should make inquiries to find out just what the situation is to avoid spending time and money on a deal that might not be completed when you want it. This is not to imply there has to be a problem with title transferred through an estate, but it is a fact that sometimes it takes a long while to get everything straightened out, and such a time problem might be an important factor for you.

Shortly, we'll look at how you can make some calculations of market value yourself. Through experience you will learn to know when it might be useful to have a professional appraiser give you his or her estimate. Through some advance checking you can easily learn what such an appraisal would cost; you'll find property appraisers listed in the phone book. Perhaps your banker would recommend someone to you.

If the current owner has done some remodeling or repair, check to see if there are any warranties applicable and whether they would apply to purchasers. If the building, occupied by more than one tenant, does not have separate meters for utilities, check to see whether it is possible to convert and what it would cost. It has become more and more important for landlords to avoid having to pay variable rate utility bills whether for gas, electricity, or water. As these costs rise, and with limited incentives for tenants to conserve, the economic consequences for the owner can be devastating.

It is often suggested that a prospective purchaser should never agree to buy until there's been a chance to see the property during a rainstorm. Then you can see whether there's a drainage or earth movement problem and whether the sewage system is performing adequately. You must learn about the particular idiosyncracies of areas and neighborhoods where you are exploring investment opportunities. Problems not always obvious can come to haunt you after purchase. Most can be avoided through diligent inquiry and observation. And, finally, in some communities, sellers must present a certificate from local authorities certifying that the property meets specified building codes. As a part of your preinspection research, find out whether such is the case in your area and make certain you gain the benefit of such regulation.

As you become familiar with the inspection process, you will likely discover the need for information not specified on the form and you may devise your own version. For example, maybe in your area cable TV is a must, and properties not served by it are at a disadvantage. Keep on the alert to other matters important to your project.

Location

Previously we stated that location was all-important. So, you may now be wondering, "How do I know a good location? What do I look for to decide against a location?" Let's explore this subject further.

For property you are going to live in you will have fixed ideas about the need for schools, access to shopping, and transportation. Will you need a second car, for example, because you would be moving away from your present location where you could get to work on the bus? Or, maybe you could get rid of the second car because you'd have public transportation. Income property must be evaluated in terms of how its location meets the needs of tenants. If you are considering an investment in commercial property for retailing or office space, you will need to give location even greater attention. The very success of the business is dependent on a favorable spot. Through observation you can learn the characteristics of location that are deemed important by professionals. Study where banks, fast-food and other franchised businesses are located. Note that at intersections, for example, one corner can be infinitely better than the other three. Discover why. Landlords are subject to the success or failure of the tenants in commercial properties. You can help yourself and your tenants by having property in the right location.

Earlier we also commented on the importance of avoiding neighborhood decline. Check to see what land use is permitted in the immediate area of the property you are inspecting. Don't make assumptions based solely on observed current occupancies. You could wake up some day to find an undesirable activity taking place near your property which was fully permitted by the zoning. Alternatively, check with local authorities to see whether there is any potential for a change in zoning. There may be a new ordinance working its way through the legislative process that could, if passed, adversely or beneficially affect your investment. Arm yourself with appropriate information to avoid unpleasant surprises and to take advantage of prospective opportunities. If you are considering a property for remodeling including, for example, increasing the number of rental units, make certain your plan will not be thwarted by prohibitions at city hall. Make all offers subject to obtaining all the permits required to do what you have in mind. In this exploratory stage, find out whether it is even possible to do what you want.

Other Matters

There's no end to the information you must obtain before making a decision to invest. Here's a group of miscellaneous items.

Where there is shared ownership, such as in condominiums and co-op apartments, owners are subject to rules
and regulations beyond those normally associated with detached single-family homes. As an important part of your research when exploring this type of property, obtain a copy of
the rules and review them carefully to see if you could live
with them. Try to judge whether someone who will ultimately
buy the property from you might find them objectionable; if so
you'll have a resale problem. Whether you want to, or should,
live in shared ownership housing is a subject far too large
and complicated for this book. If you really enjoy democracy
and being subject to rules set by the majority, when you are
in the minority, you'll probably love a condominium. Buying
a condominium to rent out may not involve you directly in the
rules and regulations on a day-to-day basis but your tenants
might have a bad time; then they won't stay. Incidentally,
you may not be permitted to rent your condominium unit.

If the property is currently rented you will buy it subject to
rental agreements and outstanding leases. Be certain to obtain, in advance, copies of such agreements so you know
what you are getting into. This includes checking with tenants, face to face, not only to confirm what rent they are actually paying but also to determine whether the current owner
has made some special arrangements with them. Perhaps a
tenant has a rent concession for sweeping the halls or tending
to the garbage or garden. These concessions can affect income and expense.

You should determine, early in the negotiations, if there
are any easements. Perhaps a utility company or a neighbor
has a legal right to cross the property. Alternatively, the seller
may assert he (and hence you as the buyer) has a right to
cross someone else's property and yet that may not be so.
Legally recorded easements will be declared in the title insurance company's preliminary report, but you should follow
up any clue obtained during your initial inspections. The
matter of mineral rights may also come up in this connection.

In some areas of the country it is customary for buyers and

sellers to have the transaction handled by an attorney. In most cases this is an optional procedure. In some cases it would be imperative that you protect your rights through the use of legal counsel and you will have to learn to judge when that would be the case. Where escrows are handled by service firms or together with title insurance, many of the hazards of the transaction are minimized. As an investor your goal is to maximize the return on funds employed. Avoiding unnecessary expense is important; so is avoiding risks.

Now we've reached the end of the first page of the Fact Sheet. We're ready to move to the collection of financial information.

Financing

Because the vast majority of property purchases are made with the use of borrowed funds, we will make such an assumption for this discussion. Further, we recognize that you will want to bargain over the total purchase price if you decide to buy; but for the purpose of the analysis, you will want to enter at the top of the sheet the seller's asking price. In a later chapter we'll explore how you might persuade the seller to accept a lesser amount.

At the time you are seriously inspecting a property, you may not have firm data on financing. Whatever information you do have should be entered here. Perhaps the owner has a good loan on the property and you have been told you can assume it. You'll need to make certain of that later by checking personally with the lender. Some sellers, in anticipation of a buyer's needs, arrange for a loan commitment. This means they have asked a lender to inspect the property and state, preferably in writing, the maximum loan and terms they would make to a qualified borrower. In other cases, a real estate broker involved in the property may be able to give a good estimate of the financing available. In arranging financing you probably should get a loan for the longest term possible because the greater the time over which payments are to be made, the lower will those payments be; smaller payments require less cash flow from the property or from the family budget. Lenders and brokers usually have loan payment tables and can quickly tell you what the payment amount would be. Because you may not always be able to ask someone for this information, we have provided a set of amortization tables in the Appendix. You can use them to compute a monthly loan payment and related information.

To use the tables, select a loan term and interest rate. For the appropriate combination, you can find the monthly payment factor for each $1,000 of loan. Multiply the factor from the table against the loan amount, in thousands, and you'll have what you need.

Lenders, to compensate for mortgage interest rates below what money is really worth, charge *mortgage points*. The point charge will fluctuate as the contract interest rate stays constant. For example, you might be able to get a mortgage at 12½ percent, subject to 3 points. This means that although you will pay interest at 12½ percent per annum on the loan balance, the lender will deduct 3 percent of the original loan amount from the funds sent to the escrow. Assume you have been approved for a loan of $150,000. The lender would impose a point charge of $4,500 and you would actually receive only $145,500 in loan proceeds. To show you what your actual simple interest rate is on this loan, the lender is required under the federal Truth in Lending Law, for loans to consumers, to express the Annual Percentage Rate (APR). Here it would be approximately 12⅞ percent. Note that regardless of how the rate is stated, you must allow for the point charge when computing the number of dollars you'll need to complete the deal. The easiest way to think of all this is to just add the amount of the loan fees and point charge to the settlement or closing costs you'll need over and above what you can borrow.

All borrowing, including loans granted by the seller, is to be stated in this section of the form. Your objective here is to calculate the amount of the cash down payment, the differ-

FINANCING

ASKING PRICE $ **250,00**

Data for Mortgage Loans

Source or Lender	Interest Rate	Term in Years	Monthly* Payment	Loan Fees or Points	Loan Amount
Bank	11%	30	1.762	2 pts.	$ 185,000
Seller	12%	25	105	—	$ 10,000
					$

TOTAL BORROWING $ 195,00

Comments re prepayment penalty, etc. *No penalty*

2nd loan due in 5yrs.   CASH DOWN PAYMENT $ 55,000

*Monthly payment computation:

$$\underset{\text{Loan in \$1,000s}}{185} \times \underset{\text{Factor}}{9.52323} = \$ \underset{\text{Payment}}{1,761.80}$$

Settlement Costs

	Expense	Capitalize	
Title Insurance	$	$ 820	
Escrow Fees	$	$ 330	
Legal Fees	$	$ 250	
Appraisal/Inspection	$	$ 250	
Prorations	$ 750	$	
Mortgage Points/Loan Fees	$	$ 3,700	
Miscellaneous	$ 500	$	$
TOTAL COSTS	$ 1,250	$ 5,350	$ 6,600

TOTAL CASH INVESTED $ 61,600

Notes re damage/advance rent deposits *$1,800 Cash from seller*
for deposits.

ence between the purchase price and the borrowing. There is more to a mortgage loan than the amount, interest rate, and monthly payments. For some loans, the lender can impose a penalty if you pay it off ahead of time; this is known as a *prepayment penalty*. This practice is less prevalent now than in the past, but you should check every loan to see whether this penalty applies. It can be an unpleasant surprise when, at the time you are selling property and the loan is being refinanced, you discover that part of your anticipated gain must be used to satisfy this penalty. And there's another feature of financing to be considered. Frequently a seller will offer to take back a second mortgage, agree to monthly payments for a time, but require that on some future *due date* you pay off the balance in full. This is known as a *balloon payment*. Because this usually will call for a significant cash payment downstream, you must not overlook it; record the details in the Fact Sheet.

Settlement Costs

Until the *Real Estate Settlement Procedures Act* (RESPA) was passed by Congress in 1974, there was little uniformity throughout the country with respect to how a variety of costs associated with buying and selling homes were handled. In some areas they were called *closing costs;* now, thanks to RESPA, not only are there rules to adhere to, but the term applied universally to them is *settlement costs*. What are they? You can see a listing of the usual items on the second page of the Fact Sheet. In any specific transaction it is unlikely that you will have a cost for each and every item, but it is possible. In any event, you need to determine what these expenses would be and record them. If you are buying property to live in, lenders are required to give you estimates in advance of the closing of the deal. One of the purposes of these regulations is to prompt borrowers to shop around to see if they can gain from the resulting competition among those who provide these services. You, too, regardless of the type of property, will want to do whatever is necessary to minimize your costs.

You may need to check out local custom concerning some of these costs. For example, in some areas the seller pays the cost of title insurance; in others, it is the buyer's responsibility. There are even places where this cost is split evenly between the parties. The cost of a termite inspection report usually is borne by the buyer but the repairs required by the report will be assessed against the seller unless the parties agree otherwise.

Now what is this item, *prorations?* When you own property, there are certain expenses which are paid in advance and others in arrears. For example, property taxes may be paid twice a year so that, depending on when the property is sold, the seller may be entitled to a credit because he or she has paid up the taxes. Or, the buyer may have to pay the bill for time prior to when title passed. In that case, the buyer gets a credit. Further adjustments between buyer and seller also may be needed for rent and damage deposits. In this section your goal is to take into account all the possible reasons for which you must put up cash in order to complete the deal; the total amount is to be added to the cash down payment to give you the grand total you'll need.

A quick comment regarding the columns *expense* and *capitalize.* Many of the items on this page will be explained in greater detail in the chapter on Borrowing Money, but at this point you need to know how to decide which column to enter. The decision is determined largely by income tax regulations. Uncle Sam requires that most of the settlement costs items, especially for investment property, be capitalized. This has the effect of adding them to the cost of the property rather than permitting you to add them to your operating expenses, thus reducing current taxable income; Uncle Sam is dedicated to the open hand policy. In most cases you would enter all settlement costs in the *capitalize* column except prorations. Later we will explore the finer points of this procedure. Ultimately you may want your tax counsel to advise you in deals where substantial sums are involved and important differences in tax liability can result.

One final comment regarding costs when you are borrowing to buy a home to live in. Some lenders, depending on the type of loan, may require that, in addition to monthly payments of principal and interest, you make monthly payments toward the property taxes and fire insurance. These amounts are then collected into a loan trust fund or impound account by the lender. When the bills come in, they are paid from that account. In some areas, lenders are required to pay modest amounts of interest. If you are making monthly payments on your home loan that include these items, you will find your payment amount will change from time to time as taxes and insurance costs change. The basic part of the payment, for principal and interest, will not change unless you have borrowed on one of the special, new alternative mortgage instruments. More on those later.

So now we've completed the fact-gathering phase of the project as far as financing is concerned. But there are two major topics remaining: data on operating expenses and income and information for computing economic values and income taxes if we become the owner.

Operating Income and Expenses

In this section we must record the details of all the expected cash flows for an entire year as if we owned and operated the property. You will draw this information from the seller, from a broker if one is involved, and by speaking with the tenants if this is an income property project. Recall that this set of forms can be used for a wide variety of property and don't be surprised to find that you don't have data for every line.

Rental Income. This figure must be decided upon after considering several matters. The total maximum amount of rent can be achieved only if every unit is occupied, each tenant pays in full, and rates are at the maximum for the entire year. That total is often called the "gross scheduled rent" for the property. If leases come due at various times in the year and you plan to increase rents for renewals, such changes could be taken into account when computing the total. Above all, you want a realistic number—the operating results of the property depend largely on the amount of rental income collected. For properties where tenants pay for laundry services, for example, and the amount is other than trivial, you should include an estimate. Expenses associated with these services will be included later and the revenue should be taken into account in order to have meaningful results.

During the course of a year it is reasonable to expect to suffer some loss of rents, primarily from vacancies. You can use the past history of the property as a guide; but remember, you will be the new operator and perhaps you'll have a different experience. To get the value here, either estimate in dollars what the loss might be and enter it or use an industry benchmark such as 5 percent of gross rents and calculate the extension. When demand is not at its peak, it would be more conservative to estimate 10 percent.

If you collect rents beyond the first month—rent should always be charged in advance—such as the "last month's" rent at the time the tenant moves in, the question will arise as to how to handle it in your record and estimates. It should be counted as rental income at the time collected, according to the IRS, even though it ultimately will apply to a future month. Some property owners set the funds aside and draw them into income when the tenant's last month arrives. In that way the cash flow is evened out. For estimating purposes, you need the value for a full twelve months, exclusive of amounts in hand for advance payments and/or damage deposits. The latter, of course, are not to be considered rental income at least until they are actually applied to pay for damages incurred.

Because of the critical nature of the revenue figure, it must be accurate. Where you can, you should confirm with tenants what you have been told about rents and lease terms. Later

OPERATING INCOME AND EXPENSES*

Annual Income

Rents $ _33,600_

Services $ _1,200_

Gross Annual Income $ _34,800_

Less Vacancy At _1_ % $ _350_

NET ANNUAL CASH INCOME $ _34,450_

Annual Operating Expenses

Property Taxes	$ _2,800_
Insurance	$ _800_
Utilities	$ _1,000_
Gardening	$ _1,200_
Maintenance	$ _3,000_
Management	$ _____
Miscellaneous	$ _1,500_
TOTAL CASH OPERATING EXPENSES	$ _10,300_

Annual Financing Expenses

Monthly Payment

First loan $ _1,762_

Second loan $ _105_

Third loan $ _____

Total $ _1,867_ × 12

TOTAL MORTGAGE PAYMENTS $ _22,404_

First Year Mortgage Interest Expense

Loan in $1,000's		Factor		Interest
_185_	×	_109.778_	= $	_20,309_
_10_	×	_119.637_	= $	_1,196_
_____	×	_____	= $	_____

TOTAL ANNUAL INTEREST EXPENSE $ _21,505_

*Assume purchase at beginning of the year; use annual figures.

when you decide to make an offer, you can always condition it upon checking the rent roll and if you find discrepancies, you may have the option of backing out. For now, do whatever is necessary to obtain accurate data; otherwise all the time and energy devoted to the analysis will be wasted. Some sellers will assert that they have been reluctant to raise rents because the tenants have been there so long but that you, as a new landlord, would have no difficulty whatever in bringing rents up to market level. Go slowly in your evaluation of such a prospect. If you have been checking the market, you'll know whether the rents for the property are in fact too low and whether they could be raised. In completing the Fact Sheet, use only figures you deem to be realistic.

Operating Expenses. Whenever possible, obtain data from an authentic source. In the case of property taxes, do not be misled by tax bills shown by the seller. They often will be bills paid for a prior period and will not necessarily reflect what you, as a new owner, will have to pay in a future tax year. Visit the tax assessor's office and get correct information from the official source. In some areas those who occupy owned property as their principal residence receive tax concessions either in the form of tax credits or reductions in assessed valuation. If you buy property for which a concession has applied in the past but won't apply to you, be certain you allow for that when deciding on the amount to show for this major expense. You must have the assessed value for a computation to be described shortly, and that's another reason for not relying on an owner or a broker for property tax data. A reminder: all entries in this section are to be made for a full year. Don't make the mistake of using only one semiannual tax installment, for example.

If you find the assessed value, and hence the property tax amount, is out of date, allow for the strong likelihood that if you buy, the values will be updated. Future tax bills will be calculated according to a current tax rate applied to a current assessed value. Don't expect to fool the tax assessor, either at all or for very long.

The cost of insurance for the property can readily be determined by talking to your insurance advisor. You may be offered the opportunity to take over the unexpired portion of the seller's policy and if, for example, it's being thrown into the deal, you will want to consider it. Consider, too, whether it would be for the correct amount or type. For our estimate of operating expenses, however, what we need is the expected cost, for twelve months' insurance, for the coverage and amount suitable for the situation. Again, a realistic number is needed and it can be obtained with a minimum of effort at this time.

Take extra care to determine what utility expense you'll have. If this is to be your home you must correctly anticipate what these very important costs will be. For income property you must know exactly which expenses are to be paid by the tenants and, therefore, what your responsibility will be. Past data offered by the seller can be useful, but you will want to hedge, usually, and add something to take care of future changes and unpleasant surprises.

Especially in the case of apartment property, the landlord may face significant expense for gardening and keeping the property neat and tidy. The seller's policies may not necessarily be yours. Be sure you reflect adequately in your expense estimate what you plan to do. In some cases a tenant may receive a rent offset for doing some work around the property. Where we are making estimates, it is best to ignore such arrangements. You would include full rent in the income figures and the expected cash expense if you paid someone to do the work. Then you will have a more accurate forecast.

Once you acquire ownership, you may in your financial planning decide to set up a "reserve" for maintenance and repairs. Realize that for income tax purposes you can't use reserves, only actual expenditures. For estimating purposes in the Fact Sheet, you need a number which you seriously believe will be the actual cash expenditure incurred during the year. This will be affected by plans you may have to upgrade the property and to remedy defects. You can make a distinction between operating expenses and capital expenditures; at this point we want only the expense items.

You will make an entry for management expense only if you expect to employ someone to perform such services; you cannot pay yourself. Again, if a tenant is to collect the rents, for example, and receive a reduction in rent, treat this as before and count the amount as a cost and include it also in rental income.

For larger properties you will need several additional expense categories: advertising, accounting, legal services, and so on. For estimating purposes, these can be lumped together under the heading of miscellaneous. If you are considering a condominium unit for your own use, don't overlook the amount of the fees payable to the homeowners' association; it can be substantial. Recall, of course, it usually covers your share of the property taxes, insurance, maintenance, and repairs for the common areas; you will have a separate bill for property taxes and insurance on your own unit. When you add that all up you may be dismayed, but remember: no more lawn mowing, snow shoveling, or exterior painting!

We've now reached a total for the cash operating expense. This figure should represent your very best judgment as to the total of all checks you would issue during one year. If you are using borrowed funds, you will also have to write checks to pay at least the interest; more commonly you'll be repaying some of the debt as well.

Annual Financing Expense. Unlike rental payments, mortgage payments are made to cover time that has passed. Interest is charged in arrears and relates, therefore, to the time for which the money has been used. For estimating, all you need is the amount of the periodic payment for interest and principal for each separate loan, then multiply the amount by the number of times in the year the payment is to be made. If the lender asks for payments to the loan trust fund, discussed above, separate out the amount for that purpose so that you record only principal and interest; if not, you will be counting the expense for property taxes and insurance twice. You should have the annual costs for those items recorded in the preceding section.

Later, to project after-tax cash flows, we'll need to know how mortgage payments are being allocated between interest and principal. Now, when we are gathering data on the payments, is a good time to prepare the data. Probably the easiest way to obtain the amount of interest cost, separate from the portion of the payment applied to reduce the loan, is to use the tables in the Appendix. To find the factor to enter on the Fact Sheet, locate the mortgage amortization table for the loan interest rate and term and select the appropriate value from the column labeled *interest,* for the first year. Multiply the original loan amount in thousands by the factor to obtain the interest expense. Repeat for each loan and sum the amounts. If the loan is not being amortized, you will need to estimate the annual interest expense by applying the interest rate against what you judge the average loan balance would be for the year and thus estimate the total annual interest expense. We'll consider more of the details of nonamortizing or stipulated payment loans in a following chapter.

Summary

It is not possible, of course, to cover absolutely all of the situations you might encounter in gathering data for an investment. Through experience you will discover when you need data not allowed for in the Fact Sheets and you then can add to what you have here. In business income property, for example, if the tenants are to pay percentage rents, you will want to estimate carefully the prospects for receiving amounts over and above the base rent and then decide whether to include something in your forecast. Some investors take a conservative position and forecast on the basis of no overages and then, if they are received, that's just a bonus. In other cases, of course, an investment would not be viable without overages so estimates are vital. In any case, the task of

evaluating an opportunity is greatly simplified if you develop
all of the data needed for analysis and record it as illustrated.

Valuation

One of the most important steps is judging whether the
asking price is appropriate. Professional appraisers use a
series of computations to arrive at their estimate of fair market value and while we are not going to attempt to perform a
professional appraisal, we can be guided by how they do
their work. If we have the right information, we can even
make some rough estimates of value along the lines of their
procedure. We now come to the section of the Fact Sheets
where we record the data required.

Tax Assessments.   Previously, we discussed the need for
an accurate estimate of property tax expense. While gathering that information we have an opportunity to find out what
the tax assessor has in mind as a basis for valuation. In many
jurisdictions the assessor is required to present the property
owner with both assessed and fair market values. For the
property being evaluated, find out what these numbers are
and enter them on the form. A word of caution, however. You
need values that are applicable at the time you are entering
them. Use assessed values on which future taxes will be
based, not last year's, for example. If fair market values are
not stated on tax bills, or otherwise given, find out what the
relationship is between assessed values and the market. In
some states, for example, the assessed value must be a fixed
percentage of what the assessor judges the market value to be.
Let's say that is 25 percent. If you know that the assessed value of the land is $10,000, then the market value, in
the eyes of the tax assessor would be four times that, or
$40,000. It is true that the real market value may not be well
represented by the assessor's opinion; often the assessment
process is delayed and the market races ahead. Through inquiry, you will be able to find out the situation and make appropriate adjustments. One adjustment you might have to

VALUATION

Tax Assessments

	Assessed Value	Fair Market Value
Land	$ 12,500	$ 50,000
Structures/Improvements	$ 50,000	$ 200,000
Equipment/Personal Property	$	$
TOTALS	$ 62,500	$ 250,000

Construction Costs

Building Location or Type	Area	Current Cost per square foot	Current Construction Cost
Apartment	8,000	× $ 30.00	= $ 240,000
Garages	1,800	× $ 8.00	= $ 14,400
		× $	= $

TOTAL REPLACEMENT COST—BUILDINGS $ 254,400

Less past depreciation at ___1___ % per year for ___10___ years = $ 25,440

DEPRECIATED COST OF BUILDINGS $ 228,960

Add: Depreciated value of equipment $ 1,500

Market value of land $ 50,000

Value of landscaping $ 2,000

TOTAL ADDITIONS $ 53,500

TOTAL REPRODUCTION COST OF PROPERTY ($ 282,460)

FUTURE DEPRECIATION COMPUTATION

Buildings

$ _200,000_ ÷ _30_ = $ _6,667_
Amount to be depreciated   Years remaining   Straight Line Annual Charge

Method to be used:	Type	Factor
(Circle one)	Straight Line	(1.00)
	125% Declining Balance	1.25
	Double-Declining Balance	2.00

$ _6,667_ × _1.00_ = ANNUAL DEPRECIATION ($ 6,667)
Annual Charge   Factor

Equipment

Value to be depreciated is $ _1,500_ over _3_ years.

Method and computation of annual charge

Straight line   ANNUAL DEPRECIATION ($ 500)

make in your thinking is that it might be quite all right to pay an asking price that exceeds the assessor's fair market value. More later on how to use valuation data.

Construction Costs.   Getting the data for this section will require some digging. The goal is to find out what a contractor would charge today to build the structure you're looking at, on the land in place. Typically, these costs are measured at so much a square foot. Record the number of square feet in the structure while you are inspecting the property. You can approximate this simply by pacing off the exterior of the building; don't overlook extra floors in the main structure nor garages or other areas. The current square-foot cost should be obtained by talking with those who are building today the type of construction involved. Perhaps you are lucky and can locate the firm that built the property you're looking at. Incidentally, we have no interest in original cost; with the way costs have increased, we probably don't want to know what the cost was new—that information might be very discouraging.

Now we need to estimate the impact of the passage of time and use since the building was new. Here's where we use the age, developed earlier. For many properties it is in order to use a rate of 1 percent a year. If the property has been badly abused, or been subject to substantial remodeling, that would not apply. Assume the property was built fifteen years ago. We then would deduct 15 percent of the total replacement cost of the building to arrive at the *depreciated* cost today. For very old buildings you would not depreciate beyond 50 percent, assuming they were fully usable. To reflect below average physical condition, you might go as high as 2 percent a year.

Next, you need to estimate the value of the other components of the property. If you are buying equipment of any significance, you'll need to guess what its value is. Appliances, carpeting, and furnishings are subject to rapid depreciation as a rule and you will want to be conservative in setting values. It is easy to check what it would cost to buy comparable used items and that will guide you. Setting the value of the land is another matter.

Ideally, you would be able to locate an identical vacant lot that was for sale; its sales price would represent its value for our purpose here. More often you will have to use dissimilar land and use some common sense. Real estate brokers can be very helpful when they have experience in the area and with the kind of property you are buying. Finally, you'll have to set some value for landscaping, perhaps a swimming pool, and cement work, such as driveways and parking lots. Avoid leaving anything out of your tally. When you've done your job properly, you'll have a realistic amount for use as the reproduction cost of the property as a whole.

Summary

Don't overlook the fact that at this stage you are only gathering information; we'll treat how it is to be used shortly. But while considering valuation data, you might be wondering why you shouldn't be writing down what similiar properties are selling for as a basis of comparison. Don't let us discourage you from that activity, but you may have trouble using it to advantage. No two properties are exactly the same, except perhaps in the case of new housing tracts, and even then, depending on how the sale is financed, selling prices may not really be comparable. No; for now, forget about other market prices. You can select between two or more properties by evaluating each of them as we are doing here and, as a byproduct, you might learn something about the relationship of sales prices.

Future Depreciation

If the property you are looking at is to be used to generate income, you will be able to deduct depreciation expense when computing taxable income. This does not apply to your home, so this section can be skipped if you are analyzing a home purchase. Of course, you may be planning to rent out part of the property and if so, depreciation needs to be considered. If you plan to offer a second home for rent, you also may be able to reduce taxes through depreciation. In no case can land be depreciated, so keep that in mind and deal only with the value of structures and equipment and furnishings.

We need first to calculate the total amount to be depreciated and then select the method to be used. Our goal is to come up with the amount for use in computing net taxable income for the first year we will own the property. The purpose of all of this is to apportion fairly over the useful life of the buildings and equipment, their cost; the underlying assumption is that ultimately they will be of no value. It is obvious it would be unreasonable to charge the original cost in its entirety to the first year's income, so through the process of depreciation, the amount by which the value is being used up is appropriately offset by income. All depreciation values are estimates; the final adjustment comes when property is sold. The net effect is to transform current income into long-term capital gain, thus minimizing income taxes. During the holding period, however, care should be taken with respect to the depreciation method chosen because some options will produce more favorable tax treatment than others.

All the rules for dealing with depreciation expense are prescribed by the Internal Revenue Service. You should obtain a copy of their Publication 534, *Tax Information on Depreciation,* and thus have all the official data needed. The larger the amount of depreciation charged for the year, the smaller will be your tax liability. Through comparing results for each of the options IRS gives you, you can make a good decision. Bear in mind that the ultimate test may be a visit with an IRS agent during which you will have to explain the basis for your calculations; do your homework here.

Amount to Be Depreciated.   To obtain the initial total for depreciation, take the offering price and add to it the capitalized expense portion of the settlement costs. Then deduct a fair value for personal property (equipment), if included.

(Later, when you prepare your tax return as the owner of the property, you will use the actual purchase price and costs; remember, here we are analyzing a prospective purchase and must use estimates.) Next we must determine a fair basis for allocating the purchase price and costs between land and improvements. One satisfactory method is to use the same percentage the tax assessor did in apportioning assessed values. From the property tax data you can quickly calculate the distribution. If, for example, the amounts are:

Item	Assessed Value
Land	$10,000
Improvements	$40,000

you would conclude that 20 percent of the total value is attributable to the land. If your purchase price including costs was $200,000, you then would say that the total amount of depreciation for the buildings would be $160,000 (80 percent of $200,000).

As you look at the Fact Sheet and the Valuation section you may wonder at this point why you wouldn't just use the amount computed for the *depreciated cost of buildings*. Realize that the value there was calculated as an appraisal figure and does not relate directly to what you will actually pay for the property. True, we will use it in judging what the property is worth and what we should offer, but it is not the best figure to use for estimating depreciation expense.

By following the procedure outlined above, you will have the figure to enter for the *Amount to be depreciated*. Next we need the estimated useful life remaining for the property.

Useful Life. The shorter the life of the property, the larger will be the annual depreciation charge and the lower the income tax. Now you know what your target is. Don't forget you may have the IRS asking questions. Here are some guides along the lines of the IRS rules.

In general, the IRS considers that a new structure such as an apartment or commercial building will have a life of forty years. From that you can estimate a reasonable remaining life for used property. Take its age and deduct it from forty. Here's where we use the age of the property as determined earlier. If, for example, the property is ten years old, you then would use thirty years for its remaining life. But what if the building is already forty years old and going strong? You then would likely use ten years, or even more if the property was in good shape. The loan term may also provide a basis. Certainly if a lender agrees to a twenty-five year loan, it would be inconsistent for you to use a fifteen year remaining life, unless you know something about the condition of the property the lending officer didn't discover. Note now that the amount you enter after dividing the years remaining into the total is termed the *straight line annual charge*. This will be used in computing the ultimate depreciation expense.

Depreciation Method.   Your choice here will directly affect the amount of income taxes you pay both each year and finally on the long-term capital gain or loss. The minimum depreciation amount will be the straight line annual charge; under some conditions this can be increased. To do so you must determine if your property is eligible for a form of accelerated depreciation.

If you buy new property and are the first user, you can elect to use, for example, the 200 percent declining balance method for residential income property and 150 percent for all other types. This would allow you, for example, to take twice (200 percent) the straight line rate the first year you owned a new apartment. If, instead, the property is already in use and at least 80 percent of the rental income is generated by residential tenants, you can choose to use the 125 percent declining balance method. For all other types of used property you are restricted to using the straight line method. After you've studied the IRS rules and made your choice, apply the appropriate factor to the *Annual Charge* and enter the result in the box for *Annual Depreciation*.

If your goal is to maximize tax sheltering, you will want to use accelerated depreciation if you can. Be aware, however, that there are some other factors to consider when you do.

The amount by which the accelerated depreciation exceeds the straight line charge is to be taken into account on your income tax return when determining whether you are subject to the 15 percent minimum tax on perference items. Further, by increasing the amount of annual depreciation, you increase the amount of gain to be taxed when the asset is sold. You may need to judge what change may take place in your tax rate to decide whether this might be a disadvantage. When in doubt consult with professional tax counsel.

Equipment. When buying property that includes appliances and other items of personal property, you must estimate its fair market value, what its remaining useful life is, and what the salvage value will be. Consult the IRS materials for options regarding depreciation methods. Note that it is necessary to use a figure for salvage here; we did not when computing depreciation for real property. Further, it is common to use accelerated depreciation, such as the sum-of-the-years digits method to reflect the fact that equipment tends to depreciate more quickly at first. If you buy new equipment, under current rules, you can take, in the first year, an extra 20 percent of the cost as depreciation expense. Let's assume you are looking at an investment opportunity where you will replace all the equipment with new items at the time you take over the property. You estimate this will cost $15,000 and you plan to use a five-year useful life. Here's how you would calculate the amount to be depreciated for use with either the straight line or sum-of-the-years digits method (SYD):

Total cost	$ 15,000
Less 20%	3,000
	$ 12,000
Less salvage	2,000
Depreciation total	$ 10,000

The annual straight line amount would be 20 percent or $2,000. The first year under the SYD method would be

$^5/_{15}$ of \$10,000 = \$3,333. See the IRS materials for how this is computed.

Summary. The way you calculate depreciation expense can be critical in determining your investment results. For complex properties you will want professional assistance both in selecting the method and in computing values. For the majority of properties, however, you can do the calculations yourself simply by following what is written here and using the IRS publications; you might even visit the IRS and ask them for help. Don't be afraid.

CLOSING THOUGHTS

The purpose of digging up information and recording it on the Fact Sheet is to provide you with all the data needed to analyze the investment property selected. Once completed for each opportunity to be considered, you'll be able to determine which is the better place in which to invest your money. By now you will see that there's obviously some work and effort required. Because you will face so many properties from which to choose, make the selection carefully to avoid spending time on those for which the prospects of being satisfactory, for your purposes, are slim. Each time you do an analysis, you are investing part of yourself. Each one you do will, of course, enable you to do the next one faster and better. Get started.

Before you get carried away, however, we need to review where and how to borrow money. Then we'll go over the procedure for using the Fact Sheet information to reach decisions.

5

Borrowing Money

*It's not a sin to use other people's money, with their
permission. It may be a sin not to pay it back, however. In order to increase your investment opportunities and the likelihood for acceptable returns
using real estate, you should borrow—prudently, of
course. This means you must know how much can
be used profitably, where to find lenders, and how
to handle a borrowing transaction. And, above all,
you must have a satisfactory plan for repayment
and not jeopardize your financial well-being.*

LEVERAGE

Perhaps you were brought up to believe you ought to be
conservative in financial matters and that you should use
only your own funds. In that way, if things go badly, you are
risking only your own assets. Unless you have unlimited
funds, however, you will miss out on opportunities to
achieve substantial returns that often are possible only
through the use of leverage. You simply can do much more
when you stretch every one of your dollars by borrowing
three or four more to go with it. Be assured there is nothing
here that will require special persuasion on your part. Lenders are attracted to making loans when the security is an interest in real property; the mortgage loan business is huge
and all you need to tap it is a little know-how. That's the purpose of this chapter—to provide you with instructions in
how to arrange to borrow money to use with your own in
making an investment in real estate.

MORTGAGING THE FUTURE

A loan is a substitute for cash you don't have or don't wish to commit. When used to acquire an ownership interest in real estate, the property becomes the collateral or security for the loan. If you default in repaying the money, the lender expects to be able to take the property, sell it, and use the proceeds to pay off your debt. You, of course, do not expect not to be able to pay off the loan so this need never happen. If the investment is in property that generates rental income, that revenue is expected to be enough to cover the loan payments of principal and interest as well as the operating expenses. If you decide to sell the property before you have repaid all the indebtedness, loan balances will then be paid out of the proceeds of the sale. As long as the value of the property has not diminished to the point where it is less than the unpaid loan balances, there should not be any problems. As we will see, lenders must evaluate loan opportunities according to the risk of loss. By understanding the procedure, you should be able to maximize your chances of using borrowed cash.

Terminology

In all cases the borrower executes a promissory note for the total amount of the loan; the terms of the note will include the interest rate, length of time for which money is borrowed, and the terms of repayment. We then say that the note is secured by a security interest in the real property by means of the terms and conditions of the mortgage loan agreement. Hence the expression *mortgage loan.* The word *mortgage* refers to the contract in which the lender, called the *mortgagee,* is given the right to *foreclose* in the event the borrower, the *mortgagor,* fails to meet the obligation to repay or violates some other provision of the loan agreement. When that occurs the borrower will be declared to be in *default.* In some areas, the mortgage has been replaced by a *deed of trust* or *trust deed.* In the deed of trust contract, the borrower signs a deed in which title to the property is passed to the lender. This is held by a trustee, such as a bank or title insurance company, which will use it to actually allow transfer of the title to the lender only when there is a default. The procedure is designed to simplify and speed up the foreclosure process to enable the lender to recover the loan balance. For our purposes we will consider mortgage and trust deed to mean the same thing and, therefore, they will be used interchangeably. A mortgage is also called a *lien* or an *encumbrance*.

Priority. Mortgages are referred to as *first, second, third,* and so on. The numbering indicates the status of the lender's rights to payment in the event of default or foreclosure. Foreclosure means action taken by the lender, through legal procedures, to seize the property, sell it and apply the proceeds to what is owing. The holder of a second mortgage may not receive anything if there is a default and the property is worth no more than enough to pay off the first loan. Mortgage loans other than first are often called *junior* loans because the right to foreclosure proceeds are subject to the rights of a preceding mortgage interest. In recent years a new type of junior mortgage has been introduced, the *wraparound or all-inclusive* trust deed. Shortly, we'll discuss how this works and you may quite likely structure your financing in this way.

Credit. Next we look at the terms used by lenders when considering mortgage loan applications. The lender's risk is that the borrower will fail to make payments on the loan and foreclosure will be required. The borrower's reputation for meeting obligations, often called *credit-worthiness*, is an important matter. You maximize your credit-worthiness by always paying your bills on time. Credit bureaus and other reporting agencies will then say all the right things about you when a potential lender inquires. Next comes the measure of the collateral.

Equity. The lender will have a loss ultimately if, after paying all the costs of foreclosure and receiving the proceeds of the sale of the property, not enough cash was realized to pay off the loan balance. The key here then is the amount of the original loan relative to the potential liquidation value of the property. But there's another aspect and it has to do with motivation. If the borrower has very little to lose through default, if there is a problem, he or she may have little reason to do whatever is necessary to solve the problem and keep up the loan payments. The measure of what a borrower has to lose is called *equity*. It is the difference between what the property could be sold for and the total of all the debts outstanding against it. Lenders are more comfortable if the borrower stands to lose a lot if he or she defaults; experience shows that the greater the equity, the less likely this is to happen.

Loan Ratio.   As stated, lenders are concerned about the relationship of the loan amount to the total value of the property. An important part of the loan transaction, therefore, is the appraisal. Lenders employ professional appraisers to provide estimates of fair market value. That value may or may not be the same as the proposed purchase price. Next the lender will apply a *loan-to-value ratio* according to the type of property and borrower. For most financial institutional lenders for loans on income property, the ratio will not likely exceed 75 percent. If the appraised value is $300,000, the most the lender would loan is $225,000. But don't values change? Indeed they do. You hope and expect the value of your property will increase. If in fact it does, the lender will see its protection against loss increasing. Lenders must, however, be aware of the possibility that values can go down. They can be very helpful in identifying situations where there is a real chance this could happen; you need that help *before* you make a deal.

Deficiency Judgment.   If a lender has a legal right to pursue a borrower for an unsatisfied debt after the security has been liquidated, we say that the borrower is exposed to the possibility of a *deficiency judgment*. In many areas lenders are not allowed to do this. You should inquire locally to see what the situation would be for you. Your risk is limited if a lender can look only to the value of the secured property.

Insured Loans.   Lenders can reduce their risk of loss through the use of mortgage insurance. Both public and private mortgage insurance programs are available.

Until recently the best known and most widely used mortgage insurance was provided by the federal government through the Federal Housing Administration (FHA) section of the Department of Housing and Urban Development (HUD). This continues to be a very important matter in the financing of single-family homes and apartments. Similarly, eligible veterans have the benefit of the GI loan program administered by the Veterans Administration; it insures mortgages. Some states also have special veteran loan programs in which lenders are protected, or the state makes the loan directly. Government-insured or assisted loan plans, however, are of limited use for investments. If you are exploring a home purchase, you certainly will want to ask your bank or savings and loan association about this type of financing—the benefits by way of lower interest rates and liberal terms are very attractive.

Typically, loans for investment real estate are termed *conventional*, thus designating that no government insurance is involved. There may be private mortgage insurance instead, however. Through private enterprise, insurance against loss arising from mortgage defaults is used by lenders to make it possible to lend larger amounts, or for longer terms and more favorable rates. The cost of the insurance is borne by the borrower. All this works well for home loans, too, serving to reduce down payments. Again, if you need a loan to buy a house to live in, ask your lender about it.

Secondary Market. As you explore the world of real estate finance, you may encounter the expression *secondary market*. You will not likely ever deal directly with it, but you do need to know about it. Lenders, after making loans, may wish to sell the mortgages to obtain funds to make more loans. This is done through the secondary market; the loans are sold to other financial institutions and investors and the original lender often continues to collect the payments and service the loans in their behalf. Because of this, the mortgage loan money supply is more liquid than it might otherwise be.

Financial Institutions. Whom do we mean when referring to a financial institution? It could be a bank, savings and loan association, savings bank, life insurance company, or pension fund. All of these entities are big in making mortgage loans. Many, however, operate through intermediaries that deal directly with borrowers. An important group is known as *mortgage bankers*. These firms function as mortgage loan correspondents throughout the country and may be approached directly.

Short-term Loans.   Generally a mortgage loan is made for a term of several years, perhaps as many as thirty or even longer. There can be an occasion when you need to borrow for a very short time, however, and a mortgage lender won't be able to solve your problem. This can arise, for example, when you are selling one property and buying another and there will be a gap between the times when funds are available from the sale and when you need them for the other property. Private lenders and some banks lend cash for this purpose; they are called *gap, bridge,* or *swing* loans.

Now that you have acquired this new language, what's next?

SOURCES

To some extent the source for your financing will be dictated by the particular deal you are working on. Most of the time, however, choices are available and you will want to explore them. If you are using a real estate broker, you should expect substantial assistance in finding the best financing, both in terms of the maximum amount and the most favorable repayment terms. When dealing directly with the seller, you may have to make all the financing arrangements yourself. Some sellers, of course, are experienced and will have everything arranged. If you make it a practice to keep in close touch with the mortgage loan market through reading financial pages and through contact with banks and other mortgage lenders, you will be able to judge proposed financing and know what you should do about it. This awareness is required also, of course, in connection with market prices, trends, and availability of property. Let's look now at the major sources for financing.

Sellers

Perhaps you believe that all sellers are anxious to cash out. That is, they expect buyers to come up with the total price in cash. Not so. In the first place, even if the seller does state that he or she requires all cash, that doesn't have to mean you need that much money. When you obtain a loan on the property and add that to your cash, as far as the seller is concerned, it is a full cash deal. Note that when you obtain financing, it doesn't matter either whether the property is mortgaged or clear; your purchase funds will be used to pay off the existing debt if there is one. Let's look now at the situation where the property is owned free and clear.

Seller Financing.   It is quite possible the owner would be interested in financing the sale by taking back a first mortgage. You might even persuade the seller to provide 100 percent financing, thus eliminating the need for you to put up any cash except perhaps for settlement costs. You'll never know if you don't ask. On the other hand, a prudent seller would want you to have the usual equity position of at least 20 percent and you should be prepared for that. Incidentally, mortgage insurance is available only to institutional and not private lenders.

Where the seller is facing the prospect of a substantial capital gains tax, the down payment may be limited to 29 percent of the purchase price with the seller carrying the balance as a mortgage loan or sales contract. This is known as the *installment sale* and will be described in more detail later.

Existing Loans.   But what about loans already in place on the property you want to buy? Do you always have to refinance? Not when the current lender is agreeable to either a *substitution* or an *assumption*. Consider the following example. Assume the purchase price is $300,000 and there is a first mortgage balance of $160,000, payable at 9 percent. One of the customary provisions in a mortgage relates to the action of the borrower such as that of selling the property. In some cases the lender can require the seller to pay off the loan balance in full if that occurs. This is called the *due-on-sale* or *acceleration* clause. If the lender enforces this provision, the buyer has no opportunity to take over the $160,000 loan and a new loan would have to be obtained. In recent years some courts have struck down these rights and it will be worthwhile for you to check the situation in your area. For if you could have this loan transferred to you, you would have the benefit of what is often a much more favorable rate than what you'd have to pay for a new loan. How can this be done?

The lender may insist that you sign *assumption* papers in which you obligate yourself to repay the loan, but this will not relieve the original borrower from paying up if you don't. The seller, of course, would prefer that the lender accept a *substitution* so that you completely replace him or her and thus eliminate any further responsibility for the seller. Recall this when the time comes for you to sell under conditions where existing financing is to be taken over by the borrower.

Some other factors should also be considered, however. As a rule, the amount of the existing loan is probably less than the amount you could get with a new loan. You will then be on the horns of a dilemma: take over the present loan at the favorable rate but put up more cash, or get by with less cash but pay more interest. Sometimes you can get the seller to come to the rescue.

Second Mortgages.   When there is a gap between the total that can be borrowed plus your cash and the purchase price, you then will need to explore how you can increase your borrowing. The usual way is to tell the seller that you are prepared to complete the purchase but that the only way you can swing it is for the seller to take back a second (or a third, or a fourth, etc.). Returning to our previous example, assume you can take over the existing $160,000 loan; you have $50,000 in cash and so you are short $90,000 to make up the $300,000 price. We'll ignore settlement costs here but in real life you can't. If the seller is very anxious to complete the sale and not hard pressed for cash, such a plan in which he or she would accept a $90,000 second may be acceptable. Most sellers in this situation are not interested, however, in having this type of loan strung out for many years. To avoid that, it is common to include a *due date* in the second mortgage loan agreement; it is often set at five or seven years hence. This means that the buyer must be prepared to pay off the loan balance on the due date and that might require refinancing at the time. When you use this type of financing you certainly will want to plan for the due date carefully. Don't assume that automatically you will be able to get a new loan just when you need it.

The interest rate on second mortgages may be controlled by your state's usury law, so you will want to check to see what its terms are. In some cases when the loan is used to purchase the property, there is no limitation on what buyer and seller-lender can agree to. Apart from the rate, some second loans may involve only payment of interest so that the full principal amount is payable on a due date; these are termed *interest-only* loans. Some lenders ask for a stipulated payment such as a fixed percentage, perhaps just 2 percent of the loan instead of the amount needed to fully amortize the debt in a specified term. Note that the loan payment tables in the Appendix are for amortizing loans only and will not provide the allocation of principal and interest for stipulated payment loans. For those, you would need to calculate the interest payments according to the loan terms.

Wraps. Previously, we referred to a new type of junior loan: the *wraparound* mortgage. Inflation is one of the major reasons this type of financing has developed, together with a shortage of institutional lending capacity. The wrap can be used in a number of situations, but we can illustrate easily how it works by means of our current example.

Let's assume that the seller is interested in helping to finance the deal but is concerned that if he takes back a second and you default on the first, he will not have all the protection he wants against loss. So he offers to finance the sale through a wraparound mortgage in the amount of the purchase price less your cash down payment. You are to take over the existing mortgage so the lender's permission is obtained. Note that a very important feature of this is the need for the existing loan to be transferable to the buyer, otherwise a lender could enforce a due-on-sale clause and upset the whole transaction. You now sign a note and loan agreement for $250,000 and put up your $50,000 cash. Your obligation is payable to the seller but it includes the $160,000 owing to the first mortgagee; this action cannot alter the first lender's rights. You will then make payments to the seller who will in turn keep the payments current on the first mortgage. It's possible that the payment on the wrap might be less than the combination of the first loan payment plus the amount payable on the second for $90,000. You will have saved loan fees and perhaps other refinancing costs. You may, of course, be paying a higher rate of interest. It is that feature which provides the seller with the motivation to enter into the deal, as well as providing extra protection.

When market interest rates are high, the buyer can't object to paying a healthy rate on the wrap; there may be no alternatives. Here's how the seller-lender gains the benefit. He can earn interest on the full amount of the loan yet pay interest, at a lower rate, on the smaller first mortgage balance. Assume here the wrap is written at 12 percent; recall the first is payable at 9 percent.

First month's interest on the wrap:	$ 2,500
The month's interest on the first:	1,200
Return on the $90,000 equity	$ 1,300
Yield: 17.3% per annum	

Further, the seller would be receiving a monthly repayment of principal out of which he would pay down the first mortgage; the difference would be his principal repayment on the $90,000 equity. All told this can be a superior way to provide financing in place of a straight second mortgage. From the buyer-borrower's point of view, careful consideration must be given to cash flow. That is, you would want to see that the total of your payments on the wrap was not significantly larger than what you'd have to pay on the two loans separately, or else you might be aggravating a negative cash flow.

Land Contract.   Up to this point we've assumed that when the seller is involved in the financing, either through taking back a first loan or providing a second or a wraparound, the title to the property passes to the buyer. The significance, of course, is that if there is a default, foreclosure action will be required. Well, why not find a way for the seller to keep the title so that if there is a default, the seller-lender can just take the property back? Although it's not quite as simple as that, there is a way that comes very close. It's by using the *land* or *sales* contract.

The land contract works best when the property is free and clear and the seller is willing to take a down payment and carry the balance. The buyer enters into a contract to buy at the stated price and agrees to make periodic payments on that price less the down payment, at an agreed rate of interest for a given time period. The terms usually will be quite similar to those payable on an equivalent mortgage loan. Once the debt is retired, the seller will then give the buyer a deed to pass title. Meanwhile, of course, the seller retains title and thus controls it. Certainly the buyer could not sell the property and give clear title to someone else.

It's possible to use the land contract even when there is an existing loan; in that case the seller continues to make the mortgage payments, using the money coming from the buyer. The contract purchaser is taking some risk here. What if the seller fails to make the payments on the first loan and there is a foreclosure? The contract purchaser may then be out of luck. Some of this risk can be reduced by making certain that the contract is filed with the county recorder so that its existence is officially recognized as an interest in the real estate. This could discourage the seller from either further encumbering the property or even trying to sell it to someone else.

But what happens if the seller disappears or dies and is unable or unwilling to execute a deed in the future? A contract purchaser does have some opportunity to go to court to obtain title but it can be expensive and time consuming to do so. All told, millions of land contracts have been used throughout the country and the vast majority have not involved this difficulty. Individuals who have had trouble undoubtedly would say they'd never buy again on contract. As a buyer you are better off getting a deed and giving a mortgage; as a seller you are better off using a land contract if you may ever have to face foreclosure proceedings. In most states, however, under a land contract, you still must declare default and follow procedures outlined in the law; contract purchasers are protected against those who would abuse them. In spite of all of the foregoing, the land contract retains the appeal of a simple process; it has its use and place so you should keep it in mind.

Land.   It is common for the owner of raw land to carry the mortgage in conjunction with the sale. If the buyer plans to subdivide the property, it is customary for the mortgage holder to agree to partial releases so that lots can be sold. The developer agrees to apply the proceeds of the sale of lots to the mortgage. If you buy land to hold for capital appreciation, you may also persuade the seller to take back a mortgage, of course. Because there are few other sources available to provide loans on vacant property, the seller may have no choice. As a rule, financial institutions do not make loans secured solely by raw land. Perhaps you should have all this in mind when you are considering this type of investment.

Financial Institutions

When you think of getting a mortgage loan you probably think of going to a bank or savings institution; most people do. Whether you need financing to buy a place to live or to finance your investment in income property, these lenders are easy to find and to approach. They will understand what you are talking about; whether you get the loan is another matter.

Your Home. If your project involves a house, condominium, or co-op apartment, you have a wide range of potential sources for borrowing from a commercial lender. For minimum down payment financing, aim for an insured loan such as FHA or GI, if eligible. Many lenders are more interested in making conventional mortgages (nongovernment insured) and it will pay to shop around and compare terms. Under the rules for government-insured loans, lenders and even sellers are subject to some limitations that serve to restrict the availability of these mortgages. In some states usury laws, suspended by the federal government for a short time, limit the interest rate and have made it impossible for home buyers to get mortgage financing when market rates have been high. These conditions are subject to change, however, so you must keep aware of what is happening.

When a lender is limited to a maximum interest rate, as in the case of FHA and GI loans, it may charge a fee called *points*. (Realize that a commercial lender makes these loans, not the government. The governnent insures the loan.) The point charge amounts to a discount and, therefore, increases the cost of borrowing. When loans are made to consumers, the federal Truth-in-Lending Law requires that the lender disclose the Annual Percentage Rate (APR) basis for the interest charge. Here's an example to show that as well as how points are charged.

Assume a savings and loan association will make an FHA loan at the allowable rate of 12 percent. The rate is set by the FHA and is changed from time to time. If, at the time, the market rate is higher, the lender may then stipulate, for example, a three point charge. This means that 3 percent of the loan amount will be deducted from the loan proceeds to make up for the below-market rate of 12 percent. If this was not permitted, lenders probably wouldn't offer any FHA or GI loans. If you had applied for an $80,000 loan, you would receive $77,600, reflecting the three point charge. This means you would need $2,400 more for settlement costs. You would sign a note for $80,000 and pay interest at 12 percent on that amount. Your monthly payments would also be based on

$80,000, even though at no time did you have that much in hand. When this is taken into account, the lender would state that your APR was approximately 12⅜ percent per annum.

When using FHA financing for your home, you are not permitted to pay this point charge yourself, and it will be assessed against the seller. You may find it difficult to locate someone willing to sell to you under these conditions. Although it may be argued that the seller will simply raise the price, because the FHA loan is subject to the lender's appraisal, in theory at any rate, the seller cannot offset the point charge through an increased price. There are also maximum amounts imposed by the FHA and the VA on loans and, as prices continue to increase, less of this financing is likely to be used. One of the purposes of government-insured loan programs is to make low down payments possible. You may be able to get by with as little as 5 percent down under FHA and nothing down for a GI loan.

Until recently all mortgage loans were fixed rate and level payment. There now are a number of alternative mortgage loan plans; not all are available everywhere just yet but you can learn about those available to you by asking around locally. The *Graduated Payment Mortgage* (GPM) provides for a fixed interest rate but smaller than normal monthly payments during the early years of the loan, increasing to amounts above the regular amortizing payment later. In this way, those with limited income can qualify for loans otherwise not available and, presumably, as earning power increases in the future, the higher payments can be handled easily. If you are a prospective home buyer, look for this plan and see if you are eligible for it.

The supply of mortgage money ebbs and flows as does the market interest rate. As interest rates to be paid for money go up, lenders who have made loans at lower fixed rates can be caught in a bind and be unable to make new loans. One remedy for this situation is the *Variable Rate Mortgage* (VRM). Under this plan, the home loan borrower agrees to the interest rate being adjusted periodically, such as once a year, according to changes in a government index of market interest rates. The loan rate can go up, but it also can go down; and there are limits to the upside. One of the conditions of a VRM loan is the guarantee by the lender that the loan is transferable to a new buyer and that can be of value, as pointed out previously, to a homeowner. Although these alternative mortgage instruments are currently available only to finance owner-occupied homes and condominium units, there's no reason why in the future they could not be used for income and other investment properties. You may want to challenge a lender with such a proposal after you find a suitable property.

The leading sources of home mortgage financing are mutual savings banks, savings and loan associations, and mortgage loan correspondents for life insurance companies. Yes, in some areas commercial banks are active in making home mortgage loans, but you will probably want to check first with a savings institution—that's their primary business. There's substantial competition among lenders from time to time so plan to shop around for the best deal.

Income Property.   If you are planning to construct a new building, you should make your financing arrangements well in advance. As a rule, the money to cover costs during the building phase, known as a *construction* loan, is separate from the permanent financing; the latter is called a *take-out* loan. In fact, it is probable there will be two different lenders, one to finance the construction and another to provide the long-term mortgage loan. Financial institutions are prime sources for both types of loans, with banks more active in most areas in construction lending. When discussing the project with a lender, make it clear that you are looking for a loan *commitment*. This refers to a guarantee by the lender to provide the long-term loan once the building is completed. Construction lenders usually require firm evidence that long-term financing is available. You will have to pay a fee for a loan commitment.

The FHA has a number of programs designed to encourage people to develop apartment projects. These include rebilitating older urban structures for residential use. Some of the features are reduced interest rates, subsidized rents for tenants, and the opportunity to write off through depreciation the cost over five years. FHA-insured loans are also available to finance existing apartments. To learn more about these plans, contact commercial lenders and the FHA.

Financial institutions are a leading source of conventional loans to finance the purchase of existing apartments and other types of income property. Discuss your needs with more than one to determine where the advantages lie. There are many variables in mortgage financing and you will want to obtain the best possible terms. The person you will deal with is a lending officer. That person may have authority to grant loans or may present your application to a committee. Be sure to give the person who may represent you with others all the ammunition possible.

Private Lenders

The least organized segment of the mortgage industry is that composed of individuals and small informal groups who lend money on real estate. Some people become private lenders because a real estate broker offered them the opportunity. In some areas mortgage loan brokers are very active, especially in arranging second mortgages. You can find private lenders by looking for their ads in your local newspaper. You could place an ad soliciting funds yourself. Consider looking to a private lender whether you need a first, second, wrap, or bridge loan. The more sophisticated the individual lender is, the easier it will be to arrange terms to suit your needs. Only you, however, can judge the terms offered, so you should keep informed about the money market on a continuing basis.

As a borrower you need to be concerned that you don't agree to terms in a mortgage instrument that you'll regret. Not only do you need an independent escrow agent, but you should also have legal counsel to draft or check the papers. You will want to safeguard against forfeiture of the property because of failure to make payments on time. You should also avoid agreeing to unreasonable late payment and other charges. Finally, there must be a clear understanding of the terms of the loan, the interest rate, and how the periodic payment is to be apportioned between interest and principal. There's nothing wrong with being guided by the terms and conditions of a mortgage contract used by a commercial lender. Why not ask your banker for a sample copy?

Earlier we discussed the wraparound second mortgage. Some private lenders can be interested in making these loans because of the potential for above average yields. Let's look at this again but now for a third-party private lender rather than the seller.

Assume a sales price of $200,000, an existing loan that can be taken over by the buyer in the amount of $100,000. You wish to put up $40,000 cash down payment. The private lender will put up $60,000 in cash and will ask you to execute a wraparound mortgage for $160,000. You will make payments on the wrap to the private lender who will in turn make the payments on the underlying loan. Note that the lender will be receiving interest on $160,000 but only put up $60,000. As a rule the interest rate for the wrap will be larger than on the underlying first mortgage. Let's assume here the wrap was made at 14 percent and the first loan rate was 10 percent. In this case the private lender will earn a full 14 percent on the $60,000 put up and the excess of 4 percent on the existing $100,000 loan. How's that for an investment yield? You, in the meantime, should also come out well, assuming that you are obtaining rents adequate to handle the mortgage payments and through equity build, capital appreciation, and probable tax sheltering. Of course, don't be misled by examples like this. The higher the interest rate, the more will be your interest expense and, therefore, the higher will the rental income have to be. There's a limit on what you can charge tenants, and when rents get too high, units sit empty. Only through careful forecasting of potential results can you know whether you can live with any specific mortgage financing plan.

It is obvious that most mortgage loans are needed for relatively long periods of time. Private lenders, generally, like to hedge their bets, minimize the risk, and lend for short terms. Earlier we spoke of your prospective need for a bridge, gap, or swing loan—money to use until a deal is closed. Realize that the best source of these loans is individual investors or small groups.

During your search for investment opportunities you may encounter individuals who express an interest in lending money. Build a file in which you can place information of that nature; no telling when you might find it very useful. Individuals can be much more flexible than commercial lenders and you may obtain what you need on just the right terms.

Credit Unions

For many years credit unions were restricted in making long-term loans suited to real estate, but this has changed recently. Loan policy is set by each credit union for itself, so don't expect all to look at this subject in the same way. The regulations now permit them to make mortgage loans, and some have become very active. It would be worthwhile to inquire, if you do belong to a credit union. However, you will probably find it easier to borrow here to finance a home purchase than for an investment project.

REITs

In putting together financing for a medium- to large-scale project, new construction or existing property, residential income, commercial or industrial, don't overlook the possibility that there's a real estate investment trust eager to make mortgage loans. At one time REITs were a prime source for this type of financing, but then came a period of very adverse conditions brought on by rapidly increasing interest rates. Many REITs collapsed and it has taken several years for the surviving mortgage trusts to recover. Valuable lessons were learned, and today there are more than 100 REITs functioning well and providing funds for real estate both by way of loans and through equity acquisitions. Not all make mortgage loans so you will need to check to see whom you should approach. Some advertise in the *Wall Street Journal*. For detailed information on the REIT industry contact the National Association of Real Estate Investment Trusts, (NAREIT), at 1101 Seventeenth St., N.W., Washington, D.C. 20036.

Mortgage Bankers

If you find that none of the local financial institutions can serve your borrowing needs, you may be able to obtain funds through a mortgage banker in your community or a nearby city. Life insurance companies and savings institutions, instead of dealing directly with prospective borrowers, use representatives, often called mortgage loan correspondents, to solicit and process loan applications. In addition to newspaper advertising, you should check the telephone yellow pages under *Real Estate Loans*. More information about mortgage bankers can be obtained from the Mortgage Bankers Association of America, 1125 Fifteenth St., N.W., Washington, D.C. 20005.

Finance Companies

Finance companies are commonly used for personal and automobile loans, but did you realize that many also make real estate loans? This source is probably better used to refinance property you already own but could be approached for a purchase money mortgage. How do finance companies compete with the more traditional lenders? Some companies do not impose prepayment penalties or charge mortgage points, and thus the cost of obtaining the loan may be quite competitive. They advertise fast service and simplified processing and those features could be important to you. The next time you see a finance company office, go in and get pertinent information for possible use in the future.

Mortgage Loan Brokers

A mortgage broker may be an individual or a firm operating to match lenders (usually private individuals) and borrowers; they charge a fee for the service. In some cases the business is advertised as a *mortgage company*. Some firms raise capital and use it for real estate loans as well. You can locate this source through newspaper advertising and, again, the yellow pages. Because the borrower pays most or all of the expenses for financing arranged here, you will want to be certain you have complete information before making a decision to accept a brokered loan.

LOAN APPLICATION

As you might expect, institutional lenders will have the most formal procedures for handling mortgage loans. Many private lenders, owing to a lack of knowledge, may be quite informal, and through lack of care they create problems either for themselves or the borrower. No one should be intimidated, however, by getting a loan. There's nothing mysterious or threatening about the process. The borrower should expect to disclose basic information to the prospective lender so that the decision to make the loan can be properly judged. All parties benefit when the loan application is complete and properly presented. We'll review its elements here and cover the loan process in a following section.

Application Form

What information must you disclose when applying for a mortgage loan? We'll assume you are dealing with a financial institution and, therefore, will discuss the typical data requested by commercial lenders. Most lenders use one form of application for home loans and a different set for investment or commercial type loans. In both cases the lender needs financial information relating to the borrower as well as information about the property to be used as security. For income property the borrower must present expected cash flow and other investment analyses to show the lender how the expected return has been computed and, therefore, how secure the loan is likely to be.

Home Loans. The lender needs a copy of the purchase contract and the details of how you plan to finance the purchase. Of great importance, also, is your financial statement and data concerning your employment and sources of income. You must be prepared to list all your resources such as bank and savings account balances and where they are. The lender is concerned that you will have a stake in the property and will not look with favor on your application if it is apparent you won't have much to lose through default. If you have borrowed the cash for the down payment, you may have trouble qualifying for the loan.

Be sure to list cash values of life insurance policies, stocks and bonds, and all other property that has a value. The lender will consider primarily only items that can readily be converted to cash and will place little value on such personal property as clothing and furniture. Show all of your debts and obligations and be accurate and truthful. Many key items on your application will be verified. One purpose in listing your assets and liabilities is to give the lending officer a chance to judge whether you have sufficient financial resources to fall back on if you encounter financial difficulties. If you have built up a significant amount of resources, it also demonstrates your ability to handle financial matters—that's good. The lender is also interested in evidence of stability and judges this by how long you've had your present job, whether you have moved around a lot, and whether you are overextended by debts.

Probably the most immediate issue is your income and ability to meet the loan payments and costs of owning a home. Because the lending officer will relate your after-tax income to the size of the loan and monthly payments, you must present on the application all data to justify your case. If both you and your spouse have incomes, the total can be used to meet the lender's requirements. Finally, every credit extender is anxious to know how the applicant has handled previously granted credit. You will be asked to state where you have used credit, and it is likely this will be verified. When you have a good credit record, you should never have any trouble getting a loan for amounts and purposes that are reasonable.

Income Property. The lending officer will be concerned not only with your personal financial data but also with the projections of income and expenses for the property. Most of the information about yourself may be checked and mistakes or omissions may be construed as an attempt to mislead. Plan on giving the lender a copy of the purchase agreement and other details of the deal. If it appears favorable, a professional appraisal of the property will be made to substantiate the values used in making the purchase and to determine the maximum loan to be authorized. Although the lender clearly is not going to be a partner and is assuming only the risk related to repayment of the loan, you may wish to adopt the attitude that you want the lender to know as much about the deal as a partner would need to know. Lender cooperation in this event will likely be greater than otherwise. In this connection, after you learn how to perform the analysis described in the next chapter, you may see a virtue in giving the lender a copy of what you prepared using this technique. It will be impressive.

Credit Checks. To emphasize a point stated before—lenders will verify much of the information you give them. This is done both by direct contact by the lending officer and through the use of credit reporting agencies. If you are applying for a home loan and the lender turns you down because of adverse information in a credit report, under federal law, the lender must show you a copy of the credit report and give you the name and address of the company that prepared it. You then have the right to discuss the report with the firm that issued it; and if you dispute the information, the reporting agency must advise each entity to whom the report was given of the details of your explanation. None of this applies to business loans.

Private Lenders.   Although you may not object to giving information about your income and assets to a commercial lender, you may be reluctant to disclose confidential data to individuals who make loans. Don't be; a private lender is entitled to the same amount of information. After all, they are about to entrust their cash to you. If you were a lender, wouldn't you want to know enough about a borrower to judge appropriately?

LENDING PROCESS

Between the time the lending officer receives your completed loan application and the time when funds can be sent to the escrow agent, several weeks may pass. Timing can be a most important matter in real estate transactions, so you should plan accordingly. If you have a deadline to meet, such as one set by a seller, be sure that the lending officer is aware of this; ask whether he or she can act quickly enough in the circumstances. To better understand why it may take so long, let's look at what is involved.

Initial Interview

It is always a good idea to make advance contact with lenders to acquaint them with your prospective needs. In many cases, if the lending officer assumes you are serious and will be making a formal application for a loan in the near future, he or she may set up a file and order a credit report; all of this is more likely if you are talking about money for an investment rather than to buy a home. Once you've narrowed your search and found a likely investment property, prepared the analysis, and made the decision to buy, subject to obtaining financing or other matters, you should then go to one or more likely lenders. At that time you should be able to present all the information we've been discussing: copy of the purchase agreement, financial statements, and a completed loan application. You can save time by picking up blank forms beforehand. Otherwise, the initial interview will end with a request to fill in the forms and bring them back.

Review

Once the lending officer has enough information in hand, it will be reviewed to determine whether further action is appropriate. He or she may decide to go and look at the property or order the appraisal. Even though these actions are taken, you must not assume that your loan application has been approved. At least, however, your application has not been rejected on its face.

One of the very critical matters considered by the lending officer is whether to grant the loan in the amount requested. Here, the loan to value ratio is used. Once the lender has a statement of the appraised value, it is easy to calculate the maximum loan amount. The ratio will be governed by the type of loan, the nature of the borrower, and whether mortgage insurance is to be used. For FHA and GI loans the loan amount is set by federal regulation. For conventional home loans, as a rule, the loan will be equal to 75 to 80 percent of the lender's appraised value. Note that this value may or may not be the same as the purchase price. Some lenders are conservative and may use even lower ratios. But how do you get a 90 or even 95 percent conventional home loan? This can be arranged by the lender requiring mortgage insurance, assuming your income and financial condition otherwise justify the amount. The premium for the private mortgage insurance is added to the monthly payment. Don't confuse this, incidentally, with mortgage redemption or credit life insurance—it has nothing to do with that. Nor does it take the place of fire insurance on the property.

Most home loan borrowers are anxious to get the maximum loan and for the payments to be stretched out over as many years as possible. They also want to be able to qualify for the smallest down payment. Just how are these things decided? To find out, consider the following.

Your cost for housing will consist of the mortgage payments, mortgage insurance perhaps, property taxes, and fire insurance. You will also have expenses for repairs. Lenders try to use a rule of thumb in checking loan applications as a rough screening device. In most cases the applicant's take-home pay, including a spouse's earnings, should be enough so that one-third of it will cover the costs stated. Example: Assume you and your spouse have a combined after-tax income of $2,000 a month. Unless the lender is very conservative, you would be judged as being able to spend up to about $700 a month for housing. How big a loan could you get? Well, a $50,000 mortgage, to be repaid over thirty years at 12 percent interest will require a monthly payment for interest and principal of $514.50. To this would be added amounts for the other costs to see if the total runs more than $700. If not, you would have met the requirements. Whether $50,000 is enough to make the purchase of the property you've chosen, or the loan to value ratio would justify a loan in that amount, are separate matters, of course.

From all of this you could determine the maximum loan for which you might qualify by starting with your take-home pay. As you check out properties, you'll learn about required down payments and maximum loan amounts. It will be easy then to see whether it is practical to pursue the matter.

Back now to income property investments. The majority of institutional lenders will lend on the basis of between two-thirds and three-quarters of the appraised value. It is possible to increase the amount borrowed beyond these by the use of second mortgages. There's room for negotiation by financially strong borrowers for properties that have excellent investment potential.

Loan Terms

During the review, the lending officer will make decisions about the interest rate, points and loan or origination fees, loan term, prepayment penalties, acceleration clause, and late payment fees. To protect yourself, you will have considered each of these in your offer to buy, making the completion of the purchase subject to the terms you have stated. This may mean, therefore, that if the lender will not lend as much as you need, or at as favorable a rate as you have stipulated, you would not be bound to go ahead. Once the lending officer has made these decisions, you will be notified. You then will know where you stand and whether all your terms have been met.

The outcome at this stage can be: an OK as requested, a blanket turndown, or a compromise. If you are turned down, find out why. Perhaps the lender has run out of funds and he would have made the loan otherwise. On the other hand, you may have presented an unworkable deal. Because you will want to approach another lender (always be prepared for this step), you will want to know what changes you ought to make to ensure success the next time. You may even find it wise to have an alternative prepared to offer the first lender if you don't get approval initially.

Making the Loan

Once the decision to make the loan is reached by the lender, a title search or abstract, if not already in hand, will be requested by the lender. Next, if a home loan, you will be given a completed settlement statement estimate, as required by the Real Estate Settlement Procedures Act, so you will know how much you are going to be charged for each of the items. There is some opportunity to shop around for these services. One of the ideas behind this federal law is to ensure that home loan borrowers realize that they don't have to just accept as fixed, fees quoted by various service providers such as escrow agents, title insurers, and real estate lawyers. A little inquiry might save you big dollars. For nonhome loans you should also get estimates and perhaps do some bargaining; lenders are not required to be involved in giving you the information, however. It is illegal for providers to agree among themselves to fix prices, but it will take some research for you to locate the best source for your purposes.

The lender will prepare the promissory note, mortgage, or trust deed and other documents related to the financing.

These will be sent to the title insurance company or escrow agent where, usually, you will execute them. The deed will be prepared according to the buyers' instructions as to how title is to stand. It will be sent for execution by the sellers and returned to the escrow or lawyer handling the transaction.

You may wish to obtain legal advice with respect to how the title is to stand. You can take title in joint tenancy with your spouse, for example. On the death of a joint tenant, the surviving co-owner(s) automatically acquire the decedent's interest. Holding title as tenants in common permits a cotenant to pass his or her interest through a will or an estate; the other cotenants do not automatically acquire the decedent's interest. If your state has a community property law, that may dictate, depending on the source of the funds used to acquire the property, how title should be taken. If the purchase is being made by a partnership, title should be vested in the name of the partners. Corporate buyers take title in the name of the corporation.

Closing Date

One of the most important points in time in a real estate transaction is known as the *closing date*. This refers to the date on which the escrow is closed. Buyers, sellers, and lenders all send their documents, instruction, and funds to the escrow. The deed and mortgage documents are to be recorded in the public record to ensure the lender's security interest in the property. Once the documents are on record, the funds can be released to the seller, the commission paid to the broker, and the surplus, if any, returned to the buyer. There may be other disbursements made then or later to inspection firms, contractors, insurance agents, and others involved in the deal. If there are some prepaid items such as property taxes or insurance, they will be prorated in the escrow and credits made to the seller. In short, all the loose ends in the transaction are tied up in the escrow as of the closing date. Note that these transactions can only take place after everything needed has been delivered to the escrow officer.

Depending on local procedure, at some time following the close of escrow, the documents will be distributed. The purchaser will receive the deed and a copy of the mortgage contract; the lender will receive the original mortgage to file with the executed promissory note. You should file your documents in a safe place, but one to which you have ready access. Note that the deed by itself is not a valuable document, as is a stock certificate, for example. Because the deed has been recorded, there is a public record of it, so original documents are not really of much consequence. If a deed is not recorded, that is quite a different proposition, however. Whenever you buy property, make certain the deed is recorded immediately. Otherwise you expose yourself to the risk that someone could obtain title to the property and you could be out in the cold.

If there is no commercial lender involved, you may have your attorney prepare the documents. Title insurance companies and escrow agencies are also prepared to do some of these things. Regardless of who prepared the loan documents, besides your counsel, you may wish to have them reviewed by a legal advisor.

Now that we have the escrow closed, you have title to the property and you owe a mortgage. What's next? Repaying the loan, of course.

REPAYMENT

The vast majority of mortgage loans involve monthly payments. The amount is calculated to pay off both the principal and interest over a stated term of years. These are termed fully *amortizing* loans. While the payment amount remains the same during the repayment period, the allocation between principal and interest varies. For an investment project, you may choose to arrange for an interest-only loan so that the principal remains the same until it is time to pay it back in full. Many second mortgages are arranged on the basis of a *due date* which is often set only a few years away. The borrower is then obligated to pay off what is owing in full; this is termed the *balloon* payment. The periodic payment may either be the amount to apply for a fully amortizing loan for an extended term or an arbitrary stipulated amount. Some loans made on commercial properties require payment of a share of the profits of the business venture over and above a normal interest rate. These are known as *participating* loans.

Computations

In order to forecast the returns from an investment where you are using borrowed funds, you will need accurate data for the loan payment and for the unpaid mortgage balance due at the time you plan to liquidate the investment. During the holding period you will also compute the interest expense to calculate income taxes.

The easiest way to determine the payment amount is to ask the lender with whom you are negotiating the loan. During your search for properties and when you are doing preliminary analysis, you will likely be making assumptions about the financing and may not be able to speak with a lender or someone else who has a loan payment book. To overcome this problem, two tables have been included in the Appendix. You may want to look at them now. Table One provides the monthly payment factor along with other factors to be used to calculate interest expense and unpaid mortgage balances. Recall that we used these previously. When you need only a monthly payment, you may wish to use Table Two. For a variety of interest rates it gives factors, for specified loan terms, to be applied to the amount of the loan. Here's an example of how to use Table Two.

Assume you need a loan for $120,750 and you expect to pay 11¼ percent interest; the loan is to be fully amortized over twenty-five years.

$$
\begin{aligned}
\text{Monthly Payment} = \quad \$\ 120 \times 9.98 &= \$\ 1,197.60 \\
.75 \times 9.98 &= \underline{\quad 7.49} \\
\text{Total} \qquad & \quad \$\ 1,205.09
\end{aligned}
$$

How about a repayment plan that does not fully amortize the debt? Such a *stipulated* payment will be negotiated by the parties. As a rule it is intended that payments be made for a limited time only and that the unpaid loan balance be paid in a lump sum on the due date. When interest rates were the single-digit variety—9 percent, for example—it was customary for the payment to be 1 percent of the loan. Once interest goes over 12 percent, that payment would not be enough to cover the interest, let alone provide any principal repayment. Currently the payment might be set at say 1½ percent or even 2 percent of the amount borrowed. When you borrow money from other than an institutional lender (they typically lend only on a fully amortizing basis), be certain you understand exactly how the repayment terms apply.

Allocation

When your loan payments cover both interest and principal, you and the lender must be able to make the allocation correctly. For a fully amortizing loan, the monthly payment will be precisely the amount needed to extinguish the debt in the time stated; but during that time, the amount paid on the principal will be different each month. Here's how it works.

Assume you borrow $100,000 at 12 percent for twenty years.

Table One:	Monthly payment is $1,101.09
First Month:	Interest at 12% for one month = 1%
	1% of $100,000 = $1,000
	Payment to principal = $101.09
	New unpaid balance = $100,000
	less $101.09
Second Month:	Interest at 1% of unpaid balance
	1% of $99,898.91 = $998.99
	Payment to principal = $102.10

This procedure is repeated for each payment. Note that the interest portion reduces as the amount allocated to principal repayment increases. The interest charge in this type of loan is based on the declining unpaid principal balance. When you need the total of the interest expense for a full year, you may be able to use Table One. In this example:

First year interest = \$1,000 × 119.31 = \$11,931

Now let's see what happens if the loan payment is not the amount required to fully amortize the debt. Assume you are borrowing \$50,000 at 12 percent payable at \$800 a month, unpaid balance due in full in five years.

First Month Interest Expense:
    12% per year = 1% per month
    1% of \$50,000 = \$500
    Payment to principal = \$800 less \$500 = \$300
    New unpaid balance = \$50,000 less \$300
Second Month:
    1% of \$49,700 = \$497.00
    Payment to principal = \$800 less \$497 = \$303
    New unpaid balance = \$49,700 less \$303

This procedure would be followed each month for the five years; the ending unpaid principal balance would be the balloon payment. Note that Table One does not apply to stipulated payment loans. From the foregoing example you may be able to estimate, for analysis purposes, what the balloon payment would be in a specific situation.

The guiding principle in the allocation of loan payments is that the amount paid is to be applied first to the interest owing and the balance, if any, applied to the amount of the debt. If a payment is not enough to cover the interest (this would not occur for a fully amortizing loan), it is not proper to increase the loan amount by the deficiency and charge interest on such increase. Instead, the interest shortage should be recorded separately and arrangements made with the borrower to pay it off quickly and get up to date with the obligation.

If your loan is one of the alternative forms, a Variable Rate Mortgage (VRM) or Graduated Payment Mortgage (GPM), the allocation process described above for a fully amortizing loan would apply. That is, the payment is applied first to the interest charge for the preceding month. In the case of the VRM, however, if the rate changes you will be given a choice by the lender. Assume, for example, that the rate is increased; it can't be more than one-half of 1 percent in any one increase. You can pay a higher monthly payment to reflect the new interest rate, or you can continue the same monthly payment but have the loan term extended. Similar options will apply if the rate goes down; that is, you would be offered a lower periodic payment or a shorter term. See why it's called *variable?*

REFINANCING

Up to now we've treated borrowing primarily in terms of financing the purchase of property. There are other times when you must know how to get a mortgage loan. When you already own the property on which there is a loan and you arrange new financing and pay off the existing indebtedness, this is called *refinancing.*

Many people who have owned property for several years now find that their equity is substantial. As they have been quietly reducing the loan balance, the market value of the property has skyrocketed and the difference between the two, called the equity, may now be quite large. How can you get your hands on this without selling the property? You do it by refinancing. In fact, you may even be stimulated by what you are reading here to use this equity for a real estate investment program. Or, you may see a way to rearrange your present loan to give you cash for some other purpose. As interest rates decline, as certainly some day they will, you may want to refinance to reduce your interest expense. Finally, to make it easier for someone to buy your property, you may want to refinance before putting it on the market. Let's look at what's involved here.

Home Equity

Assume you bought your home a number of years ago with a mortgage at 7 percent and monthly payments of $167. (That was good planning, wasn't it?) The balance is now such that the difference between the potential appraised value and the loan is $100,000. You have two choices:

Get a new loan, pay off the old, and use the cash; or

Get a second mortgage and use the proceeds.

To choose wisely you need to look at both the interest cost and the effect on your monthly payment. There are always other costs, too, in refinancing and they must not be ignored. Not only will there be appraisal fees, but probably title insurance and escrow costs and, in most cases, loan fees or mortgage points.

Let's say that new first mortgage loans are going at 11 percent and second mortgages at 12 percent. Either type of loan will be available up to an amount such that the total debt is not greater than 80 percent of the appraised value. Assume the property is appraised at $120,000; loan term twenty-five years.

New loan:	$ 96,000	monthly payments:	$ 940.80
Pay off old loan:	20,000	monthly payments:	167.00
New cash:	$ 76,000	increase of:	$ 773.80
Second mortgage:	$ 76,000	monthly payments:	$ 836.76
Existing loan balance:	20,000	monthly payments:	167.00
New money:	$ 76,000	total payments:	$1,003.76

You now can consider carefully the effect of the increase in the monthly payments and the fact you will be paying much more interest. As interest expense is tax deductible, of course, you will have some offset providing you itemize deductions on your tax return. The key to whether you should proceed with refinancing lies in how you can employ the funds it would produce. In this example, $76,000 in cash would enable you to do a lot in real estate. Whether your investment would adequately take care of the increased monthly payments is a critical matter and must be examined carefully.

And now a word about prepayment penalties. In the past it has been customary for lenders to include a provision in the loan agreement calling for a penalty if the borrower pays off the loan before its regular maturity. The basis for this lies in the fact that the lender has incurred expenses to make the loan and they will not be fully recovered unless all the loan payments are made as scheduled and there will be more cost to reinvest lump sums received. The prepayment penalty terms vary widely; there is no standard. A popular form calls for the borrower to pay 1 percent of the outstanding loan balance at the time of the payoff. If you now have a mortgage, why not get out the contract to see whether you are subject to this penalty? In any case, whether you are refinancing to spring your equity or your loan will be paid off as a result of a buyer's financing, you need to know ahead of time what penalty, if any, will be imposed. It can be a significant amount and might prompt a person to go the second mortgage route instead of arranging to replace the present first mortgage with a new one.

One last item. If you refinance with a loan that has a due date and balloon payment, be certain you fully allow for the possibility that when it comes time to meet that obligation, you may not be able to get a new loan; you'll need one if you don't otherwise have access to cash to bring the balloon down to earth.

Prior to Sale

The subject of refinancing can come up at the time you are thinking about selling your property; it may even be something to propose to a seller whose property has caught your attention. In the latter situation, if there's a chance the seller could get more favorable loan terms than you could as a buyer, you may want to try to persuade the seller to obtain a new loan on a basis whereby you could take it over.

Assume you are getting ready to sell; you've built up a substantial equity and want to cash out. You are concerned that this may mean that buyers would be hard to find when a lot of cash was required because new mortgage loans were hard to come by. You wonder whether you should refinance the property and thus cut down on the cash a buyer would need; the new loan, of course, would have to be assumable by the buyer. Note that in some cases when mortgage money is tight, lenders will make refinancing loans to their current borrowers whereas they might have to turn down new applicants. By discussing all this with your present mortgage holder, you can determine which course of action to take. Some lenders would prefer not to refinance if they thought it was for the purpose of setting the property up for sale. Consider that when devising your strategy. In any case, if you refinance, don't overlook the need to raise your sales price by enough to offset the costs you will have.

TITLE INSURANCE

We've referred frequently to title searches and title insurance but have yet to discuss what it involves and why you should know about it. As a buyer or lender, always obtain the benefits of title insurance. If you are using funds borrowed from a financial institution, it will insist on title insurance to protect its interests; your protection can be bought at additional cost.

When buying real estate you acquire a legal right to ownership and use of property; the property has a legal description to identify it from all other property. The record of ownership is maintained by a govermental office, typically the *county recorder* or *land title office*. To learn who holds title or who has a security interest in a particular parcel of real estate, it is necessary to search this public record for all transactions relating to it. As a rule, property is indexed according to its legal description and is not always cross-indexed by its street address. Legal descriptions appear on tax bills, deeds, and mortgage documents. It follows that only legally recognized owners of property would have the right to sell or encumber it. And this is where the trouble can arise.

Assume you arrange to buy property from someone who appears to be an owner. You trade your money for a deed and believe all is in order. Next, along comes the real owner. Where do you stand? Just where the last person who bought the Brooklyn Bridge stands—in the soup! Or try this. Assume the seller tells you the property is free and clear so you buy it, pay a lot of cash, accept the deed, and then run down to the recorder's office and have it recorded. You may now appear to be the legal owner but that does not affect the rights of persons to whom money is still owed and for which the property was pledged as security, assuming they in fact recorded their security interest. You will now have to pay them off to gain clear title, notwithstanding what the seller said and how much you paid. Yes, you may have a cause of action against the seller for fraud but that may not do you much good, especially if he has taken your cash and moved to Tahiti. So, how do you avoid these pitfalls? It's not hard to do.

At the time you make an offer to buy property, an escrow should be opened and you should insist that your deposit or earnest money be placed in it. This means turning over the cash to an independent third party who is to protect everyone's interest. In many places, this escrow service is operated by a title insurance company. The title insurance company will search the public record and prepare a report to show how title stands and what liens and other encumbrances there are against the title. From this title search or abstract of title, you can see whether the seller, in fact, can give you title if you proceed and whether the property will, in fact, be free and clear of prior debts. If all appears in order and you instruct the escrow agency to close the deal, you should also ask that title insurance be issued to protect you. When the title insurance policy is issued, you will then be protected against unpleasant surprises.

Suppose, for example, in searching the title records, the examiner missed an outstanding lien. The lien holder would have to be paid off but that expense would be carried by the title insurance company, not you. If other flaws in the title appear, including the existence of other owners, you will be indemnified against loss. Be aware, however, that title insurance doesn't necessarily cover all problems you could have, so you will need to talk this over at the title insurance company. The policy doesn't guarantee, for example, that the lot lines are just where you think they are. You'll need a survey for that possible problem. In complex title matters you can employ legal counsel and the insurance policy can be extended to cover some of the items excluded in the basic form.

But who pays for title insurance? The practice varies so you will want to ask locally. This is negotiable and you may want to start from the position of asking the seller to pay; anything to cut down on your own costs. And just think, if you don't ask, you'll never know what the answer might have been. The premium is a one-time expense. Even though you obtained title insurance at the time you bought property, a new policy will be required when you sell. If there is a short time between such transactions, some title insurance companies reduce the price to reflect the saving in work.

NONPARTICIPATIVE INVESTMENTS

Can you borrow money to buy shares in a REIT or a partnership interest in a real estate syndicate? Probably yes, but as a rule, what you buy will not serve as collateral for the loan. An exception to this might be found if you have a margin account with your stockbroker and you purchase listed shares. Some investors, however, use other assets, including stocks and bonds, as collateral to obtain cash to make a nonparticipative investment.

Some REIT shares do generate current income. Whether this will be enough to pay borrowing costs should be examined carefully. It is quite unlikely the rate of return would be even close to the interest expense for a loan for the full purchase price. It may be sound, however, to look to the potential capital appreciation as justification for using leverage. If it is lacking, it would be difficult to support the case for buying with borrowed cash.

CLOSING THOUGHTS

Typically, those who invest in real estate employ leverage; it readily can be shown what a difference using borrowed funds can make. Your first step is to locate an investment vehicle that appears to make economic sense and will likely meet your investment objectives. You must then compute how much cash you'll need to borrow. By keeping informed about the money market through continuing contact with real estate brokers and lenders, you can decide where to go to discuss your borrowing requirements. You will need to disclose fully your personal financial affairs including all your income and its sources. For an investment property, be prepared to discuss your forecasts and profit analysis with the person whom you are asking to make the loan. Through careful planning, if you are turned down by a lender, you can quickly decide where next to apply; always have a contingency plan. If you find a property that fits your needs, don't be thwarted by a lack of financing. Knowing how to reach private lenders as well as commercial sources is essential. Above all, don't be intimidated by the thought of a large mortgage debt. By the proper use of borrowed funds, the property itself, whether an investment or as a home, will provide a basis for making the periodic payments. As long as you make the payments, the lender can't take the property from you. And in an inflationary period, the value of the collateral for the mortgage will continue to increase. If a problem arises, you have every right to be able to sell the property for at least what is owed, and thus you can pay off the debt. Try it. You'll probably like it.

6

Analyzing Investment Opportunities

Because there are so many properties to choose from, your big problem is judging which is best for you. Through analysis it will become quite clear which choice to make.

FORECASTING

Now we come to a review of how to use the facts you have gathered for each property under consideration. This information is needed to compute probable values, what your cash returns might be, possible capital gains, and yields—if things go as you assume. There are many decisions to make and assumptions to apply as you forecast the future. You must learn as much as you can about some aspects of income tax regulations so you can select ways to treat your investment that will minimize taxes and maximize the ultimate return. Depreciation is an important topic and we'll take a close look at it. You can readily prepare a cash flow forecast, using the data corralled on the Fact Sheets; this will enable you to see whether you can expect tax sheltering from a specific piece of property. Of course, you never want to pay more for something than it is worth. Here we'll take the steps, one by one, needed to arrive at good estimates. After that you should be able to have confidence in your selection of an investment vehicle. While most of what is covered here applies to each of the major types of real estate, emphasis is placed on analyzing an investment in an apartment house or commercial property such as an office building or retail premises. Even though you follow exactly all that is stated, we offer no guarantee of your success; but we certainly are convinced that you will do better than if you don't take these steps.

OBJECTIVES OF ANALYSIS

The purpose of the analysis is to produce a realistic forecast of financial results from making an investment under the conditions assumed. Once you have all the details such as the offering price, cash required, rental income, and expense data, what do you need to know? Well, what is the property really worth? Will the income cover the expenses, including the mortgage payments? How much can you expect to gain by holding it for a few years? What are the conditions over which you have little control that could affect the value of the property? Yes, you need answers to each of these questions and much, much more.

Indicated Economic Value

There are three basic values to calculate which will help you reach a decision whether to reject a property or pursue it further. For this purpose we need only reasonable approximations, so don't expend too much energy digging up unnecessary details. Use that energy to find property to buy.

First, we can compute the current *reproduction cost* and thus compare the offering price to what the property would cost to build today, less depreciation. Next, we can compare the property against comparable opportunities as to market value. This is done by measuring rental income through the *gross rent multiplier*. We might decide the property is overpriced when compared to others and use the multiplier as a basis for making a more realistic offer. This is a widely used measure and acts as a good barometer of what is happening in the marketplace. Finally, we can prepare a measure that is a favorite of professional appraisers, *capitalization of income.* These calculations will tell us the maximum price we ought to pay for the property. The bargaining will take place after that.

Cost Approach.   Appraisers refer to the *cost approach* as the method for determining current value based on what construction and land costs are today. From that is deducted an estimate of various forms of depreciation such as physical, obsolescense, and use. In Chapter 4 we reviewed the section of the Fact Sheet where you record construction cost information and make the calculation of replacement and depreciated reproduction costs. You may wish to refer to that now. On the following page you will find an illustration of how you can pull all the valuation data together. You start by entering the previously computed reproduction cost in the first box. If you can buy the property for less than this figure, you should feel comfortable. It would not necessarily be improper to buy it for more than this figure, but you would want to have some compelling reason for doing so. But this is only one measure; there are others.

Market Approach.   Cost is not the only measure of value. What does competition do to values? Well, it generally forces prices down when the supply is greater than the demand and up when there's a scarcity relative to what buyers offer. If you are looking at houses, you should be able to get some idea through comparing offering prices, provided you can compare like properties; that's not easy. When judging raw land, you'll likely have a price-per-acre to use in making comparisons but it's obvious one acre can differ vastly from another. Still, if similar properties are offered at quite different per-acre rates, you will want to find out why. Vacant lot prices are much affected by location, and very much by terrain, relative to construction cost. If you see what appears to be a bargain price, you might expect it will cost more than usual for foundations, driveways, and so on. These factors should be re-

INDICATED ECONOMIC VALUE

A. *Cost Approach*

TOTAL REPRODUCTION COST OF PROPERTY $282,460

B. *Market Approach*

$$\frac{\$ 250,000}{\text{Asking Price}} \div \frac{\$ 34,800}{\text{Gross Annual Income}} = \frac{7.18}{\text{Gross Rent Multiplier}}$$

$$\frac{8}{\text{Your Multiplier}} \times \frac{\$ 34,800}{\text{Gross Annual Income}} = \text{MAXIMUM PRICE} \quad \$ 278,400$$

C. *Capitalization of Income*

Net Annual Cash Income $34,450

Less Annual Cash Operating Expense $10,300

Net Cash Operating Income $24,150

$$\frac{\$ 24,150}{\text{Net Cash Op. Inc.}} \div \frac{.09}{\text{Cap Rate}} = \text{MAXIMUM PRICE} = \$ 268,333$$

$$\frac{\$ 24,150}{\text{Net Cash Op. Inc.}} \div \frac{\$ 250,000}{\text{Asking Price}} \times 100\% = \text{CAP RATE} = 9.66\%$$

CASH FLOW FORECAST

Before-Tax Cash Flow

Net Annual Cash Income $34,450

Less: Total Cash Operating Expenses $10,300

Total Mortgage Payments $22,404

Total Cash Expenditures $32,704

NET ANNUAL BEFORE-TAX CASH FLOW $1,746

flected adequately in the proposed sales prices and competition is supposed to keep everything in line. For rental income, property comparisons of market values are much easier to make because of the widespread use of two measures that reflect competition: gross rent multiplier and the cost per rentable foot. We will concentrate on the multiplier and compute it according to the steps shown on the form illustrated.

You will probably agree that a building with $800-a-month apartments is going to be worth more than one for which rents are $300 a month, given that the total building size is comparable. A store building renting at $1 per square foot per month ought to be worth more than the same size structure that commands only $.60 a foot. Recognizing this, we can do a little arithmetic to get an idea of value. The relationship between gross rental income (expressed, as a rule, on an annual basis) and market value of the property is provided through the factor called the multiplier.

EXAMPLE: Gross annual rent $\times$ the multiplier = market value.

$$\$18,000 \times 8 = \$144,000$$

But, you ask, where did the "8" come from? You will find what the multiplier should be by researching similar properties and comparing rents to offering prices. Because market factors such as demand and supply are not the same throughout the country, there will be different multipliers. They will vary also from one neighborhood to another and from one size range to another. Note that the multiplier is computed by dividing the gross annual rents into the offering price. Here we have:

$$\frac{\$144,000}{18,000} = 8 \text{ times}$$

By getting rents and asking prices for a number of properties in the area and by calculating the multipliers, you will soon have a good idea of what the marketplace is saying. With that benchmark as a guide, you can quickly measure each property in which you have a serious interest and see how it stacks up. The smaller the multiple, all other things equal, the better is the offering price. This can be a very useful tool in screening opportunities. Through it you can isolate the one with the smallest multiplier and look into it first. On the basis of preliminary checking, you should be able to come up with your target multiplier and say, for instance, "I'll concentrate on properties for which the multiplier is not above six." Whether you can find something that is otherwise suitable is another matter, but inasmuch as your goal usually will be to find property to buy at less than the market value, you can identify likely candidates through the gross rent multiplier.

If you are exploring medium- to large-size apartment projects, you may be able to use, in addition to the multiplier, the rentable foot measure. This comes in two varieties: cost and rental income. Here we are interested in its use as a measure of income. You take the gross monthly rent for the entire building and divide it by the number of square feet of space that can be rented. The result will give you a measure of the tenants' cost. By making this calculation for each property you are exploring, you will have an additional value to use in narrowing your search. The property with the largest number would be the most desirable, all other things being equal.

A word of caution at this point. Rental income is only one factor. While it obviously is best to own property that generates the maximum rents, what really counts is what you have left over after meeting the expenses. The market approach deliberately ignores operating costs and you will need to keep that in mind when using it. The measure that does consider net income comes next.

Income Capitalization.   The end result of applying this valuation approach is a percentage that will resemble an investment yield. Look now at the illustration to see the information needed to compute it. An investor must arrive at a standard or target yield, called the *cap rate*. As we know already, there are several ways to measure returns from an investment in real estate and it is a tricky business to compare them with non-real estate yields. Don't confuse the cap rate with prospective yields from stocks or bonds. Let's see why that is the case. Just as with the gross rent multiplier, you can calculate what is being used in the marketplace for capitalizing income and thus have a benchmark. You will use it to judge whether a specific property may meet your objectives or not, according to its offering price. Again, we are seeking to set a value in order to judge how much, as a maximum, we should pay. We can arrive at such a value by dividing our target cap rate into the net operating income. It is called a desired yield only in terms of how it is used to compute a maximum price to pay, not as a measure of actual investment return. Perhaps an explanation of the concept, using a savings account, will provide further insight.

Assume you have $10,000 at work in a savings account. At the end of the year you find that $850 interest has accumulated. Your yield, before income taxes would be:

$$\frac{\$ 850}{\$10,000} \times 100\% = 8.5\%$$

Now consider an investment in income property. Ignore how it is financed and assume there is no mortgage; ignore also income taxes and depreciation. From the gross rental income subtract all the operating expenses to calculate how much cash you'd have in hand after they were paid. Assume this net operating income amounted to $12,000 for the year. If you had a cap rate of 10 percent, how much should you pay, as a maximum, for the property?

$$\text{Maximum price} = \frac{\text{Net Operating Income}}{\text{Desired Yield}}$$

$$= \frac{\$ 12,000}{.10} = \$120,000$$

Note how this compares to the savings account example. If you put $120,000 to work and earned $12,000, you would agree that your yield was 10 percent. This is the cap rate. Once you decide on yours, divide it into the net operating income of the property you are considering and the result will be the maximum price to pay to earn the rate chosen. This is known as the *capitalized value* of the property. It is a very good measure of what you should consider paying as the top amount.

Because the cap rate deals only with the net operating income, we cannot consider it a measure of investment return. Real estate prospectively also will provide returns from equity build and capital appreciation and, in some cases, tax shelter benefits, so we need other ways to measure yields. We'll come to them shortly.

We've shown that you can use a cap rate to calculate a maximum purchase price, given that you know the net operating income. Remember, do not include mortgage payments in the computation of net income. If we are given an offering price and net income, we can use them to compute a cap rate. Then you can compare it to your desired rate. What do you look for?

Assume you have decided that you will use 8 percent for your cap rate. You check out a likely property and find it has a cap rate of 9 percent. What does that mean? By examining how income, cap rate, and price are related, we can see that for a given amount of income, the higher the rate, the lower will be the purchase price. (Try your hand at a few examples to see how this works.) If you select a cap rate that is above the market, you will probably reject properties because the asking prices will be too high for your standard. If you are too low, you may agree to pay more than you should. So, when you compare cap rates, the property with a rate that is higher than yours may be a bargain.

Some investors like to use the price-earnings concept from the stock market as a guide. If you divide the offering price by the net operating income, you obtain a factor that represents the number of times earnings you are paying. It is clear you want the purchase price to be the smallest multiple. If, for example, a property is producing net income (as defined here) of $12,000 a year, a purchase price of $96,000 would be at eight times earnings; $120,000 would be ten times. So, as a variation on the income capitalization approach, you could divide an offering price by the net operating income to get the times earnings figure. In comparing properties on this basis, the one with the smallest number would be the better buy.

Our objective was to use the three standard approaches to valuation. Once computed for a property, the amounts should be compared to the offering price. If in each case the valuation is greater than the seller's price, you may conclude the property is not overpriced. If there is much discrepancy, once you've eliminated computational errors, you will want to look for reasons the seller is not asking more. He may know more about the property than you have been able to learn. Beware of bargains—but buy one when you can. Later we'll see how the three values reached here can be recorded on a Summary Chart to make comparison simple.

But there's still more; indicated economic value isn't everything. How about cash returns? Perhaps the best property for you is one that throws off the largest amount of spendable cash or tax shelter benefit even though its indicated economic value is not as favorable as others. Let's look now at what else we need to analyze.

Cash Flow Forecast

Now we come to the analysis of the property in terms of its ability to generate cash income. You should refer to the previous illustration to see the first portion of the calculation. To measure cash returns we want to know, ultimately, how many dollars the property will produce each year after all expenses, including income taxes, are paid. This ending figure, known as *net spendable,* is the best measure of current yield. You will not necessarily choose the property that gives you the greatest net spendable, however, unless your investment objective was to maximize current income. Net spendable in no manner reflects capital appreciation potential nor does it include equity build. Nonetheless, judging a project on the basis of aftertax current return is quite important.

On the Fact Sheets we calculated the Net Annual Cash Income. This figure allows both for nonrental income, such as from services, as well as a deduction for vacancies and lost rents. That is the source for the entry in the Cash Flow Forecast section. From that cash income we will make all cash expenditures. These include all operating items and the total amount of the payments made on the mortgage loans, both principal and interest components. The amount remaining out of the cash income is the net annual before income tax cash flow.

For many properties today, this cash flow figure might be negative. If you maximize leverage, for example, at high interest rates, you may find the rental income isn't enough so that each month, and for the year as a whole, you'll have to put up more cash to pay the bills. Is this any way to make money? Don't shy away at this point. When you have to add more cash, think of it as simply increasing your investment in installments. This, of course, will be prudent only if the final result is satisfactory. We'll calculate that shortly and then we can see. So much for the *negative cash flow*. You should want to avoid it, if possible, but don't reject opportunities out of hand solely because of it.

But what about our silent partner, the Internal Revenue Service? We now must calculate how much income tax, if any, we'll have to pay if we own the property for a year. The taxable income for the project will be combined with income from other sources when we file our tax return. We start again with the total cash revenue and subtract the cash operating expenses, but then we deduct only the mortgage interest payments, not dollars applied to reduce the principal balance. In anticipation of the need for this figure, recall that we calculated it at the time we were gathering data.

At this point we deduct the annual depreciation charge for the buildings and for the equipment. Once again we turn to the Fact Sheets as the source for the amounts needed here. It pays to plan ahead, doesn't it? Now we have the total annual taxable income for the first year; it may be either positive or negative. If the cash income is large enough to more than cover all the deductions, we will have a tax liability and therefore be subject to income tax, assuming we have other taxable income as well. On the other hand, as shown in the illustration, when the deductions exceeds the income, the result is a minus quantity and will produce a tax shelter benefit if we have other income offsetting this loss.

To calculate either the tax benefit or liability you need to estimate what your combined federal and state income tax rate will be for your top bracket. Remember that federal tax rates increase as your total taxable income increases. Here we are assuming you have other income—from employment, for example—and this investment result must be considered as coming on top of it. For that reason you need to use the marginal rate for the bracket you reach with the combined figure. Don't spend too much time arriving at this figure. A reasonable estimate is all that is needed, but you will want to use the same procedure for calculating it each time you apply it. Note that depending on the size of each project you are analyzing, a larger taxable income may take you into a higher tax bracket. In the illustration we can see that the negative taxable income, or operating loss, will be worth $2,035. This is the amount by which our total income tax bill is reduced by reason of owning the property. That saving is to be counted in the return from the investment. And now we are at the end of the cash forecast: we have a figure for the *net spendable*. We take the cash surplus from rental income less cash expenditures and add the amount of the tax shelter benefit. Because this is cash in hand after all expenses and tax responsibilities, we are free to spend all of it if we wish. This is truly the after-tax cash return for the first year due entirely from owning this property.

Let's pause for a moment to consider some of the implications of these computations. First, we'll look at the tax shelter benefit. Note that in the example we actually had a surplus of

TAXABLE INCOME COMPUTATION
FIRST YEAR

Net Annual Cash Income $ _34,450_

Less: Total Cash Operating Expenses $ _10,300_

Total Annual Interest Expense $ _21,505_

Depreciation—Buildings $ _6,667_

—Equipment $ _500_

Total Deductible Expenses $ _38,972_

TOTAL ANNUAL TAXABLE INCOME FIRST YEAR $ <_4,522_>

TAX LIABILITY OR TAX SHELTER BENEFIT

If the taxable income is positive, you will have a tax liability. ☐

If the taxable income is negative, you will have a tax shelter benefit. ☒

$ _4,522_ × _.45_ = $ _2,035_
Taxable Income   Tax Rate

NET SPENDABLE

Net Annual Before-Tax Cash Flow $ _1,746_

Less: Tax Liability or (add) Tax Shelter Benefit $ _2,035_

NET SPENDABLE FIRST YEAR $ _3,781_

cash after paying the bills, yet for tax purposes we had a loss. What's the reason? It lies in the way we can deduct depreciation from income as an expense. It is the best of all kinds of expense: we have the benefit of it yet do not have to part with any cash; we don't write out a check to pay depreciation. Now let's imagine that, unlike the situation for this property, we had a negative cash flow because the rents collected were less than the total amount we had to pay out. Often it turns out that this is more than offset by the tax savings created by the tax shelter benefit. If the reduction in your total income tax bill is greater than the negative cash flow, you won't have a shortage after all. This is why you don't want to summarily reject an opportunity on the basis of negative cash flow before completing the computation of the balance of the cash flow forecast.

Because we expect to own the property for at least a few years, we will need to know what we can expect in the way of net spendable during the holding period. The value we computed here for the first year will be used as a basis for calculating the total return. Because the net spendable in subsequent years will not be the same amount, even if we can keep rents in line with changes in expenses, an adjustment will be needed. That will be taken care of shortly.

Finally, to explain why we treat the tax shelter benefit as cash, consider this. From the computations you can see that the tax rate multiplied against the negative taxable income produces the benefit. The other way to look at this, to get the same result, is to start with your total taxable income before you add the results of owning the property. Assume that from all other sources you have:

Taxable Income	Tax Rate	Income Taxes to Pay
$35,000	45%	$15,750

Now reduce your taxable income by the operating loss:

($ 4,522)	45%	$ 2,035
	Revised Tax Liability	$13,715

Therefore, if you have to pay only $13,715 in taxes you have saved $2,035. This is money in the bank (assuming you aren't overdrawn) and is not to be confused with tax refunds. You have the money in hand because what you owe is a smaller amount.

If the property did not produce an operating loss, such as would generally be the case when you used little or no borrowed funds, you would increase your tax liability and the extra income taxes would be deducted from the cash returns to give the correct after-tax yield.

All of this deals with annual returns during the time you own the property. But, after all, we bought it to sell at some time in the future in order to realize the other potential gains. Let's look now at how to forecast those.

Realization on Sale

A major objective in investing in any form of real estate is to achieve long-term gains both from appreciation and, if leverage has been used, from equity build. Some properties have greater potential for these gains than others. It is important, therefore, to be able to analyze each opportunity and forecast what can reasonably be expected if the property is held for a number of years. When you consider the sales expense both of acquisition and resale, unless you have an unusually high appreciation rate, it will take at least a few years to earn any above average return. We will use a five-year investment horizon. You will need to make some judgment as to what time period to use in your forecasting. Under federal income tax rules, you must hold a capital asset for at least one year to have the benefit of the lower tax rate on capital gains. Check your state rules because the time period can be much longer. In California, for instance, minimum taxes apply only when the holding period exceeds five years. Our goal in this section of the analysis is to estimate the total number of dollars by which we'll be ahead for putting our cash to work, owning and managing the property for a stated number of years, and then selling for a reasonable price. The only

REALIZATION ON SALE

Holding Period **5** Years. Estimated Annual Appreciation Rate **7 1/2** %

Expected Selling Price: **1.43563** × **$250,000** = **$360,000**
Appreciation Factor Asking Price

Less: Sales Expense at **6** % commission $ **21,600**

    Fix-up Expense $ **2,000**

    Prepayment Penalty $ _____

    Total Expenses $ **23,600**

          GROSS CASH PROCEEDS $ **336,400**

Less: 1st loan $ **186,000** × **971.647** = $ **179,755**
         Original Amount   Factor

    2nd loan $ **10,000** × **956.531** = $ **9,565**
         Original Amount   Factor

    Total Amount paid off $ **189,320**

        NET CASH PROCEEDS FROM SALE $ **147,080**

Computation of Long-Term Taxable Gain

    Beginning Book Value: Original Cost $ **250,000**

                  Capitalized Costs $ **5,350** $ **255,350**

    Less Accrued Depreciation—Buildings $ **33,335**

                —Equipment $ **2,500** $ **35,835**

          ENDING BOOK VALUE $ **219,515**

    Taxable Gain: Gross Cash Proceeds $ **336,400**

           Less Ending Book Value $ **219,515**

          GAIN/LOSS ON SALE $ **116,885**

Income Tax Liability

Federal—

$ **116,885** × **.20** = FEDERAL TAX LIABILITY $ **23,377**
  Gain/Loss   Tax Rate

Tax Rate: Use full rate if short term; 40% of rate if long term.
           Gain/loss is long term if property has been held
           for more than one year.

State—

$ **116,885** × **.05** = STATE TAX LIABILITY $ **5,844**
  Gain/Loss   Tax Rate

          TOTAL TAX LIABILITY $ **29,221**

worthwhile measure is the cash in hand after all expenses and loans have been paid, income taxes have been settled, and your down payment and other outlays have been recovered. Let's proceed to discover what it might be.

Appreciation.   You can see what has been happening to property values. Almost without exception, every property, save those that have literally fallen apart, has increased in value each year for the past several years. The annual compound rate for some has been unbelievably high. And you want to get in on this! For the purpose of forecasting you will have to decide whether this condition is likely to continue and if so, at what annual rate. The rate will vary from one type of property to another and according to location. Although you should try to determine past rates, don't assume they will continue. It is not easy to reach a realistic number. If it is too large, you will not only be disappointed at liquidation time but you might pay too much for the property initially. Once we have an annual rate, we can estimate the sales price of the property at the end of the holding period.

In reality, property values can be measured from one year to the next and the rate of increase in effect is a compound percentage. You don't have to be that fussy, of course. If you conclude, for example, that values will increase at 10 percent a year and you hold the property for five years, simple arithmetic shows that you would expect to sell it for 50 percent more than you paid for it. That would give you a conservative value, however, if the rate was in fact 10 percent annually. A more accurate computation would require that you use a compound appreciation factor. In Table Three in the Appendix, you will find just what you need.

Continuing with our example, you can see from the illustration, that if you use a five year holding period and forecast an annual appreciation rate of 7½ percent, the factor from Table Three is 1.43563. By applying that to the original proposed cost, you can calculate the expected rounded sales price. After that you may want to step back and try to judge whether this is a realistic number. This is not easy to do. In any case, you need to forecast the probable resale price. From this forecast all the other calculations will be made. If you want to see the expected appreciation amount, just subtract the original cost from the sales price. Here it is $110,000. Possible?

To estimate the actual cash we'll have after expenses we have to decide whether we will use a real estate broker to find a buyer. Even if you have at least a tentative plan to do the selling yourself to save the commission expense, for analytical purposes you probably should assume there will be sales expense. If you do save it, your returns will be larger than otherwise expected. Under current income tax rules, fix-up expense incurred just before the sale can be treated as tax-deductible expense; otherwise it would have to be capitalized. You probably should anticipate spending some money to prepare the property for the sale, so enter a figure here. Note that we have not shown that a prepayment penalty would apply. Be certain you understand fully the terms of your borrowing. You may find that at the time you anticipated selling and paying off the loan, you would be faced with that cost. If so, include it in your forecast. Recall that if the buyer takes over the existing loan, no penalty would be imposed. That could certainly influence your marketing strategy at sale time.

Equity Build.   It is assumed in the example that the buyer will, perhaps through refinancing, give us all cash so that we will be settling the mortgage balances. You can determine what the loan balance would be by using Table One. For practice, why not check the factors shown in the example against the table? Again, although we do not need a separate amount for the equity build recovery, we can compute it at this point. It is the difference between the original loan and the payoff balance. Combined here it amounts to $5,680, the result of subtracting $189,320 from $195,000. Because we are selling the property for not less than its cost, we can recover all of the payments made on the mortgages during the holding period.

Capital Gains Taxes.   To determine how much income tax we have to pay on the gain from the sale, or tax credit we would have if there is a loss, we must first calculate the amount of the gain or loss. When you buy a capital asset and later sell or trade it, you are required to report the transaction on your income tax return. The federal rules are used here and apply, of course, uniformly. Your state rules are likely to be different so you will need to determine what they are. Real estate owned either for your use or to generate rental income is a capital asset. Property you hold as a stock in trade, such as inventory, is not. The amount of gain or loss from the sale of a capital asset is not simply the difference between its cost and sale price. We need to determine what the tax people call *basis.* Here's where we see how, in the case of rental income property, depreciation is converted to capital gain. Because capital gains are often taxed at lower rates, it is beneficial to arrange your financial affairs to maximize capital gains, especially the long-term variety.

The original cost, including capitalized expenses, is the basis of the asset at the outset. As you charge depreciation expense against income from the asset, you must change the basis by deducting the depreciation from it. By the time you sell the property, the revised basis should be the original cost minus the total of all depreciation taken during the holding period. The difference then between the gross cash proceeds from the sale and the revised basis, called *ending book value* by accountants, is the taxable gain. Note that this gain is more than it would be if you could simply deduct original cost from what you receive from the sale. The extra amount of the gain is due to depreciation and thus it has been converted to capital gain.

You will recall that we have computed depreciation separately on the buildings and the equipment; the process for determining taxable gain is the same for both. As you can see in the illustration, when the sales proceeds apply to the property and the equipment, to get the gain or loss, the total of all depreciation is reflected in the *ending book value.*

All along you expected to share at least part of the gain from appreciation with the tax collector. You may also expect that the taxable gain is the amount by which the property has appreciated. Not quite. Let's calculate the gain in another way to understand how it is arrived at as well as to double-check our computations. The original cost of the property in the example was a total of $255,350, counting the part of the settlement costs that were capitalized. This total must be reduced, as stated previously, by the amount of depreciation charged each year. In this example it is $35,835. If we can sell the property for $360,000, it would seem that the total appreciation is $360,000, less sales expense of $23,600, less original basis of $255,350, thus amounting overall to $81,050. On the face it would seem to be the net amount by which we're ahead, before taxes; in short, the net amount of appreciation. Well, not quite, from the income tax point of view. To this must be added the amount of depreciation. When that is done we arrive at $116,885 ($81,050 plus $35,835 = $116,885). Thus we have confirmed the earlier figure. Now comes the calculation of the amount of tax to pay on this part of our investment return.

Earlier we stated that gains from the sale of capital assets held more than a year, for federal tax purposes, are taxed at reduced rates. It's all a matter of definition: short- and long-term gains. Under current rules (and they are subject to change so you should keep informed about what the IRS is up to, not to mention Congress), when the sale takes place more than a year after the purchase, the gain (or loss) is deemed *long term*. Long-term results are subject to 40 percent of your regular current income tax rate, thus what you have to pay out of a gain is substantially less than for a short-term transaction. Stated another way, 60 percent of long-term gains are exempt from capital gains taxes. All short-term gains are taxed fully as current income.

Returning now to the illustrated example, let's see how this is applied. Because you've held the property for more than a year, five in this case, the gain qualifies as long-term. If your federal tax rate on current income for the bracket in which your taxable income lies is 50 percent, including 40 percent of the long-term gain, then the federal long-term capital gain tax would be calculated at 20 percent (40% of 50% = 20%).

To this you must add an amount for state and city income taxes. Assume here that amounts to another 5 percent. Now we have the total amount of taxes to be paid on the gain. Well, at least we have a figure for use in estimating results and choosing one investment opportunity over another. The actual amount of taxes to be paid may be affected by whatever liability you have under the rules for minimum taxes on tax preference items such as capital gains and accelerated depreciation. See IRS publication 525 and your tax advisor. We do not have to be concerned with such matters when analyzing a property, however.

Yields

When you invest for both current and long-term gain on the sale, it is customary to measure the yield on a combination of these, called the *total return*. It also is customary to express investment yields in annual percentage terms. As a part of the analysis of each property, following the cash flow forecast, you will want to determine these measures. They make it easier to compare one opportunity against another and reach a decision for action. You will notice that there are different ways to calculate yields so make certain when doing a comparison that you are judging apples against apples. Don't be misled, either, by someone else's statements about investment returns—find out how they made their calculations before making a judgment.

Total Return. If you own securities, you will find that in the investment community, people speak of the total return from an investment as the sum of the dividend yield and the annual appreciation rate. If a stock is paying an 8 percent annual dividend and is appreciating in share price by 10 percent a year, the total return is said to be 18 percent. It is possible to measure a real estate investment that way but it is not generally done because it is too cumbersome to estimate each of the sources of return. Instead, we speak of the total return as being the amount of cash, in hand, by which you are ahead through investing in the property. Look now at the illustration on the following page.

From a prior sheet we can determine the net cash proceeds and enter it here. The amounts to be deducted are also found in earlier sections of the analysis. Note that we did not show any additional investment during the time the property was held. If you make capital improvements, thus increasing the amount of your investment, such sums would be recorded. They would also affect the book value or basis of the property and the amount to be depreciated. At this point we compute the amount we'll have in cash flowing from the sale. But, what about the cash returns during the holding period? In this example, we assumed there would be a positive after-tax cash flow; this would not necessarily be true for all investments. If you had a great deal of willpower you might put aside, each year, the net spendable so that when you sold the property and had all those cash proceeds in hand, you could add the annual returns and see what a really big pile the property produced. Well, whether you decide to accumulate the net spendable or not, it must be added in to give us an accurate picture of the investment results.

When you use borrowed funds and pay off the loans with periodic payments of principal and interest, each year the total tax deduction for interest expense will go down, thus increasing your tax liability. If you are getting a tax shelter benefit, it will be reduced for this same reason. But we need a basis for estimating what our after-tax return will be each year and it would be convenient to use the net spendable computed for the first year, all as shown in the example. To reflect the change in the income tax when leverage is used, we can adjust the net spendable and use it in the forecast. Here we suggest you simply reduce it by 10 percent (take 90 percent of it) and multiply the result by the number of years you expect to own the property. Add the total of the annual returns and now you have the grand total of cash, in hand, the amount you truly are ahead after all obligations are settled and all cash employed has been recovered. All this will be so, of course,

TOTAL RETURN

Net Cash Proceeds from Sale $147,080

Less: Total Cash Invested $61,600

    Less Prorations $750 $60,850

    Tax Liability $29,221

    Additional Investment While Owned $ 0

    Total Recoveries $90,071

      NET GAIN AFTER-TAX AND RETURN OF FUNDS INVESTED $57,00

Add Annual Returns

$ 3,781 × 90% = $ 3,403 × 5 = $17,015
Net Spendable   Years
First Year*   Held

      TOTAL AFTER-TAX GAIN FROM THIS INVESTMENT $74,024

YIELDS

A. *Annual After-Tax*

$ 3,403 ÷ $ 61,600 × 100% = CASH ON CASH RETURN 5.5 %
Net Spendable   Total Cash
First Year*   Invested

B. *Average Annual Total Return*

$ 74,024 ÷ 5 = AVERAGE ANNUAL RETURN $14,80
Total After-Tax Gain   Years Held

$ 14,805 ÷ 61,600 × 100% = AVERAGE ANNUAL YIELD AFTER-TAX 24 %
Average Annual Return   Total Cash
                      Invested

*If funds are borrowed, multiply by 90% to reflect reduction in mortgage interest as loan is paid down and income tax is increased as a result.

only if the assumptions used in the forecasts hold true. This is the total return from this property. But how do you use this value, apart from contemplating how sweet it is?

If you could invest exactly the same amount of cash in each of several different properties, then the one that produced the largest total return would be best. In real estate, rarely is this the case. Each opportunity takes a different amount of cash and has differing risk characteristics. You need a measurement of returns in percentage form and there are a number of ways to calculate them.

Cash-on-Cash Return.   Ignoring returns from equity build and capital appreciation, let's calculate what the investment will do for us on a current basis. What's a good measure of annual after-tax returns? Remember, the only worthwhile dollar is the one left after taking care of income taxes. If you take the adjusted net spendable and relate it to the actual cash dollars you committed to the project, the percentage result is a fair measure of what those dollars are earning. Because we are dealing with cash in hand, we call this the *cash-on-cash return.* You can compare this against alternative ways to employ the cash. Of course this is not the only source of prospective gain from this type of investment, so be careful how you use it.

As a modest refinement here, if the amount of the settlement costs used for prorations is relatively large, you may want to deduct it from the total of the cash invested figure used in calculating the cash-on-cash return. During the first year you own the property, you will recover the prorations from the operating income.

Average Annual Total Return.   Now we come to a percentage expression that covers all the sources: net spendable, equity build, and appreciation. You can see from the illustration how to compute the average annual return in dollars and how to relate those dollars to what you have invested. There are some objections against this computation but, nonetheless, it can serve as a valuable measure for comparison of one property against another. It is likely you'll see that the bulk of the return used here, the total after-tax gain, is available only as a result of the sale and hence comes into your hands only at the end of the line. To state that as your *average* annual yield tends to imply that you've been receiving more return each year than actually has been the case. Be that as it may, because we refer to investment results in terms of annual percentages, we need this measure. If, after analyzing each of several properties, you find that the average annual yield after taxes for one property is significantly greater than all the others, you obviously will want to pay attention to what that suggests.

Yield Including Equity Build.   Some real estate investors argue that net spendable understates the real return from the property. With each mortgage payment from rental income, the investor's interest in the property is growing and the amount should be treated as a return. On the other side of that argument is the fact that you do not get your hands on the equity build unless and until you sell, and sell for not less than you paid. Given those two caveats, let's see how you would arrive at this additional measure of current yield.

To get the annual after-tax yield, including equity build, you simply need to add to the net spendable the amount by which the mortgage loans were reduced for the year. This can readily be determined from the entries on the Fact Sheets for the operating income and expenses. There you can deduct the total annual interest expense from the total of the mortgage payments. This difference is the amount by which the loan balances have been reduced; this is the equity build. Now take the total of net spendable and equity build and divide it by the total cash invested. The result, as a percentage, is the yield that reflects the equity build for the year.

We now must find a way to pull together the key items in the forecasts to judge which of the several properties analyzed is the best for our purpose.

Analysis Summary

On the following page you can see how to display, for each opportunity, the data important to selecting the property

ANALYSIS SUMMARY

| Property Location | Asking Price | Cash Required | Indicated Economic Values | | | | Yields | |
			Cost	Market	Income	Net Spendable	Cash on Cash	Average Annual
220 Ambus Cres	$250,000	$61,600	$282,460	$278,400	$268,333	$3,781	5.5 %	24 %
878 Regal Road	300,000	76,000	305,000	295,000	274,000	1,050	1.4 %	81 %
McCarthy Apts.	400,000	59,000	420,000	414,000	415,000	4,000	8.0 %	14 %

which will most likely produce maximum results. All this presumes, of course, that not only have you avoided arithmetic errors, a feat in itself for many, but have based your forecasts on appropriate assumptions. The more often you analyze property, the better you'll get at the process.

Can you properly select an investment property solely on the basis of numbers such as these? Looking at the illustration, which would you put your money on? Ask yourself, "How do I feel about current yield versus long-term appreciation?" It appears that the potential for capital gain is greatest for the Angus Crescent property. If you prefer more birds in the hand to those in the bush, you might want to own the McCarthy Apartments. That project takes less cash and produces the largest cash-on-cash yield, but it seems to have limited upside potential. If you do have your act together with respect to your investment goals, the numbers displayed in this manner will make the task of choosing relatively easy. But what about the intangibles? You have more things to think about.

Prospective Changes

Forecasting is a risky business. At the time you are analyzing a specific property, you should sit back and thoughtfully list all the conditions that could change and reasonably be expected to affect the value of your investment, both plus and minus. Here are some examples.

The prospects for rent control are of vital concern if you are considering investing in residential income property. This is not a factor, of course, for commercial properties, raw land, or for your own home. On the other hand, changes in zoning or land use regulations could make a difference no matter which type of property you're looking at. The impact, of course, could be greater for one property than another. Limitations on your selection of tenants, such as the application of fair housing laws and ordinances banning refusal to rent apartments to families, may apply to property under study. What could these things mean to you or to a future buyer when it comes time to resell?

Then there are some items directly related to the specific property, not necessarily to all properties in the community. What is the risk of earth movement, flooding, earthquake, windstorm, and other physical perils? Yes, you can usually buy insurance but there are always costs beyond those to which the insurance applies. Would you be better off investing where these risks are minimized? How about the employment prospects for your tenants? Perhaps the present tenants are substantially dependent on employment at a nearby factory, air base, or other government installation. What is the outlook for employment stability? How about existing lease agreements? You may want to remodel or further develop the property but would be stymied because of the rights of the present tenants.

In general, the foregoing points suggest possible adverse results. It is equally important to look for those factors uniquely present that will provide the basis for above average returns. There may be such a shortage of rental units in the area, with no reasonable basis for assuming people will leave the area and no likelihood that newly constructed property could be rented for moderate rents, that your investment will be extremely secure. Here, of course, you'd have to make certain you didn't pay too large a premium.

If in the process of analyzing all your alternatives, you have done your best and reached a conclusion, then relax. Once done, rest easy. If a mistake has been made after all your efforts along the lines outlined here, remember that you're human after all. Just avoid being both human and stupid.

CLOSING THOUGHTS

This chapter contains probably the most important part of the entire book. Your success as an investor in real estate depends on your ability to choose the right property. Once you have developed the information for a specific opportunity and recorded it on Fact Sheets, what you do next is critical. Forecasting cash flows, computing indicated economic values, and projecting what is reasonably likely to be obtained when you sell are essential to the ultimate decision-making step. There can be no question but that your returns from employing cash in real estate can be substantial if you employ what you have learned.

But you aren't through learning yet. We need to discuss how you negotiate the purchase of the property your analysis directs you to, how to manage it once you've "stolen it" from the seller, and how to develop strategies for selling that will minimize taxes and enhance your financial security. Let's get on with it.

7

Negotiating the Deal

Now that you've narrowed your search to only a few properties and have analyzed each, what's next? This is the time to make a decision—choose one, make an offer, and be prepared to complete the purchase.

Once you have finished a set of Fact Sheets for each property, you should enter the highlights on an Analysis Summary as discussed in the preceding chapter. Then, almost at a glance, you will be able to judge which property is likely to be the best. Now comes the double checking, the soul-searching, and the big step—making an offer the seller can't refuse. But be careful, if your offer is readily accepted, maybe it is too generous.

The investment begins with the *purchase agreement*. This is a formal contract presenting all of the terms and conditions which buyer and seller agree to by signing. This agreement contains the purchase price, financing, and other contingencies, such as time for performance, penalties for failure to complete, and many other items. Once you've made up your mind you want to buy a property, you then should have the purchase agreement prepared. In some areas this is done routinely by a real estate lawyer, and in other areas the real estate brokers do it in behalf of buyers and sellers. Realize that you are making an offer, not the seller inviting you to accept. Your offer can be legally accepted only when all parties with an ownership interest in the property sign the agreement.

For protection of all when it's time to exchange money and deeds, it is best to have an independent third party perform an escrow service. The escrow agent receives cash from buyers and lenders, and title transfer documents, such as a deed, from the seller. Once the deed is recorded and title transferred, the lender's interest secured, funds given to the sellers, and keys handed over, the deal is complete. The escrow is *closed* and the *settlement* is made.

THE PURCHASE DECISION

You may find looking at property, gathering facts, and musing on potential profits to be very exciting. For any profits actually to be realized, you ultimately will have to choose a property and take the steps needed to make it yours. There are many factors to be considered in reviewing your information, and your emotions may play a role. Don't make the mistake of allowing unjustified enthusiasm for unrealistic expectations to be dominant. Not only must you remain objective about the property itself, but also about the financing and other economic aspects. Finally, especially if this is to be your first venture, you must not be intimidated by the unknown and apparent great magnitude of the financial commitment. Many are hesitant to borrow funds to buy real estate because they fear the possibility that they will have trouble meeting their obligations. While it is healthy to be a prudent borrower, remember that when the property is security for the loan and you really do have financial difficulties, it is unlikely that you would have to pay off the debt without, at the same time, being able to liquidate the property. The cash to meet the loan would come from the sale of the real estate itself.

It is possible to reach a point where, after foreclosure, there is only enough from the sale to pay off the indebtedness.

Note, however, that in such a situation, the buyer has lost only the original cash investment. Except in some very unusual circumstances, the lender can look only to the security and cannot make a successful claim against the borrower for any deficiency arising from default. As a practical matter, during an inflationary period, the value of the collateral will be increasing so that an owner will likely be able to find someone to take over the property, avoid foreclosure, and recover some, all, or more than the cash invested. If you develop information accurately and completely, make the analysis described here, and prudently use the data to make your selection, you can expect to avoid pitfalls.

Making the Choice

Let's first consider property to be your home. This can be a single-family home, condominium, or co-op apartment unit. Previously we discussed the rules of thumb that can be used to judge your income against the cost of owning your home. Now that you have settled on your dream house, you need to ask yourself this question once again: "How much house can I afford?" The most satisfactory way to answer that is to make out a family budget, making certain you have included all expenses you'll have. If your take-home income covers them, including an allowance for unexpected bills, then you're all set. On the other hand, this calculation may tell you it is premature to buy now if it means significantly increasing your cost for housing and stretching your income beyond reason. No matter how much you'd like to have a big house in a fine neighborhood, perhaps your current income and obligations simply preclude moving up at this time. Maybe you need simply to lower your sights. In any case you should, however, be prepared to make some sacrifices in order to own your own home. Judging where these should come is the hard part.

But let's assume you do see how you can handle the financial aspects. Now you need to check out the property once more. Take another look at the neighborhood. Talk to your prospective neighbors, not only to judge compatibility, but also to learn more information that might be pertinent to your selection. If at all possible, check out the property on a day when it is raining or snowing. Are there drainage or earth movement problems not readily apparent? Consider the layout of the house. Will it really give you what you and your family need? What compromises are you making and are there enough offsets to make them worthwhile? How about furniture? Will it fit in the new house or will you have to spend a lot to make the home livable? And will you have any cash left over after the deal is closed to buy things you'll need? Try to imagine yourself all moved in. Can you anticipate any problems that should be resolved *before* you commit yourself to buy? Once you've done all this and are still convinced it's right to buy, then check over the financing plan once more. See if the mortgage that you'll need is realistically obtainable. If not, don't waste your, or others', time. If so, then decide on an offering price and terms.

If you are considering income property, what action is needed at this point? First you need to reconfirm your investment objectives and make your choice from the properties analyzed according to which one best fits your goals. Consider all the assumptions made concerning prospective growth in value. Are there any hidden physical problems? Are you really ready to assume ownership and managerial responsibilities? Do you have all the beginning cash required to make the deal? How about cash reserves for emergencies? Just what will it mean to your life-style to be an owner and landlord—and are those changes acceptable? Before making an offer, try to ensure that every aspect of the deal is practical and reasonable. This, however, should not deter you from making an offer the seller might reject because he or she does not consider it reasonable. It's your money you are spending.

Financing

The purchase price is one thing; the amount of cash you need when you make the offer is quite another matter. Prior to putting the offer in writing you should review your proposed financial plan and check to make certain you can perform if required.

Assuming you plan to use borrowed funds, the total cash you will need to complete the transaction will be the sum of the down payment (the difference between the purchase price and the amount to be borrowed) and the settlement costs. Now's the time to confirm that you do, in fact, have all that is needed. But must you hand over the full amount of the down payment, or the purchase price if there's no borrowing, at the time the offer is made? No. It is customary for the purchase agreement to be accompanied by *earnest money* or *purchase deposit*. The amount will depend on local custom, to some extent, and on your evaluation of the specific situation. Basically, this sum is intended to convince the seller that you are a serious and responsible prospective buyer and to justify the seller in taking the property off the market while you are completing the deal. Most real estate offers involve contingencies and many transactions are never completed. The seller is taking some risk and your deposit will be taken as an indication of your intent. Under appropriate circumstances, this deposit is subject to forfeiture for nonperformance by the buyer, and thus represents the potential recovery by the seller for damages suffered. If you put up only a nominal amount, the seller may not wish to go along with you. If you are offering less than the asking price, a larger deposit might be more persuasive.

To avoid tying up a large sum, you may wish to tender a modest deposit with the offer but agree to increase it substantially if the buyer accepts. Generally, there will be some lapse of time before you have to present the down payment. That usually happens only at the time of the close of the escrow, coincident with the disbursement of the loan by the lender. Although local customs differ throughout the country, it is best, regardless, for all deposits and other cash payments to be made to the escrow agent. In some cases, of course, it is quite acceptable to pay the deposit to a real estate broker who, if the seller accepts the offer, will then transfer the money to the escrow. As a rule, deposits should not be simply handed to the seller; what could you do about getting the money back if the deal falls through? This is not to malign sellers, but buyers must be realistic. When people disagree over a business deal, money becomes a bone of contention. If you put your deposit in the hands of an escrow agent with instructions that it is to be returned if the deal is not completed, you will have minimized prospective difficulties.

Is your proposed financing plan feasible? Are the lenders you've lined up still interested? If you obtained a written commitment, as long as the time limit has not expired, you have little to worry about. If things still appear favorable you will want to proceed, but protect yourself nonetheless. To avoid being committed to making a purchase even though your financing plan falls through, you should make your offer *subject to* being able to obtain specified loan terms. This requires precise language in the offer. As you make up your mind about the deal, you need to decide just what conditions you want in the agreement. What is the minimum loan amount required? How soon is the balloon payment due and can you live with that? Take another look at the loan payment amounts for the mortgage you've been considering to see whether the cash flow will really be adequate. Maybe this is the time to try for a longer term loan to reduce the payments. Formulate the best possible financing terms for your purposes and incorporate them in the contingencies. You can always agree to less favorable terms if what you ask for isn't available. But as long as the seller accepts your conditional offer, if the terms can't be met, you can back out and recover your deposit.

Timing

There are many steps to be taken and you will find it desirable to prepare a timetable that will lay out clearly the necessary sequence of action. This means deciding on how much time is to be allowed for certain decisions and performance on the part of both the seller and yourself. Here are the critical items.

1. Time for seller to accept your offer. This usually is limited to as little as forty-eight hours but can be any time the parties agree on. It is best to designate it so that there can be no question as to the precise time the offer expires; use an hour and date such as "...offer expires if not accepted before 8 p.m., April 18, 19xx." If you are offering exactly the terms stated by the seller, there should be no delay. On the other hand, the seller may have to weigh all the contingencies you present and evaluate the likelihood you can perform. The seller may also want to see if he can get a better offer from someone else. Note that during the time your offer stands open the seller is free to consider, and even accept, other offers. For that reason, if you are really keen on the deal, you will want to make your offer subject to acceptance within a very short time period, thus prompting the seller to action, hopefully acceptance. Once the time period for acceptance has expired and the seller has not acted, you are no longer bound by the offer. If later, the seller says he or she will now accept, you are free to reject such acceptance. At that point, perhaps, the negotiations could start up all over again.

Assume now that you are dealing through a real estate broker and the property is available to other brokers, such as through the Multiple Listing Service (MLS). Once an offer has been presented to a seller, on an ethical basis, no others are to be communicated to the seller until he or she has made a decision on the first. You need to be prepared, however, to find that, in fact, your offer will be competing with other offers which have indeed been communicated in the interim. Such is the way in which competition operates. To the extent this may be a factor in your dealings, the shorter the acceptance time is, the less likely your offer will face others.

2. Once the offer is accepted by the seller signing the purchase contract, the next time period for performance will be when you put up the balance of the down payment. In your plan for the property you will have set a time by which you

want possession. This means that the escrow must be closed in time to make that possible. It is customary for possession to be withheld until all money has been paid and documents recorded. Realize that when you state a date for closing, this means you will have to have performed all parts of your obligation.

Throughout our examples we have assumed that property is purchased with borrowed funds. The purchase deposit usually is considered to be a part of the down payment, hence the reference above to putting up the balance. In actuality, the buyer must put up all of the remaining cash needed to close the deal and this will include not only the rest of the down payment but also the settlement costs. Recall how all this was calculated when completing the Fact Sheets.

When buying income property, the time for closing the deal and obtaining possession is not as critical, as a rule, as for a home purchase. In making an investment you may want the transaction to close on a specified date to accommodate income tax considerations, but other than that the prime concern probably will be the time when the lender will put up the loan funds. If you are planning to move out of one home and into another, timing may become a most serious matter. Camping out in the city park for a few weeks may appeal to the kids but how about you and your spouse? Here are some suggestions.

When all the terms of the deal are set, don't let delays jeopardize it. If, for example, you discover that you won't be ready to occupy the new house until sometime after the deal can be closed, you might ask the sellers if they would like to be your tenants. Perhaps the sellers, in their anxiety to make a deal, find that they don't really have a place to go at the time the escrow can be closed—maybe they are moving to another property that isn't quite ready. In this case, two problems could be solved. All that is needed is an agreement on the rental value of the property. The former owners then pay you for staying beyond the closing date. Be certain, however, to have a written agreement as to the basis for payment and, above all, when they are to leave. Never postpone a settlement date to cover the situation described here. Too many things could happen to prevent the ultimate completion of the purchase.

But now let's look at the other side of this problem. What if you needed to move in and the seller was able to give up the property, all before the close of the escrow? As a buyer, you have little or no risk here; the seller does face the possibility that the deal may fall through and that you may remain in residence. If you do move in before the settlement is made, expect to pay the seller rent. Sellers will agree to all of this only after being satisfied you will complete the transaction.

3. The balance of the purchase price usually is payable after certain steps stated in the agreement have been taken. These typically include obtaining assurance that the financing as defined is available, and that property is inspected and appraised. Even though the deal is not to be completed before all the contingencies have been met, it still may be useful to provide a time limit within which performance is required. As the buyer you may be asked to meet these time limits in order to give the seller adequate protection. You'll have to balance your desire to have the transaction completed against having enough time in which to do what you have to do—such as raise cash. All this can become an exciting balancing act.

The language of your offer may require the seller to perform as soon as you do things you are committed to do. An eager seller will not likely be opposed to such a provision. But, what protection does the seller have against your procrastination? Your failure to meet deadlines should give the seller the right to withdraw without penalty. There's a malady that may affect those who become involved in real estate; it is known as *buyer's remorse*. This is the condition the buyer finds himself in the morning after making a commitment to buy. It leads to strange and wondrous actions all designed to wiggle out of a deal at no cost. Sellers must be careful to see that purchase agreements contain adequate protection against the ravages of this ailment. This is not to say there haven't been reported cases of *seller's remorse*. These have been observed immediately following the presentation of a better offer. The known antidote for buyers' remorse is forfeiture of the deposit; you may have to sue the victim of seller's remorse for specific performance.

What do you do if you must sell one property in order to buy another? Can you make such a sale a contingency in an offer to buy? Yes. Some of the greatest excitement can be found in transactions where one or more parties are participating subject to the sale of other property. Although not limited to home purchases, that's what we'll use as an example to illustrate. Assume you find another house and make an offer to buy it subject to the sale of your currently owned home. Now you have to hustle to find a buyer. Perhaps a prospective buyer offers to purchase your house subject to the sale of his or hers. Note this could go on and on. Each seller has to evaluate the likelihood that the proposed buyer can actually sell the other property within a stated time limit. Timing is critical. Some experienced real estate investors, having been burned, refuse to become involved in such contingent deals. This may mean turning down an otherwise perfectly acceptable offer, and soul-searching is needed. Note that failure to perform within the time limit usually means the deal is off. Whether there are any damages to pay will depend on the terms of the contract and the nature of the failure to perform.

4. At what time is possession to be granted? Good business practice dictates that possession should not be given the buyer until the deal is closed. It is customary to make such a provision in the purchase contract. Often keys to the property are turned over by the escrow agent as a part of the settlement. The parties are free, of course, to reach other arrangements.

Summary: Time limits are essential and they should be stated clearly in the agreement. Because performance can be inhibited by conditions beyond the control of the parties, it is customary to allow for extensions to avoid inequities. When a real estate broker is involved in the transaction, for example, it is commonplace for both buyers and sellers to delegate to the broker the authority to extend deadlines, within limits. If you do not wish to be bound by such an arrangement, make certain it is not in any agreement you sign.

All told, then, when you are putting together the terms of an offer, you should exercise great care in deciding how much time you want to have to do your part, and what limits you wish to impose on the seller. This and all the other aspects of your offer will have to be communicated to the person who drafts your offer when you are not doing it entirely yourself.

PURCHASE OFFER

During preliminary negotiations and the fact-gathering phase, you may have very little in writing. But once there is a possibility of making a purchase, steps must be taken to commit the offer, and its acceptance, to writing. Oral agreements to buy or sell can lead only to trouble! Nor should there be any oral agreement with respect to any written provision. Once an offer is made in writing, any and all revisions must also be in writing and be signed by all parties. This procedure will minimize misunderstanding and will lead to more satisfactory relationships. A written contract is essential in the event legal action is ever taken. It is recommended that purchase agreements be drawn by experienced people; this is usually accomplished by qualified legal counsel. Many real estate practitioners are qualified through training and practice to prepare purchase agreements and frequently this service is simply part of handling the transaction. You must decide for yourself in a given case whether to engage an attorney to draw your agreement and represent you in the negotiations. Although many investors have found it practical to handle these matters themselves, this is not a risk-free activity for the inexperienced.

The purchase offer agreement provides all the terms and conditions to which each party chooses to be bound by the act of signing. The seller, before accepting, must consider whether he or she is fully aware of what is being agreed to. The buyer must, among many matters, be satisfied that the seller does, in fact, have the legal right to sell. Because any flaws in the seller's right may not appear until after the money has been exchanged, it is essential that the buyer be protected. This can be accomplished by stipulating in the offer that an escrow agent is to be used and that title must be in a form acceptable to, and insurable by, a title insurance company. As long as there is some reasonable indication that

CALIFORNIA ASSOCIATION OF REALTORS® STANDARD FORM

REAL ESTATE PURCHASE CONTRACT
AND RECEIPT FOR DEPOSIT

THIS IS MORE THAN A RECEIPT FOR MONEY. IT IS INTENDED TO BE A LEGALLY BINDING CONTRACT. READ IT CAREFULLY.

_____ , California. _____ , 19 _____

Received from _____

herein called Buyer, the sum of _____ Dollars $ _____

evidenced by cash ☐, cashier's check ☐, or _____ ☐, personal check ☐ payable to _____

_____ , to be held uncashed until acceptance of this offer, as deposit on account of purchase price

_____ Dollars $ _____

for the purchase of property, situated in _____ County of _____ , California

described as follows: _____

1.	Buyer will deposit in escrow with _____ the balance of purchase price as follows

_____

_____

_____

_____

_____

_____

_____

_____

_____

_____

_____

_____

_____

_____

_____

_____

_____

_____

_____

_____

_____

_____

_____

_____

_____

_____

_____

Set forth above any terms and conditions of a factual nature applicable to this sale, such as financing, prior sale of other property, the matter of structural pest control inspection, repairs and personal property to be included in the sale.

2.	Deposit will ☐ will not ☐ be increased by $ _____ to $ _____ within _____ days **acceptance of this offer.**

3.	Buyer does ☐ does not ☐ intend to occupy subject property as his residence.

4.	The supplements initialed below are incorporated as part of this agreement.

Other

____ Structural Pest Control Certification Agreement   ____ Occupancy Agreement   ____   _____

____ Special Studies Zone Disclosure   ____ V A Amendment   ____   _____

____ Flood Insurance Disclosure   ____ FHA Amendment   ____   _____

5.	Buyer and Seller acknowledge receipt of a copy of this page, which constitutes Page 1 of____ Pages.

X _____   X _____
BUYER   **SELLER**

X _____   X _____
BUYER   **SELLER**

A REAL ESTATE BROKER IS THE PERSON QUALIFIED TO ADVISE ON REAL ESTATE. IF YOU DESIRE LEGAL ADVICE CONSULT YOUR ATTORNEY.

For these forms, address California Association of Realtors®
505 Shatto Place, Los Angeles, California 90020
(Revised 1978)   FORM D-11-1

REAL ESTATE PURCHASE CONTRACT AND RECEIPT FOR DEPOSIT

The following terms and conditions are hereby incorporated in and made a part of Purchaser's Offer

6.   Buyer and Seller shall deliver signed instructions to the escrow holder within _____ days from Seller's acceptance which shall provide for closing within _____ days from Seller's acceptance. Escrow fees to be paid as follows:

_____

_____

7.   Title is to be free of liens, encumbrances, easements, restrictions, rights and conditions of record or known to Seller, other than the following: (1) Current property taxes, (2) covenants, conditions, restrictions, and public utility easements of record, if any, provided the same do not adversely affect the continued use of the property for the purposes for which it is presently being used, unless reasonably disapproved by Buyer in writing within _____ days of receipt of a current preliminary title report furnished at _____ expense, and (3) _____

Seller shall furnish Buyer at _____ expense a standard California Land Title Association policy issued by _____ Company, showing title vested in Buyer subject only to the above. If Seller (1) is unwilling or unable to eliminate any title matter disapproved by Buyer as above, Seller may terminate this agreement, or (2) fails to deliver title as above, Buyer may terminate this agreement; in either case, the deposit shall be returned to Buyer.

8.   Property taxes, premiums on insurance acceptable to Buyer, rents, interest, and _____ shall be pro-rated as of (a) the date of recordation of deed; or (b) _____
Any bond or assessment which is a lien shall be ___paid___ by _____ . _____ shall pay cost of
                                       assumed
transfer taxes, if any.
9.   Possession shall be delivered to Buyer (a) on close of escrow, or (b) not later than _____ days after close of escrow or (c) _____
10.   Unless otherwise designated in the escrow instructions of Buyer, title shall vest as follows: _____

_____

    (The manner of taking title may have significant legal and tax consequences. Therefore, give this matter serious consideration.)
11.   If Broker is a participant of a Board multiple listing service ("MLS"), the Broker is authorized to report the sale, its price, terms, and financing for the information, publication, dissemination, and use of the authorized Board members.
12.   **If Buyer fails to complete said purchase as herein provided by reason of any default of Buyer, Seller shall be released from his obligation to sell the property to Buyer and may proceed against Buyer upon any claim or remedy which he may have in law or equity; provided, however, that by placing their initials here Buyer: (**   **) Seller: (**   **) agree that Seller shall retain the deposit as his liquidated damages. If the described property is a dwelling with no more than four units, one of which the Buyer intends to occupy as his residence, Seller shall retain as liquidated damages the deposit actually paid, or an amount therefrom, not more than 3% of the purchase price and promptly return any excess to Buyer.**
13.   If the only controversy or claim between the parties arises out of or relates to the disposition of the Buyer's deposit, such controversy or claim shall at the election of the parties be decided by arbitration. Such arbitration shall be determined in accordance with the Rules of the American Arbitration Association, and judgment upon the award rendered by the Arbitrator(s) may be entered in any court having jurisdiction thereof. The provisions of Code of Civil Procedure Section 1283.05 shall be applicable to such arbitration.
14.   In any action or proceeding arising out of this agreement, the prevailing party shall be entitled to reasonable attorney's fees and costs.
15.   Time is the essence. All modifications or extensions shall be in writing signed by the parties.
16.   This constitutes an offer to purchase the described property. Unless acceptance is signed by Seller and the signed copy delivered to Buyer, in person or by mail to the address below, within _____ days, this offer shall be deemed revoked and the deposit shall be returned. Buyer acknowledges receipt of a copy hereof.

Real Estate Broker _____   Buyer _____

By _____   _____

Address _____   Address _____

Telephone _____   Telephone _____

ACCEPTANCE

The undersigned Seller accepts and agrees to sell the property on the above terms and conditions. Seller has employed _____
_____ as Broker(s) and agrees to pay for services the sum of
_____ Dollars ($ _____), payable as follows:
(a) On recordation of the deed or other evidence of title, or (b) if completion of sale is prevented by default of Seller, upon Seller's default or (c) if completion of sale is prevented by default of Buyer, only if and when Seller collects damages from Buyer, by suit or otherwise and then in an amount not less than one-half of the damages recovered, but not to exceed the above fee, after first deducting title and escrow expenses and the expenses of collection, if any. In any action between Broker and Seller arising out of this agreement, the prevailing party shall be entitled to reasonable attorney's fees and costs. The undersigned acknowledges receipt of a copy and authorizes Broker(s) to deliver a signed copy to Buyer.

Dated: _____ Telephone _____   Seller _____
Address _____   Seller _____

Broker(s) agree to the foregoing. Broker _____ Broker _____
Dated: _____ By _____   Dated: _____ By _____

For these forms, address California Association of Realtors®
505 Shatto Place, Los Angeles, California 90020 (Revised 1978)   FORM D-11-2   Page _____ of _____ Page:

the seller has a legal right to sell and can pass clear title, it is in order to present an offer. Here are the major points to be considered in preparing it.

Price

As a rule, the seller will stipulate a sales price together with the terms; in some cases all cash is required. How you obtain that cash has nothing to do with the seller. You are free to use the property as security, presuming you plan to have the title transferred free and clear of encumbrances. If there already is a loan on the property and the seller stipulates all cash, that simply means that if the loan is to be assumed he wants all cash down to the loan. Alternatively, the buyer is expected to come up with a new loan and pay off the existing debt. So, all cash means only that the buyer does not want to be involved in participating in the financing. Because you can borrow, you could still buy even though your cash resources fell far short of the asking price.

Amount.   But what about the price you should offer? Should you just accept or reject the seller's asking price? Never! Using the procedure discussed in the preceding chapters, you should come up with your own price for the property. If it happens to be higher than the seller's, fine. But don't conclude you should, therefore, agree to pay exactly what the seller wants. If your evaluation produces a lower price, it should strengthen your conviction the property is overpriced. Once you have made a decision as to what the property is worth to you, you should make an offer of an amount that is both *less* than your value and *less* than the asking price. In negotiating you can always raise your price but rarely will you have a chance to lower it and gain acceptance. Because valuation of real estate is anything but an exact science, you must realize there is no such thing as a *correct* price.

If the seller is desperate for a buyer, you may be able to drive a very hard bargain. If the seller is not really serious about wanting to sell, the asking price may be ridiculous and you'd be a fool to pay it. But, it is a waste of time making an offer that couldn't possibly be acceptable to the seller. Discovering the point that lies in between requires skill, perseverance, and imagination. Even if you are extremely enthusiastic about acquiring the property, never forget that if you don't present the lowest price you believe is reasonable, you may never know whether the seller would have accepted it. Wouldn't that be frustrating? Just think, you might have been able to buy for less than you offered. The way to find out is to offer price and terms that are rejected, then inch up until a satisfactory deal is made. If your offer is accepted without question, you may have given something away. That will be an especially nagging thought if your offer is accepted *immediately*.

Financing.   We must not overlook the great difference financing can make on the overall purchase price. That is why judging prices paid for property can be difficult and even misleading. Assume there are two identical properties, such as those found in a housing subdivision. In one case the property is placed on the market by the original owner who, over time, has developed a substantial equity. The other property has been refinanced through a prior sale. The loan balance on the first house is $30,000 and the second, $65,000. At present, mortgage money is very scarce and interest rates are at their peak. Should these identical properties carry the same sales price? Probably not and let's see why.

Assume we have a buyer with $20,000 in cash. If the $65,000 loan can be assumed by a qualified buyer, a total price of $85,000 is feasible. Obviously the property must have a value at least in range of this for it to be a realistic price. But let's say the buyer is attracted to the other house for some personal, non-economic reason. Unless refinancing can be obtained under conditions where the buyer's monthly expense will not be drastically different from that for the second house, he could not buy the first at $85,000. The seller's equity would be $55,000 and the buyer's $20,000 cash would be inadequate. If the seller offered to provide the $35,000 additional financing needed through a second mortgage, that still might not solve the problem. It's more than likely that the sum of the first mortgage payments plus that for the second mortgage would far exceed the debt service on the $65,000 loan on the second property. And it's unlikely that the seller would really want to go for the $35,000 second mortgage anyway; many would not be able to if they were going to buy other property. So what happens, especially when it's tough to get a new first loan, to the price of high-equity property? The asking price is reduced, relative to comparable properties for which high loans are in place.

In our example, the owner of the first house would probably ask $70,000, thus making it necessary for a buyer to come up with a down payment of $40,000. Because this appears to be a bargain price, some buyers would scratch around and do whatever was necessary to come up with the money for the down payment. The seller could help things along with a second mortgage for $5,000 or $10,000, but that's better than one for $35,000. The net result would be that the seller with the large equity would not obtain what might otherwise be considered the market price for the property. To point to that house and say that because the seller agreed to the $70,000 price, the second house is not worth $85,000 would be stating an improper conclusion. How a deal is financed can make a big difference!

Perhaps the moral of the situation just described is: don't let your equity become large if there is any chance a buyer with enough cash cannot be found or the supply of mortgage funds is limited.

Cash Down: In making an offer, you are agreeing on two things: the total price you will pay, and how you will pay that price. Basically, the offer should show how much you intend to borrow, when the financing is one of the contingencies, and how much earnest money is tendered with the offer. Here's an example of a typical proposal. The language used is for illustrative purposes only and is not offered as legally sufficient, necessarily, for use in a real-life transaction.

> The buyer agrees to buy the property described for a total purchase price of $200,000 payable as follows:
> $500 as earnest money accompanying this offer; a further $4,500 to be paid within twenty-four hours of the time this offer

is accepted by the sellers; and the balance of the purchase price to be paid within forty-five days of the acceptance of this offer, subject to the buyer obtaining financing on the following terms —a first mortgage loan for at least $175,000 fully amortized over a term of not less than twenty-five years, at an interest rate not to exceed 11½ percent and a loan fee not to exceed two points, and the loan to be free of any prepayment penalty after the first year of the mortgage term.

Once these terms are accepted, the buyer would have to scurry around to get the loan on the terms stated. He or she would have the option to back out of the deal if, for example, after a good faith try, the only loan available was at 13 percent or at 11½ percent but with loan fees of four points. In effect, the seller has agreed that the buyer can be relieved of the obligation to complete the purchase if any one or more of the terms cannot be met. It must be clear that this gives the buyer lots of opportunity to fall victim to buyer's remorse. A seller would have to rely on the buyer being well-motivated to do everything possible to obtain the terms stated and to accept a compromise if this were not possible. In most cases, buyers who really want to obtain the property willingly accept loan terms less favorable, if they have to, and thus complete the deal.

Once you've decided on the price, down payment, deposit amount, and loan terms, you or your advisor can prepare the language to insert in the purchase agreement. Don't be surprised if this section has to be rewritten a few times to hit upon terms acceptable to all concerned.

Personal Property

Furnishings and equipment are not a part of the real estate and must be treated specifically in the language of the purchase agreement. Unlike realty, title to personal property is passed through a *bill of sale*. There is no requirement that there be a separate purchase price and some sellers throw in the furniture without any extra payment. Where the value is important, there should be a clearly stated separate price and a statement of how and when it is to be paid. This will be important information for the buyer to use when computing depreciation. All personal property, whether paid for specifically or not, should be described in a bill of sale formally executed by the seller. This will eliminate any question as to ownership in the future. In the case of a going business, the transfer of inventory and equipment is usually subject to notification to creditors by way of legal notice in a newspaper.

When you are buying a home and the seller agrees to include the drapes, appliances, and so on, great care should be taken to specify such items clearly in the purchase contract. Those who rely on verbal understanding may later have reason to revise their views of humanity. Buyers and sellers have been known to come to blows in a disagreement as to exactly what was included in the deal. The difference in the recollection of each other's statements is remarkable.

Property Description

A parcel of real estate may have more than one identification. A structure such as a house, apartment, or commercial building will typically have a street address. It is used primarily for the convenience of the postal service and the public in general. Every plot of land, however, has an official *legal* description. It is the legal description that is required for any transaction involving the transfer of an interest or its use as security for a loan. It is the legal description that appears on the title document, usually called a *deed*. The description is set by local authorities and is widely used by tax assessors, tax collectors and, of course, the county recorder who maintains the official records of property ownership. It is essential when preparing a purchase contract to use the precise and correct legal description for the property involved. As a rule, it is readily obtained from the deed held by the seller. The legal description is a matter of public record and you can get it from the county records or land title office.

It is important to realize that the legal description does not, by itself, guarantee that you can determine exactly where the physical boundaries of the property are, unless you are a trained land surveyor. Where property has been divided into lots and blocks, as is true for most urban areas, there is little opportunity for confusion as to which property is involved in a purchase transaction. There may be a serious question as to where the actual lot lines are and fences are not reliable guides. Where there is a doubt, the buyer should employ a surveyor and have stakes set. Where land is still described according to a *metes and bounds* description, there may be less clear understanding as to where boundaries are and it will not necessarily be clear from the legal description even where the land is. In any event, when making an offer to buy, you must be satisfied that the description used in the agreement is accurate and that there is no room for error or misunderstanding as to which property you are actually proposing to purchase.

Contingencies

We've already discussed at length how you can condition your offer on obtaining financing specified in the contract. There are many other items you can make your offer contingent upon. Recall that any provision in the offer designated as a *subject to* involves the possibility of the buyer being released from the obligation to proceed. In general, you want to have the right to back out, at your option, without forfeiting anything. Don't be at all surprised to find sellers less enthusiastic about making these concessions; you'll be a seller someday yourself. But which contingency comes first? None; each and every one will be of equal importance unless the contract stipulates otherwise. Even the most minor provision could serve to release the buyer.

The objective of a contingency provision is to relieve a buyer from having to do something he or she is unable to do as a result of conditions beyond his or her control. Incidentally, sellers may introduce contingencies too, but that is less common. Unless care is used, the agreement may be written simply to give the buyer an out regardless of whether there is a genuine difficulty. Here are some examples.

Physical Condition. The buyer may be concerned about the condition of the property from a structural point of view, or because of potential pest damage. It is not enough simply to include in the offer a condition that "the offer is subject to obtaining a structural engineering report" or similar inspection. The intent, undoubtedly, in using this language is to make it possible for the buyer to back out or seek a price modification depending on what a report shows. But look again at the statement. It does nothing more than place a burden on someone to obtain a report. It certainly doesn't provide a basis for revoking the offer on the strength of what is said in the report. To provide suitable protection to the buyer the language should include, for example, "the offer is subject to the review of a soils engineering report by the buyer; and unless the condition of the property as stated in the report is satisfactory to the buyer, this offer is null and void." Note that this now gives the advantage almost fully to the buyer. The argument could ensue with regard to what is meant by "condition . . . is satisfactory to the buyer." All this affords employment for attorneys and judges.

Buyers must be concerned about the possibility of physical deterioration and damage caused by dry rot or termites. It is customary in most areas for each purchase, especially of housing structures, to be subject to the conditions stated in a termite or pest control inspection report. Usually there is an agreement that the cost of the report is to be borne by the buyer and the repairs identified in the report are to be paid for by the seller. These arrangements can be modified by agreement of the parties. Most lenders will require that repairs recommended in these reports be made and will even require that funds for that purpose be set aside in the escrow. If you wish to buy property to fix up, the offer should include a provision whereby you agree to take the property on an "as is" basis. That would relieve the seller of any responsibility for conditions you might discover after taking possession.

Verification of Records.   All offers for investment income property should be conditioned on inspection of the rent rolls and verification of the data provided by the seller, or the determination of income if not otherwise provided. The importance of having accurate income data cannot be overemphasized. It is customary for a buyer to have access to the rent collection record, to talk with resident managers, and even to talk to tenants. Because the value of income property is a function of the actual money collected, it is essential that an offer be based on facts, not fancy. Here again it is important that the language of the offer accomplish what is intended. It's not enough to state that the offer is subject to review of the rent records. So what? If the buyer wishes to have the right to withdraw an offer if the records do not substantiate what he or she has been told, then the language in the offer must so state. You could state: "the offer is contingent upon verification by examination of the seller's records that the annual rents collected for the period January 1 to December 31, 19xx, was $22,000. If it is then found that the actual income was less, the buyer reserves the right to withdraw this offer."

Warranties.   When buying property from the contractor, or if you've had the structure erected under contract, you may want to include in the agreement a guarantee that the property is free from defects and that the seller will make repairs for a stated period of time. If you are buying a home, newly constructed or otherwise, you should explore the Home Warranty programs. These are available in most parts of the country. Typically, home building contractors pay the cost of an insurance policy to cover defects in the major components of the building and the appliances. In the used-home market, many real estate brokers make similar policies available to sellers. If you are to have this benefit, be certain there is a provision in the purchase agreement that obligates the seller. In some instances, home warranty coverage may be bought by the purchaser.

New Construction.   Virtually everywhere, building construction is supervised by local authorities and work is inspected as the building is put together. When finished, there will be a final inspection and a certificate of occupancy issued. The buyer should see that the offer is conditioned upon delivery of the certificate of occupancy. Here the expectation is that the builder has met the municipality's building code and other requirements which have been established for the protection of occupants.

Title.   All purchase offers should be conditioned upon the seller delivering title that is free and clear of all encumbrances except those specified that the buyer is content to assume. Through the process of abstracting the title or the title search, the existence of unpaid liens, tax liabilities, and names of those with an apparent interest in the property, all will be uncovered. This information will be set forth in a preliminary report of title or in the abstract. At this point, the buyer may have a basis for withdrawing from the deal. More commonly, the seller does whatever is necessary to clear the title and the transaction can be completed.

Review.   Depending upon the circumstances in which the offer is prepared, a buyer may wish to include in the offer a provision that the purchase agreement " ... is subject to the approval of the buyer's legal counsel." Assume that the seller has prepared the purchase contract and it is presented to you to sign, thus making an offer on the terms you presume to be satisfactory. You want to commit the seller, so you are anxious to sign the offer and get the seller to sign as well. But you're cautious and unfamiliar with these matters. That's when you should use the provision quoted above. This gives you an opportunity to back out if your attorney discovers something in the contract that you don't wish to accept. It should be clear that this surely gives the buyer a wide-open opportunity to back out of the deal. No attorney would find it hard to discover something unsatisfactory in a contract drawn by someone else.

Other Terms

There are a number of very specific things to be settled before money changes hands. All matters requiring agreement by the parties are to be treated in the purchase contract.

Possession. In the discussion of timing we treated the matter of the buyer obtaining possession of the property. Once you've settled on the date, that should be clearly stated in the offer to avoid confusion. Ordinarily, possession is granted coincident with the closing of the escrow, but the parties are certainly free to agree otherwise.

Inventory. In conjunction with obtaining possession, if there is personal property to be transferred, the buyer should insist upon taking an inventory in the presence of the seller and seeing that all is delivered before authorizing the settlement. You will have very little leverage, once your cash has been paid over, if the seller has failed to perform. In the case of apartment property, for example, the extent of the personal property can be great. Be certain you get what you have paid for.

Deposits. It is customary for landlords to require tenants to make cash deposits against possible damage or as payment for cleaning when the tenant leaves. Customs in this regard vary and you will want to find out what they are in your area. It also is good business to have the tenant pay not only the first month's rent in advance but also give you, before moving in, an amount to be credited to the last month of tenancy. In this way you will have some hedge against delinquencies. As a buyer, you should be given all such deposit funds by the seller. The purchase agreement should contain a provision to this effect. Typically, the money is credited in the escrow. You may also wish to include a provision permitting you to verify with the tenants the deposit amounts, if not already taken care of when verifying the records.

Prorations. It is regular procedure for the purchase agreement to provide that the buyer and seller prorate expenses such as property taxes, insurance, utilities, and other items. The buyer thus will reimburse the seller for prepaid items and be credited with any expenses that are paid in arrears for time prior to the close of the escrow.

Repairs.   If the property is to be repaired by the seller as a condition of the sale, completion of the transaction can be delayed, at the insistence of the buyer, until the work has been approved. An alternative is to provide for a sum to be withheld from the sales proceeds to cover the repair cost. As the buyer, you would want to reserve the right to approve the work before payment is made. The funds can be held in the escrow or delivered to an independent third party. The danger to the buyer is that once the bulk of the purchase price has been handed over to the seller, there may be limited motivation for the seller to do what remains. In any event, the agreement of the parties in this matter must be stated in the purchase agreement if enforcement through legal action is ever required.

Offer and Acceptance

A lawyer will tell you that there are many aspects to the creation of a contract and, although the parties may think they've entered into a legally binding agreement, this may not be so because of some failure or deficiency. We will avoid being preoccupied with all the fine points of law but emphasize that the best thing for buyers and sellers to do is put in writing what they are agreeing to, then sign the document. In such circumstances, the chances are quite good that they will have created a valid contract. If there never is a disagreement that cannot be resolved through discussion, no one will ever know (or care) whether the contract met all the niceties prescribed by law. It is when there is an argument that the legal technicalities arise—and enter the lawyers.

We have now reached the point where you have prepared your offer and are ready to present it to the seller. You will need enough copies so that everyone involved has one. As a minimum, a copy is needed for each of the sellers, lenders, escrow agent, real estate broker, and the buyers. Copies made by photocopying one original are the most satisfactory; that way every copy is assured to be the same. The next step is for the seller to sign the purchase contract, thus accepting the offer. It doesn't always, or even usually, work quite that way.

COUNTEROFFER AND ACCEPTANCE

If the seller is agreeable to all your terms, he or she will sign the contract copies, keeping one or more, and deliver one or more to you. Much of the procedure depends on who is controlling the transaction. Throughout we have been assuming that you, the buyer, were taking the lead. Real estate brokers, of course, should conduct the negotiations in behalf of all the parties and thus will control the paperwork. Experienced sellers, especially when dealing with inexperienced buyers, will see that all the necessary steps are taken.

More than likely you will have made an offer that is not exactly in line with what the seller wanted so there will have to be further negotiation. The result of that activity will be either a termination of all dealings or the preparation of a counteroffer. Once this has been put in writing and signed by all parties, you will have an acceptance.

Counteroffer

The seller may reject the offer completely and dismiss it. In that case you may not be able to find out why and it may be difficult to prepare a new offer if you continue to be interested in the property. If there's a real estate agent involved, it is likely he or she will be able to learn what the seller's objections are and can develop a new proposal. Once you know what the problem is, you can decide whether to proceed further. In some cases only a very minor adjustment to the original offer is needed. If so, you can put together a brief addendum to the contract and have the seller sign both the basic agreement and the attachment. You must sign or initial the addition, too.

If the revisions to be made in the original offer are extensive, do not attempt to modify the agreement by adding slips of paper to it. Start all over again and do it properly. Otherwise, the arguments over unclear intentions can be expensive to resolve.

You must adopt a strategy in dealing with counteroffers that will assure that you do not lose the war even though you win the battle. Try to evaluate the relative importance of the items in contention and try not to be unreasonable in insisting on your position. It could be folly and cause you to lose an otherwise good deal. Maybe the sellers did say the drapes were included and now they are going back on their word. If it really is a good deal, don't plant your feet and refuse to go ahead. Don't risk losing a lot over a very little. With practice, of course, you might be able to know when people are bluffing; you'll probably do some yourself.

If the seller rejects your offer, do your best to get him or her to give you a basis for a counteroffer. If the price is too low, ask, "How much too low?" Get the sellers to commit themselves if at all possible. Let them sweat it out by not pursuing them right after the rejection. Of course, you may run the risk that there's another buyer in the works. Note that regardless of how the conversation may go, technically, it is you who are to make the new offer even though it looks as though the seller is countering your original—hence the expression *counteroffer*. All of the negotiation will be vastly improved if you gain knowledge of the marketplace and know what properties are selling for and what financing terms are available. If you do your homework along the lines stated in this book, you will be well-equipped to deal with sellers, including even those who have also read all this.

Acceptance

Once the purchase contract has been properly signed, steps must be taken to close the deal. The buyer should determine either in advance, or now, who has an interest in the property and, therefore, must sign the acceptance. Find out beforehand if there are going to be any complications as far as the sellers are concerned. In most situations an agreement to sell cannot be enforced if someone who has an ownership interest has not formally accepted the offer. With a valid acceptance in hand, you now must proceed to open an escrow, arrange financing, check out the contingencies, get your cash together, and prepare to assume ownership. We strongly recommend the use of an escrow agency and title insurance. Buyers and sellers will deliver funds, documents, and keys to the neutral party, the escrow agent, who represents all concerned.

Property Inspection.   The buyer should inspect the property once more and, where pertinent, review the records, talk to the tenants, and otherwise confirm all the items involved whether provided for in the purchase agreement or not. Even if you discover a condition that cannot be used as a reason for withdrawing, it is important to know about it anyway. You can make a list of all the things to be done and set target dates. While up until now the thrust of your energies has been to get the seller to act, you now must act too. Your failure to perform in time may result in a loss to you.

Insurance.   What will your position be if, during the time between acceptance of the offer and the closing of the escrow, the property is damaged or destroyed? Whose loss is it? Fundamentally, while you may have lost an expectation, the title holder is the entity that has suffered this loss. If serious enough, the damage could be the basis for releasing the seller and buyer from the agreement. Obviously, the seller should act prudently and have adequate insurance. It will apply up to the exact moment at which title is passed. In anticipation of this problem, the buyer may wish to stipulate in the offer that the seller carry insurance. You do not have an insurable interest until you take title. It is not up to you to buy insurance to cover the property prior to the closing. You must make advance arrangements, however, for insurance to become effective once the property is at your risk. If there is a mortgage lender in the picture, you can expect he will insist on insurance to cover its interest. Earlier, in discussing prorations, we suggested that the seller may offer to turn over the insurance coverage to you, with or without payment for the unexpired portion. Note that no policyholder can transfer the coverage; that can only be done by the insurance company accepting the new insured party and endorsing the policy. Those arrangements must be made in advance of the date of closing. Appropriate papers are to be delivered to the escrow in time. If you obtain new insurance, you need to instruct your insurance advisor as to how the policy is to be drawn to meet lenders' specifications as well as your own, and where to send the policies.

Financing

Because the vast majority of real estate investment involves the use of borrowed funds, we are stressing throughout the book the procedures to be followed for mortgage financing in all parts of the transaction. Once you have a signed purchase agreement, you will proceed to apply formally for the mortgage loan, giving a copy of the agreement to the lender. It often takes several weeks to get an answer from the lending officer. Before setting your time limit in your offer for getting the loan, you certainly would want to do some advance negotiating to determine just how much time might be required to process your loan application. You do face a prospective serious problem if you are turned down for the loan and have to then go through the same procedure with another lender. All this points to the virtue of making preliminary arrangements for the loan *before* you make an offer to buy that is conditioned on financing.

Failure to Perform

There is no way to record data accurately but it's a fair assumption that a significant percentage of accepted offers do not result in closed deals. Buyers may find more suitable property and sellers may receive better offers. If both parties want out, there is no problem, unless it is with a real estate broker looking for the commission he or she earned by getting the parties together. Trouble does arise, however, if one party is going to suffer when the other is permitted to withdraw.

Under the law you can seek damages for breach of contract. In doing so, in addition to proving there was a valid contract and that the other party did in fact breach it, you must also demonstrate a measure of your loss as a basis for being awarded damages. Assume you had your heart set on a piece of property, made an offer, and the seller accepted it. Then the seller changed his or her mind and refused to go ahead with the transaction. What is your financial loss? How can you measure your disappointment in dollars? It's not easy. If you are quite serious about all this, you can hire an attorney and pursue your legal rights. You may sue for damages or for specific performance. If the latter, you would ask the court to order the seller to complete the sale.

But let's look at the result of the failure of the buyer to proceed. This can come about simply because the buyer changed his or her mind and refused to go ahead or it may be due to an inability to obtain financing or meet other requirements. If the contingency language in the agreement is inadequate to protect the buyer, the seller may wish to force the issue. Here again it becomes a matter of demonstrating the amount of the financial loss suffered. The seller's loss usually arises from the fact that after accepting the offer the property is removed from the market. That action brings all sales activity to a halt and may prompt other potentially interested buyers to go elsewhere. It is very difficult for sellers or their real estate agents to get things going again when the property is put back on the market. Basically, the seller's likely loss is that of a sale to someone else, at least for the present. What's that worth? Although this argument can be settled in court, such litigation can be time consuming and expensive. One way to avoid it is to provide in advance for a measure of the loss if it occurs. This is known as *liquidated damages*; it is covered in a provision in the purchase contract.

When buyer and seller agree to a liquidated damages provision, they have set a basis for payment to the seller by the buyer for failure to complete the deal. We're concerned, of course, only with situations where there was no contingency language permitting the buyer to withdraw without penalty. Assume, for example, that the buyer just changed his mind and refused to put up the money. In general, the typical liquidated damages clause provides for forfeiture of the earnest money or deposit to the seller. This avoids any further argument about how much the buyer should be assessed for his or her failure. It also means that the seller should think twice about accepting an offer that is accompanied by only a token deposit.

Agent's Commission

In most jurisdictions a real estate agent will have earned a commission by bringing the buyer and seller together regardless of whether the deal is consummated. As a result, the seller may be asked to agree that, if the buyer or seller backs out, all or part of the deposit be paid to the real estate agent in satisfaction of the obligation to pay the commission. Language to this effect needs to be included in the contract if it is to be enforced.

CLOSING THE ESCROW

The term *escrow* applies to the process in which an independent entity represents the parties to a purchase and sale transaction. The buyer turns over cash and related documents, and the seller delivers the deed and bill of sale for personal property, if any. Both parties give the escrow agent written instructions regarding acceptance and release of documents and money. As a consequence, the buyer can be assured he or she is getting proper title and the seller will get the cash in exchange for the deed. The escrow service can be performed by a lawyer, banker, an escrow service firm, or by a title company; real estate brokers may also handle escrows. The fees for this service are paid by the buyer and seller according to local custom or negotiation.

Instructions

Title insurance and escrow service companies typically provide printed forms to be used by buyers and sellers in stating what the escrow agent is to do. The buyer must specify the manner in which title is to be vested; that will govern how the deed is to be drawn. When the seller's document is delivered, the escrow officer must make certain it meets the buyer's requirements. The buyer may also indicate to whom funds are to be paid for services in connection with the transaction. Lenders send loan proceeds to the escrow together with the mortgage papers. If not taken care of previously, the escrow officer may have the borrowers sign the promissory note and mortgage agreement. The seller may be paying off existing indebtedness and will authorize the payment from the sale proceeds. The entity to whom money is owed will be contacted and asked to send a demand for payment together with the evidence of the debt. The escrow officer will not release the borrower until payment is assured. It is also customary for real estate brokers, inspection and appraisal firms, construction companies, and real estate lawyers to be paid out of the escrow. All told there can be a large number of people waiting, sometimes impatiently, for the escrow to close. Not the least of these is the buyer, anxious to pick up the keys.

Documents

The escrow officer is responsible for seeing that deeds and mortgage documents are sent to the county recorder for recording. Lenders will rely on the escrow process to produce signed and legally effective notes and security interest contracts. Once recorded, the original documents will be sent to the appropriate party. Once the documents are recorded, the title insurance policy can be issued. But how much time does all this processing take?

The escrow cannot be fully processed and closed until all the forms, instructions, and money are in hand. Even the most minor of items, if not in order, can delay the settlement. Once ready, the actual processing need not take more than an hour or, in many cases, just a few minutes. Much preliminary computation can be made while waiting for papers to arrive. It is important, of course, to set a target closing date in the purchase contract so that everyone is on notice as to the date by which they are expected to perform.

POST CLOSING ACTION

The seller may have planned ahead and be on the plane to Tahiti moments after the check is received from the escrow. How about the buyer? You now may have many things to do. If the property is your home, you'll have packing, movers to arrange for, utilities to check, and maybe even an overdrawn checking account to mend.

If you have bought income property, you will need to give official notice to each tenant that you now own the property and that rents are payable to you. It can be helpful if you are able to arrange for the seller to join with you in signing such a notice. Unless you plan to collect the rents in person, you must give clear instructions as to where rent payments are to be sent. If not done before now, you will need to arrange for utility services to be provided in your name and continued without interruption. This may involve making deposits, so be prepared for that outlay.

At this time you will also need to establish a record-keeping system if you don't already have one. As we will discuss briefly in the next chapter, except for very large income properties, you probably can maintain all the needed accounting records yourself. It will be important to start out correctly with an appropriate set of record books and a bank checking account to be used only for the property.

CLOSING THOUGHTS

As with almost everything in life, practice makes perfect. It is not unusual to be apprehensive when contemplating your first investment in real estate. There appear to be so many details and unknowns, and often the financial risk is intimidating. In reality, buying real estate is a well-defined and straightforward transaction and you will have all the help you need from real estate practitioners, lenders, and escrow services.

Choosing the property on which to make the offer is all-important. Next come the terms: the price, the financing, the contingencies, and the timing. Don't expect to get something for nothing other than something worth nothing. By careful analysis you can determine what the property, as a maximum, is worth to you. If the seller won't agree, go on to another deal. Always offer less than the asking price or your value, whichever is smaller. Otherwise you'll be left wondering for the rest of your life whether you could have bought for less.

When there are elements of the deal yet to be determined, be certain to state such contingencies in your offer. There's no excuse for being bound to a deal you can't live with. If the seller won't agree to your safeguards, and they are reasonable, go on to another deal. Great care needs to be exercised in formulating the terms and stating them in the offer. Develop your skills and you'll go on to become a real estate tycoon.

Finally, include in your negotiating strategy the use of an escrow service and the purchase of title insurance. These safeguards will help ensure the financial success you set out to achieve.

8

Managing the Investment

After using all your skills to buy property at a bargain price, you may run the risk of losing your advantage through mismanagement. Real estate requires continuing attention. You must constantly work to maximize your return and govern your actions by the potential effect on the resale value.

THE PROPERTY OWNER

Your home is more than a house (or condo unit). It's an investment to be nurtured and protected as it grows in value. Keeping it well-maintained, making improvements to increase its livability, and improving its appearance should all lead to greater ultimate investment return.

When you are a landlord you must give your attention to your tenants. If you need tenants, you'll have to search for the right ones. You may have to spend money to keep good tenants and be prepared to do what is needed to evict the others. You'll need to keep up with your competitors and be certain you always know what fair market rents are and how yours compare.

And then, in order to know how you are doing and be able to file an accurate tax return, you need to be somewhat of a bookkeeper. Keeping the records of income and expenditures need not be a heavy chore; it is a necessary one, however.

Once you see what is adequate, perhaps you'll agree that it might even be fun to be a bookkeeper.

YOUR HOME

The first thing you should do in your new home is examine the property inside and out and make a list of all the things you believe might be done to improve the property or at least keep it in satisfactory shape. Determine how much each project may cost and assign priorities; you will also need to figure out where the money will come from. From this you can make up a timetable or, as a minimum, a list of the projects in the appropriate sequence. You could pin the list in a prominent place so it will serve as a reminder; fight procrastination.

Home Maintenance

Depending upon your prior experience, you will want to learn all you can about heating and plumbing systems and where the water and power cutoffs are. Be able to replace a fuse. Look for safety hazards and get rid of them. Your local firemen will be pleased to help you identify problems and advise what to do about them; they will probably recommend that you install smoke detectors. The police department will survey your home and tell you how to burglar-proof it. If you find leaky faucets, fix them. It's astonishing how much water can be wasted and what that can cost. Check the heating and cooling system; chances are the filters need replacing.

Kitchen appliances such as dishwashers and garbage disposals can develop leaks. Head off damage to walls and floors by seepage. If the motor is not sealed, it may require lubricating; you probably will be able to do that yourself. Check the laundry appliances, too. None of this should be neglected because an electric motor can easily burn out and repairs will be expensive.

Painting and decorating are often done enthusiastically by new occupants, at least the first time 'round. Be sure you realize that there is just as much labor involved in applying cheap materials as expensive. Cut-price paint may appear to save you dollars but the end result could be a disaster. As a rule you are better off going for the product that offers the longest and most satisfactory life. Check around thoroughly before making decisions both as to product and color. Cheap brushes are no bargain either.

And now for the roof. Chances are that if you have bought a used home, your first major repair will involve the roof. You can get valuable information by asking a number of roofing contractors to give you cost estimates and opinions. Watch for opportunities to have this type of work done in the slack season and thus get a better price. Roofers charge the most and are the busiest when it rains. Avoid being one of their customers at that time. From the roof, go to the basement or foundation. Check for leaks or signs of cracking and earth movement. Reroute surface waters away from the building. See that openings are secure against rodents. Remove any soil that lies against wood in order to minimize potential termite damage.

In carrying out any or all of these projects, keep in mind you are acting to protect your investment and increase the enjoyment to be realized by owning your own home.

Improvements

In most homes there are opportunities to reduce the cost of heating or cooling and, in this inflationary era, these are big items. Check out the possibility of insulating and weatherstripping if not already done. Get details from the IRS on tax credits for this type of improvement. Solar units are highly suitable in some situations and might be worthwhile exploring. Again, part of the investment can be offset by tax credits. Energy-saving features will save you money while you live in the property and will add to its resale value.

Let's assume you feel the need for more space and are considering adding a room or otherwise enlarging the living space. Perhaps you hope to generate a little rental income from space you don't need yourself. Not only should you check out alternative costs, but it's also essential that you give adequate attention to the design. Of course, if you really can be assured that you'll live in the property for the rest of your life, you don't have to be concerned about anyone else's opinion of your improvements. As a rule, however, the day will arrive when you will want to sell your property. Be sure that the changes you are planning, if made, will in fact not detract from the desirability of the house. You can employ an architectural designer who will not only give you the benefit of his or her skills in layout but can also prepare the construction plans needed for the work. When you have a set of plans, it is much easier to get competitive bids, and you can be assured of getting what you want.

As a homeowner you probably will have a chance to exercise your green thumb. There are many opportunities to improve property through suitable use of landscaping and it doesn't have to cost a lot. A pleasing garden can provide current enjoyment and add to the value of the property.

It is important to keep an accurate record of money spent on your home. Expenditures that serve to increase the value, such as structural changes, can be added to your original cost. This will reduce the amount of gain realized when you sell. This could mean lower income taxes. Later, we'll review the conditions under which you may not have any tax to pay at all on gains from the sale of your home, but they depend on actions you take in the future. Meanwhile, keep receipts and other pertinent records.

Operating Expenses

The homeowner will have some specific expenses not encountered by a tenant, such as property taxes and hazard insurance.

You will recall from earlier material that the amount of property taxes to be paid is computed from an assessed value. In many tax assessment offices, the actual price you paid when you bought the property will be used in setting the assessed value. If you have reason to believe your assessed value is too high, visit the tax assessor's office to learn what you can do about it. In most areas there are assessment appeal procedures so find out what is to be done. Be aware that there are deadlines and if you delay, you might be unable to have an error rectified. Watch also to see that you are receiving all the tax credits that, in many states, are granted to owners who occupy the property as their principal residence. You may also be eligible for veterans' property tax allowances. In the other direction, keep in mind that as you increase the value of the property through structural improvements, it is likely that such improvements will be reflected in the assessed value and hence taxes will increase. That's something to take into account when you are adjusting the family budget.

How about insurance? Regardless of whether the lender is insisting that you carry fire insurance, no one should neglect having enough of the right kind of insurance. It is easy to discuss this with a few insurance advisors and get the information you need. There are two basic risks: loss because of physical damage to your home or possessions, and being sued by someone who claims you have injured him. In either case, if there is a loss, you could find yourself losing your home and investment if you don't have proper insurance.

An insurance agent or broker can give you the cost and coverage terms for a wide range of perils, starting with fire and windstorm. You can add many more perils up to what is termed *all risks;* personal property can also be covered for loss by robbery and theft. You will have an important decision to make about the amount of insurance coverage to buy. Usually you can buy a homeowner's policy that will pay the full cost of repair, without deduction for depreciation, provided the policy amount is large enough. You will need to know what it would cost to build the house new, called the *replacement cost,* and base the amount of insurance on that figure. Most companies provide for an automatic increase in the insured amount tied to an inflation rate. Your furniture, clothing, and other personal property also are exposed to possible loss and can be insured. Your insurance advisor will explain how this coverage can be bought to cover either the depreciated (actual cash) value or the replacement cost.

If someone is hurt or property is damaged because of your activities, you may be found liable in a lawsuit brought against you. It is quite clear that if you negligently operate an automobile and cause damage, you'll probably have to pay. (Only a few states have no-fault laws and even those that do, require you to carry insurance.) It may not be as clear, but it certainly is equally so, that you can be sued for damages arising from many incidents other than auto accidents. The insurance that will protect you and your family members in these situations is known as *personal liability* coverage. Everyone needs this protection. If you own or operate a car, you also need automobile liability insurance. Your insurance advisor can help you with all the decisions that are needed. It's possible to combine the insurance on your home and personal property with personal liability coverage in one contract; as a rule, auto insurance is sold separately. You get peace of mind when you buy insurance.

RESIDENTIAL INCOME PROPERTY

No one should go through life without being a landlord— at least for a while. Rent property to others and you instantaneously become a landlord. Because of the differences between rental housing and commercial rental property, we will consider the management of these investments separately. Whether you plan to manage the property yourself or employ a property management service, you will need to deal with the following matters:

1. How do you locate tenants?
2. What forms do you need?
3. How do you set rents?
4. Is there a rent control law? If so, get a copy of it.
5. What is the procedure for evicting tenants?

Finding Tenants

The two basic methods used to prompt prospective tenants to approach an apartment owner are the *For Rent* sign on the building and the ad in the rentals section of the classified advertising part of the local newspaper. In many communities you can also list your vacancy with a rental agency. These include commercial enterprises dealing exclusively in rentals, real estate brokerage firms, and college and university housing offices. Some large industrial organizations offer employees assistance in finding accommodations and landlords are encouraged to list properties with them.

Prior to offering a rental unit, you must consider the following: rental terms; supply of rental applications; supply of rental agreement or lease forms; and the appearance of the property. Once you've taken the action required for each of these, you may be prepared to interview prospects and negotiate the rental.

Rental Terms. Your first decision involves setting the monthly rate. Many landlords do comparison shopping. That is, you go to similar properties and pose as a prospective tenant. This can be most instructive. You can see what is being offered and how it compares with your units. You can also see how other landlords handle (or mishandle) prospective tenants. Your rent will be affected by the size and quality of accommodation and the strength of the demand for rental property. In many cases, setting your rent just below the market not only will serve to attract more applications but will also tend to discourage tenants from moving out.

What is the local custom concerning advance rent payments and damage or cleaning deposits? Who pays for the utilities: the owner or the tenant? And should you offer month-to-month terms or an annual lease? Whenever conditions permit, you should aim to have the tenant pay the first and last month's rent before moving in, regardless of whether there is a lease. On such a basis you have some leeway if the tenant gets behind in making rent payments. It is understood that the last month's rent would be applied after the tenant has given notice. You will want to keep such advance rent funds in reserve and treat them as rent at the time applied, thus keeping your cash flow even.

As a rule when tenancy is on a month-to-month basis, you will want to use a rental agreement to formalize the arrangement. With or without a written agreement, it is probable you will thus have the right to give the tenant one month's notice to leave; the tenant likewise is required to give you one month's notice. Some states have laws that regulate this and other matters relating to rentals. Your notice runs from the time you give it (and do so in writing), not from the time rent is paid. Even if the tenant is late in paying the rent, the time begins with when you ask him or her to leave, not, for instance, from the time when the rent was due. Either you, or the tenant, or both of you may wish to have what appears to be more security provided under a lease agreement. Here are the advantages and disadvantages of leases.

Under a lease the rent will usually be paid monthly and at a rate that cannot be changed during the term of the lease unless provided for otherwise. For residential property the typical lease period is one year with renewal options. This means that a tenant is protected against rent increases for a stated time period and the landlord has some assurance the property will stay rented for the term of the contract. Technically, under most leases, the tenant is obligated to pay all the rent for the full term and may be sued for failure to do so. Assume, for example, that you write a lease for a year calling for rent at $400 a month. When the tenant signs the lease, he or she agrees to pay $4,800 in total, notwithstanding the privilege of paying monthly. If the tenant moves out partway through the year, he or she would be liable for whatever part of the $4,800 remains unpaid. That requirement tends to discourage tenants from moving out before the end of the lease. A landlord, of course, is free not to enforce such a provision. You may, on the other hand, need the services of an attorney to pursue your landlord's rights.

The option to renew the lease can be important to both parties. The owner must try to estimate rent levels in the future and allow for possible increases in setting the renewal terms. The tenant, to guard against having to leave before wishing to, will want to be able to renew the lease subject only to paying the agreed rent. If the renewal rent is not specified in the lease, a landlord might be able to take advantage of a tenant who couldn't move to escape unreasonable terms. One equitable choice is to set renewal terms on a basis related to some independent measure, such as a cost-of-living index. To a landlord, a lease may be of some comfort if it serves to discourage a tenant from looking for other accommodations, given the tenant is satisfactory. If there is a problem with the tenant, the owner may not be able to get rid of him or her before the expiration of the lease, and if the agreement gives the tenant a unilateral option to renew, the landlord may regret being so generous. Deciding whether to offer a tenant a lease, and what the renewal option terms might be, is not an easy matter. Some cynical landlords feel that a lease provides protection only to the tenant.

Damage Deposits.   By requiring a tenant to hand over a cleaning or damage deposit, the landlord may have some protection against future expense. The actual amount will probably be set by your competitors; if you ask for more than other landlords, you may have trouble finding suitable tenants. Above all, if you take a deposit, establish exactly in writing the basis on which it is to be returned. Check local regulations; don't violate the law. Basically the purpose of the deposit is to cover the actual cost to repair tenant-inflicted damage or the cost to clean the unit after the tenant departs. You may choose to operate on the basis that if the tenant performs satisfactory cleaning, you will refund the deposit in its entirety. An alternative is to make it clear that regardless of the condition of the property, you expect to have it cleaned so there will be no return.

But how do you establish when a tenant is liable for damage? This could be very important not only for handling the damage deposit but also for making a claim beyond it. Some owners prepare a suitable description of the premises at the time of occupancy and have the tenant sign, accepting it. This can be supported by photos if necessary. Some prudent tenants will ask an owner to acknowledge the presence of existing damage to avoid an argument later.

Rental Application.   Are you a good judge of human nature? As a landlord you'll need to sharpen whatever skills you have in this area. One way to have help in choosing one tenant applicant over another is to require rental applications. Here you ask for employment data, bank references, and names and addresses of former landlords. Information developed this way will be needed in making the original decision to accept or reject. It may also be needed if you have to locate a tenant who didn't go through the formalities of saying goodbye.

It may be customary to ask the prospective tenant to make a deposit at the time the rental application is submitted. This helps to screen out those who are not seriously interested in your apartment. The receipt for the deposit should state clearly the terms under which the deposit is to be retained or returned. Generally, if you reject the applicant, the deposit should be returned in full. If the tenant declines to go ahead with the agreement, once you've accepted the application, and you've taken the unit off the market, you may wish to retain the deposit to cover your possible loss. Whatever you decide to do, make certain your actions are fully covered by the language in the receipt and rental application form.

Above all, check out the information the tenant gives on the application. Confirmation from a prior landlord that the tenant performed satisfactorily is of great value, although it's no guarantee of future behavior. Confirmation of employment or other information related to the ability to pay rent is also important. One of the more frustrating experiences you can have as a landlord is for the tenant to occupy the unit, refuse to leave, and not pay the rent. Unless you intend to become a charitable organization, you must avoid this situation. In the ordinary course of events, you can easily screen applicants who respond to your advertising, if you have carefully thought

TENANT APPLICATION

Property Address: _____ Apt. No. _____

Name(s) of Applicant(s): _____

Other Name(s) used within last 3 years: _____

Names and Age of other Occupants: _____

_____

Pets (Number & Type): _____

Present Address: _____

    How long? _____ Reason for leaving: _____

    Name and Address of Owner or Owner's Agent: _____

Previous Address (Past 3 Years): _____

    How long? _____ Reason for leaving: _____

    Name and Address of Owner or Owner's Agent: _____

Previous Address (Past 3 Years): _____

    How long? _____ Reason for leaving: _____

    Name and Address of Owner or Owner's Agent: _____

Employment: Social Security Number _____ Drivers License Number _____

    Present Employer: _____ How long? _____

    Address: _____ Telephone: _____

    Employed as: _____ Salary: $ _____ per _____

Employment of any other Occupant: Social Security Number _____ Drivers License Number _____

    Present Employer _____ How long? _____

    Address: _____ Telephone: _____

    Employed as: _____ Salary: $ _____ per _____

Other Income: $ _____ Source: _____

Credit References (2): _____

Credit Cards: Issuer _____ Acct. No. _____ Issuer _____ Acct. No. _____

_____

Automobile License No. _____ State of Registry: _____

    Make & Model: _____ Year: _____ Color: _____

IN CASE OF EMERGENCY:

Name of Closest Relative: _____ Relationship: _____

    Address: _____ Telephone: _____

AUTHORIZATION TO VERIFY INFORMATION

I Authorize Landlord or his Authorized Agents to Verify the above information, including but not limited to obtaining a Credit Report and if this application is accepted I agree to execute the residential lease or rental agreement as set forth on the reverse side hereof.

Date _____ 19 _____ Applicant: _____

Telephone No. _____ Applicant: _____

    RECEIPT FOR DEPOSIT

        The undersigned acknowledges receipt of $ _____ in the form of ( ) Cash, ( ) Personal Check

        or ( ) _____ payable to _____ as deposit on the above described property.

Date _____ Agent _____

out this process in advance. To those who appear to meet your requirements, you can offer an application form. Tenants need prompt responses so they can go elsewhere because you can prevent them from finding something else. Don't dilly-dally trying to make up your mind; be decisive.

Agreements. Many properties are rented solely on the basis of oral agreements and no great harm ensues. On the other hand, if you are to minimize the likelihood of a disagreement that will be difficult to resolve, you will want to use a written contract. There are a few points of more importance than others and they should be stressed at the time of negotiation to avoid subsequent difficulties.

First, how many people are to occupy the premises? You probably don't want to find that although it seemed you were renting the apartment to "a nice young person," it turns out that you have provided housing for an extended family of half a dozen or more. Don't expect some people to be discouraged by cramped quarters. To avoid or diminish the chance of this happening, have an oral understanding with the prospective tenant as well as a provision in the agreement limiting the number of persons permitted to occupy the property as living quarters.

How about pets? This can be a very thorny problem. Assume you have a chance to rent to an ideal tenant: middle-age, single, employed woman whose more vigorous activities include reading and visiting the library, and who has no interest in hi-fi, motorcycles, or carpentry in the living room. What's the catch? She's devoted to her St. Bernard dog! Now, if you agree to her having such a "well-behaved" beast, you won't likely be able to turn down others. The first thing you know, your property may look like the local headquarters for the SPCA. Yes, you are going to have to come to grips with a policy decision concerning pets. How about recommending goldfish? For larger pets, consider increasing the damage deposit.

And about tenants with children? While this subject is at the end of our present list, it probably should be at the head of yours. This is going to be the most difficult matter you'll encounter as a landlord. Are you going to have an "adults only"

RESIDENTIAL RENTAL AGREEMENT

(Month To Month Tenancy)

THIS IS INTENDED TO BE A LEGALLY BINDING AGREEMENT — READ IT CAREFULLY

CALIFORNIA ASSOCIATION OF REALTORS® STANDARD FORM

_____ , California _____ _____ 19 ____

_____ , Landlord, and

_____ , Tenant, agree as follows:

1. Landlord rents to Tenant and Tenant hires from Landlord those premises described as: _____

_____

_____

together with the following furniture, and appliances, if any, and fixtures: _____

_____

_____

(Insert "as shown on Exhibit A attached hereto" and attach the exhibit if the list is extensive.)

2. The term shall commence on _____ , 19 _____ , and shall continue from month to
month. This rental agreement may be terminated at any time by either party by giving written notice 30 days in advance.
Tenant agrees to pay $ _____ rent per month payable in advance on the _____ day of each
month and $ _____ representing prorated rent from date of possession.

3. The rent shall be paid at _____
or at any address designated by the Landlord in writing.

4. $ _____ as security has been deposited. Landlord may use therefrom such amounts as are reasonably
necessary to remedy Tenant's defaults in the payment of rent, to repair damages caused by Tenant, and to clean the premises if necessary upon
termination of tenancy. If used toward rent or damages during the term of tenancy, Tenant agrees to reinstate said total security deposit upon
five days written notice delivered to Tenant in person or by mailing. Security deposit or balance thereof, if any, together with an itemized
accounting, shall be mailed to Tenant at last known address within 14 days of surrender of premises.

5. Tenant agrees to pay for all utilities and services based upon occupancy of the premises and the following charges:

_____

except _____
which shall be paid for by Landlord.

6. Tenant has examined the premises and all furniture, furnishings and appliances if any, and fixtures contained therein, and accepts
the same as being clean, in good order, condition, and repair, with the following exceptions: _____

_____

7. The premises are rented for use as a residence by the following named persons: _____

_____

No animal, bird, or pet except _____
shall be kept on or about the premises without Landlord's prior written consent.

8. Tenant shall not disturb, annoy, endanger or interfere with other Tenants of the building or neighbors, nor use the premises for any
unlawful purposes, nor violate any law or ordinance, nor commit waste or nuisance upon or about the premises.

9. Tenant agrees to comply with all reasonable rules or regulations posted on the premises or delivered to Tenant by Landlord.

10. Tenant shall keep the premises and furniture, furnishings and appliances, if any, and fixtures which are rented for his exclusive use in
good order and condition and pay for any repairs to the property caused by Tenant's negligence or misuse or that of Tenant's invitees.
Landlord shall otherwise maintain the property. Tenant's personal property is not insured by Landlord.

11. Tenant shall not paint, wallpaper, nor make alterations to the property without Landlord's prior written consent.

12. Upon not less than 24 hours advance notice, Tenant shall make the demised premises available during normal business hours to
Landlord or his authorized agent or representative, for the purpose of entering (a) to make necessary agreed repairs, decorations, alterations
or improvements or to supply necessary or agreed services, and (b) to show the premises to prospective or actual purchasers, mortgagees,
tenants, workmen or contractors. In an emergency, Landlord, his agent or authorized representative may enter the premises at any time
without securing prior permission from Tenant for the purpose of making corrections or repairs to alleviate such emergency.

13. Tenant shall not let or sublet all or any part of the premises nor assign this agreement or any interest in it without the prior written
consent of Landlord.

14. If Tenant abandons or vacates the premises, Landlord may at his option terminate this agreement, and regain possession in the manner
prescribed by law.

15. If any legal action or proceeding be brought by either party to enforce any part of this agreement, the prevailing party shall recover in
addition to all other relief, reasonable attorney's fees and costs.

16. Time is of the essence. The waiver by Landlord or Tenant of any breach shall not be construed to be a continuing waiver of any
subsequent breach.

17. Notice upon Tenant shall be served as provided by law. Notice upon Landlord may be served upon Manager of the demised premises

_____

at _____ . Said Manager is authorized to accept service on behalf of Landlord.

18. Within 10 days after written notice, Tenant agrees to execute and deliver a certificate as submitted by Landlord acknowledging that
this agreement is unmodified and in full force and effect or in full force and effect as modified and stating the modifications. Failure to comply
shall be deemed Tenant's acknowledgement that the certificate as submitted by Landlord is true and correct and may be relied upon by any
lender or purchaser.

19. The undersigned Tenant acknowledges having read the foregoing prior to execution and receipt of a copy hereof.

Landlord _____   _____ Tenant

Landlord _____   _____ Tenant

NO REPRESENTATION IS MADE AS TO THE LEGAL VALIDITY OF ANY PROVISION OR THE ADEQUACY OF ANY PROVISION
IN ANY SPECIFIC TRANSACTION. A REAL ESTATE BROKER IS THE PERSON QUALIFIED TO ADVISE ON REAL ESTATE. IF
YOU DESIRE LEGAL ADVICE CONSULT YOUR ATTORNEY.

For these forms, address — California Association Realtors®
505 Shatto Place, Los Angeles, California 90020
Copyright ©1977 California of Realtors® (Revised 1977-1978)

FORM RA-14

property? It often is argued that by restricting property to adults you can save the building from wear and tear associated with young people. There is also the matter of consideration for other tenants; children can be noisy. One solution is to try for all-family tenancy, assuming the units are large enough. If you do decide to try to restrict occupancy by children, determine first whether you can legally. Many communities have ordinances banning adults-only rentals; find out how things stand where you are. If you decide you can prohibit occupancy by children, be certain your rent or lease agreements so provide. You may face a court test.

One less important but final matter is that of storage. Apartment dwellers frequently need storage space. The landlord should make certain that whatever space is provided is clearly designated to avoid squabbles between tenants. There is a matter of possible liability for loss or damage to personal property of tenants located in storage areas not totally within the control of the tenant. You may want to include a nonliability provision in the rent or lease contract. Perhaps there are mini-warehouse facilities nearby. If so, you could direct tenants to them. Storage of travel trailers, boats, and recreational vehicles also may be a problem and should be anticipated where likely.

Don't be discouraged by all this. Being a landlord *can* be enjoyable, and owning residential income property can be profitable.

Dealing with Tenants

From the very beginning, establish firmly that rents are due on the dates agreed and that delinquencies will not be tolerated. Follow up promptly if a payment is not received on time. You are running a business, have bills to pay, and don't plan to have to make excuses to your creditors. Avoid at all costs giving tenants any basis for assuming you won't throw them out if they don't pay on time. Through your accounting records you should be able to have a complete history and know, for example, how each tenant has met the obligation to pay. This information would be very useful in the event you are

This information would be very useful in the event you are called on to consider making an exception to the rule.

Whenever possible, avoid finding yourself in the middle of disagreements between tenants. Of course, to the extent that such activities interfere with the peace and serenity of others, you may have to act. You should also have an emergency plan thought out and have telephone numbers for police and fire services readily available. If you do not live on the premises, tenants or the resident manager should know how to reach you.

Once a tenant gives either formal notice or simply hints he or she is going to leave, you should start seeking a replacement. Some owners post a sign stating: "Applications taken for future rentals." Your goal is to be able to move a new tenant in perhaps even the same day the former occupant leaves, thus avoiding any loss of rental income. But what if the tenant plans to leave before the time for which rent has been paid has run? You may have a choice: offer a refund or stand firm. This also applies to the notice requirement. What will you do if a tenant says she must leave next week and she's sorry she wasn't able to give you the required month's notice? Try to think these situations out in advance, reach some conclusions, and set a policy. In that case you will be prepared and can deal effectively with your tenants.

Now we come to "E-Day." Do you have the stomach for evicting a tenant? If you are lucky, you'll never have to find out. After all, the vast majority of tenants not only pay their rent, and on time, but never cause any trouble and, above all, never have to be forced to vacate. But there are some tenants, for reasons known maybe only to themselves, who may create a situation that can be solved only by the owner pursuing his or her rights to recover the property. The rules and regulations for eviction are local in nature. Before needing to know, you should consult with an attorney, local law enforcement office, or an eviction service organization. By simply being aware of what is involved you may, in fact, be able to avoid an unpleasant situation. Essentially, a tenant can be forcibly removed by cluding failure to pay rent. Certain time periods are involved and notices generally must be given in prescribed form and time sequence. In a number of cities, by far the easiest way to handle this problem is to use a commercially operated eviction service. These firms know all the requirements and can guide you in the steps to be taken; your cost will be their fees plus lost rent. The longer you delay, the greater may be the rent loss and even your forbearance may act to hinder your ability to take action. Be firm and, above all, be prepared.

Tenants expect rental units to be livable and may, from time to time, ask a landlord to redecorate, make repairs and so on. In a very tight rental market, where tenants have little choice, you may be inclined to be hard-nosed. Be careful. The day will come when it is clear that was a shortsighted policy. There's nothing wrong, however, with suggesting to the tenant that you will provide the materials if they wish to apply them. You would want to judge carefully what their painting skills might be, of course. Be careful with respect to colors, however. Many landlords do not permit the use of controversial color schemes because of the possibility they would make it hard to obtain future tenants for units so decorated. You should think about that, too.

Once a tenant complains about something, you'll find that the best policy is to respond immediately. When problems and complaints are ignored, they have a tendency to grow and be more costly to solve in the end. If you are handy with tools, you can quickly make repairs; if not, line up a handyman in advance so that when needed, all you need do is make a phone call. The landlord who develops a reputation for taking good care of tenants will find it easier to get new tenants; the old ones will advertise for you.

And now, what about the tenant who agreed to take care of the garden, or maintain the halls, or the garbage, or whatever? You will want to inspect the property often enough to know whether such obligations are being met. Ordinarily you will have made a rent concession so remember, you are paying for the work. If it's not being performed, find out why and make it clear that you expect the tenant to perform. To minimize conflicts, put the agreement, both what is to be done and the allowance for it, in writing.

Summary

Owning residential income property is a business and the landlord needs to be businesslike in running it. Tenants are the customers and should be treated accordingly. You may have to attract business, when you have vacancies, just like any other business wishing to prosper. You must minimize expenses and maximize revenues. And you must keep aware of what your competitors are doing and, where necessary, make adjustments in your policies to meet the competition.

BUSINESS INCOME PROPERTY

Here we are considering office buildings for business and professional occupancies, as well as buildings used for wholesale or retail activity. Shopping centers and industrial parks are included. Many investors are attracted to this type of property primarily because they would rather deal with such tenants than with individuals and families. In many cases the turnover is less than in housing and often business and professional tenants do, in fact, require less attention by the landlord. Although it's not unknown for a business tenant to fail to pay the rent, some owners view the risk of rent loss as being less.

In most areas the demand for office or commercial space may fluctuate more than for housing, however, and vacancies might be more difficult to fill. There's probably a greater risk of rent loss between tenancies than for apartments. But there are two positive aspects to business rentals: you may be able to participate in the business profits and you may be able to have the tenant pay all the operating expenses. Where customary in your area, you will be able to charge a base rent plus a percentage share of sales, known as a *participation*. The terms should be stated clearly in the rent or lease agreement but you will have to make certain, as a part of your property management activities, that you not only collect the base but also the rent that is due under the participating terms. The tenant will have to report sales volume to you on which the overage is to be calculated. You'll have to judge whether there's been any error in the data reported and take appropriate action. Under a net lease arrangement the tenant has assumed responsibility for specified operating expenses so you must be sure you don't inadvertently pay any of them. These, then, are the features of business income property to be considered when making your choice between it and residential housing.

Can an individual private investor personally manage this type of property? Yes, depending, of course, on the type of occupancy and availability of the owner. If you have a regular nine to five job, with no opportunity to leave it to take care of your property, you'd be handicapped. Business tenants are accustomed to dealing with experienced property management services and would not likely appreciate your inexperienced approach. Well, what's wrong with having a property management service company handle your affairs, either because you can't be available, or because you just don't want to? Let's see.

In managing property there are two separate activities: finding tenants and taking care of the property (collecting rents, making repairs, and so on). You can contract for one or both of these services. The cost needs to be weighed against your ability and desire to do the work yourself. Property management customs and practices vary from one area to another. In some cases it is customary for the owner to pay the cost to find the tenant and in others that is an expense for the tenant. As for the ongoing rent collection and other management functions, it is customary for the owner to pay for them on the basis of a percentage of rents collected; the rate may run between 4 percent and 6 percent. It is important for you to understand exactly what you are to get for this fee. The service agreement should spell out clearly what is to be done and the basis for paying. As a rule, the fee covers only collecting rent and arranging for repairs, subject to the owner's direction. In some cases this does not extend to the pursuit of delinquent tenants but just covers receiving rent money offered. You would have to chase the deadbeats yourself. Further, unless agreed to otherwise, the property management service will not seek new tenants as a part of the work for which a percentage of the rent applies. This is commonly misunderstood. Where it is a custom for the tenant to pay the fee levied by a rental agent, the owner need not be concerned about the expense. You do need to be concerned about keeping your property occupied. Let's look now at what's involved in locating tenants for business property.

Finding Tenants

We'll assume you are going to be active in handling the property yourself. Once you've considered what's involved, you may wish to think again about the opportunity to use a management service; usually you have a choice.

The two recognized ways to attract prospective tenants are to place a sign on the premises and to advertise in newspapers. Depending on the type, size, and potential use, you may want to use the *Wall Street Journal* as well as the local daily paper. Additionally, you could list the property with a real estate firm that is active in dealing with your type of property.

In contrast to renting housing, you must be more concerned with the creditworthiness of potential tenants and the type of activity to be conducted on the premises. For that reason you will want to obtain as much information as you can from applicants. You may also have to be somewhat flexible in negotiating terms, all of which should be thought out in advance. You could make up a rental application form to allow for the particular features of your property and the type of information needed from prospective tenants. It can be most instructive to visit similar properties when they are offered for rent to learn how other owners and rental agents operate in this field. Whenever possible, acquire copies of applications and rental agreements for use in devising your own policies and procedures. Before inviting people to rent your space, be prepared for them by making decisions as to terms, and have all the documents ready for use.

Can you ask a prospective business tenant to give you confidential financial information? After all, in a sense you are sharing some of the business risk. If the tenant fails, you will likely suffer through unpaid rent. How good a business person is the applicant and what are his or her prospects? You should ask for the information; often it will be given without question. To supplement it, or obtain it when it is not otherwise available, you should arrange with a credit-reporting organization for credit reports. Names and addresses will be found in the phone book. Choose one that deals in business as opposed to strictly personal credit reporting. Ask your banker to assist you in determining the credit standing of a prospective tenant. Just remind the bank how much you owe them and how repayment is related to your having financially stable tenants—they'll help.

Rental Terms

How about putting down your terms, along with a description of the property, in writing and pass them out to potential tenants? That can save everyone a lot of time. Let's look at the items you have to consider both to make the offer and for the terms to be set forth in the agreement:

1. Lease or month-to-month
2. Base rent
3. Basis for overage or participation
4. Share of common area maintenance
5. Net basis
6. Occupancy restrictions
7. Insurance

Perhaps you are wondering why there would be items in a rent or lease agreement that deal with the tenant's business affairs. When you use property for business purposes, all the rental terms are pertinent in one way or another to your operating costs and the desirability of the space. In making a choice, all these matters must be considered and, of course, be covered in the agreement between the owner and the tenant. To illustrate, let's assume you have bought a medium-size building that contains offices for professionals such as doctors and dentists, and retail space on the ground level; there's parking space as well. Here are some of the considerations relative to preparing terms and agreements for this property.

Lease or Month-to-Month.   It is probable that prospective business and professional tenants will want the relative security of a lease together with an equitable renewal option. Some business tenants need the ability to expand their space as the business expands and they will have an interest in knowing what additional space may be available and when. When possible, you should stagger the expiration date of the leases and try to anticipate your tenants' needs. Keep in touch with your major tenants to know what is happening and relate their plans and expectations to your own. You may have a chance to commit space for a future period and meanwhile need a short-term tenant. There is lots of potential juggling here. Your objective is obviously to keep the building fully rented at maximum rents and avoid losing a good tenant who needs more space. All this may mean you will have a combination of some tenants on leases and some month-to-month. As needed, the latter may be asked to move so you can accommodate better occupancies if the opportunities arise.

Before setting the lease renewal provisions, with respect to term and rent basis, you should ask the prospective tenants what their needs are. You have to protect yourself against rising costs unless renting on a net basis, so this prospect must be allowed for when setting renewal terms. How long into the future do you want to commit the space? What are your plans to sell? Realize that buyers take property subject to lease agreements outstanding. For some prospective buyers, having the property fully occupied and committed well into the future would be a plus. On the other hand, if a buyer was looking for space to occupy, your advance commitments would eliminate such prospects. There are many variables to consider. Given that you have resolved some of these aspects, how do you set fair rent amounts for renewal options? Here's where learning what others are doing can be very important. Essentially, you want the rent payment to reflect changes in costs and the value of the property. And you'll have to reach different conclusions if the tenant is paying a straight monthly rent or, in addition, is paying a percentage of sales. In the latter situation, the presumption is that you are already participating in any increased value of the property to the extent the success of the business has contributed to it. Many lease agreements include that renewal rents be set according to the impact of an index, either cost of living, cost of money, or some other independently prepared measure. Look around for examples of how these work. For more details of how base and participating rents are set, let's look at common practices.

Base Rent, Participation, Escalation.   Office space is often offered at so much a square foot. That will be translated into a dollar amount either per month or per year. A reminder: under a lease agreement, it is usual for the lessee to be committed to the total dollar amount for the period of the lease even though it may be payable in monthly installments. For retail space you should set a fixed-base monthly amount along with a basis for additional payments related to sales of profits. Because so many things enter into a profit computation, you are better off linking the rent overage to sales volume. This would mean, of course, that even if the firm was not making any money, as long as the sales revenues were large enough to exceed the base line, rent overage would be payable. Setting the base rent and the minimum sales volume will be a challenge for you and your tenants. The lease agreement should provide for you to have access to the tenant's records so that you can confirm the accuracy of the amounts reported and used as a basis for computing rent. Many investors have achieved remarkable rates of return through owning properties subject to rent participation agreements when businesses have been successful. You should watch for opportunities to change flat rent terms to a combination with participating overages.

With or without participation, you should consider an escalation clause under which the rent payment is changed to reflect the change in specified expense factors, such as property taxes or other services. Once your investment has been made, you must ensure that the return from revenues less operating expenses does not decrease. Look carefully to each of your prospective cost elements and determine what you have to do, through the agreement with your tenants, to protect your return.

In shopping centers and even industrial parks, it is customary to assess tenants a share of the cost of maintaining the property used by the public and the tenants in common. This is known as common area maintenance. The lease agreement should provide for the appropriate payment. Be certain you establish a system for pursuing this, inasmuch as it is customary to bill tenants separately from the rent and at different intervals, such as once or twice a year rather than monthly. In our office building example, perhaps the overall cost of the janitorial service is to be apportioned to the tenants along with the cost of maintaining the parking lot.

If you are providing utilities, you must learn how to reflect their cost in the rent. Whenever possible, arrange for utilities to be billed directly to each user. In an office building, of course, there will be heat and light for common areas even if each occupant has his or her own meter. To protect yourself, if at all possible, find a way for variable costs to be assessed to the tenants.

After reflecting on each of the foregoing potentially troublesome topics, you might be attracted to the *net lease* approach.

Net Lease.   As can be seen, one of the difficulties you may face in owning business income property is the variable expense. Variable expenses include property taxes, insurance, utilities, maintenance, and repairs. If you rent the entire building to one tenant, it would be easy to prepare an agreement under which the tenant would assume responsibility for all of these expenses. If so, the rent payment then would be termed *net*. In this connection you will associate the expression *triple net* or *NNN* lease when you see it. This can work well for the owner, of course, because the income will not be subject to these variable expenses. The tenant can minimize occupancy expense by being careful with controllable costs. Net leasing, however, does not work quite as well for multiple occupancy property because, as referred to above, there will be common area expenses for which no one tenant could be asked to assume responsibility. You, however, might try for a modified form.

Deposits. Once you've settled the foregoing matters, and before looking at some nonfinancial topics, you must decide on how much the tenant is to pay in advance. Your position is the most secure when you have, as a minimum, the first month's rent in hand before the tenant moves in. If local custom permits, ask also for the last month's rent and a damage deposit as well. Well-financed tenants may suggest you take a full year's rent in advance provided you offer an adequate discount. Technically, you should compute the present value of the rental payments for a discount rate that reflects the time value of money. For such a computation, check with your banker or accountant. Think of the single sum advance payment of the rent which, if invested at an appropriate interest rate, would grow to the same total the individual rent payments would if deposited each month and earned interest all to the end of the lease term.

Occupancy Restrictions. In multi-occupancy properties in particular it may be important to have restrictions on use and on signs. In our example, it probably wouldn't be necessary to limit the number or type of doctors, but we might be asked by the retail tenant to restrict or prohibit other retailing in the building, at least of products that would compete. In shopping centers typically there are lease restrictions to minimize the presence of competing enterprises. Certainly in the office leases there ought to be a prohibition against manufacturing or assembly work or any other activity incompatible with the intended occupancies. As in housing accommodation agreements, office leases may restrict occupancy to a stated number of persons. Whether a tenant has the right to sublet all or part of the space must also be covered in the agreement. Typically, a landlord will reserve the right to sublet, thus maintaining control over the use of the property. If a tenant proposes an acceptable sublet, an owner can readily agree, but at least is in the position to say no if conditions warrant it.

Businesses dependent upon attracting the public need an ability to install advertising signs. Lease agreements should address this matter along with structural alterations. Office occupants may be restricted to lettering on the office door. Uniformity in a building can be obtained by the owner setting forth the specifications and even arranging for the work to be done. The size and nature of outdoor signing should also be controlled. It is customary to require the property owner's permission to place signs on the exterior of the building and in the parking lot.

What if the tenant needs to rearrange the space, install fixtures, or walls and partitions? This is a negotiable matter and if there's a shortage of tenants, landlords may have to pay the cost to prepare space to meet the tenants' needs. Under other circumstances, tenants must pay the cost and often these are substantial. It's important to be aware that the value of the structural alterations accrues to the owner of the building, and the money spent by the tenant to make them is not recoverable. Because of the potential for creating a problem for future rentals, the owner needs to be careful in reaching an agreement regarding changes to be made in the building by a tenant; this includes painting and decorating. If you can foresee the need to have tenant-made alterations removed, insert a requirement in the rental agreement that the property is to be restored, at the tenant's expense, to its original condition at the end of the tenancy.

Insurance. The building owner should control the hazard insurance covering the building and the contents not owned by the tenants. This leaves insurance on tenants' property a matter for them to handle. But the liability risk is another matter. When someone is injured on a business premises, typically the claim for damages is made against everyone in sight, including of course, the property owner, regardless of the circumstances. In general, only the person adjudged to have been negligent will actually be responsible, but many others may incur substantial legal expense defending themselves. For this reason, the building owner should carry adequate public liability insurance on the property as a whole. For additional safeguard, the rent agreements should call for tenants to carry specified types and minimum amounts of insurance and to provide the owner with a copy, known as a *certificate of insurance*. This will also mean that the insurance company is obligated to notify the landlord if the contract is cancelled or changed by the tenant.

When there is a loan on the property the lender will require the borrower to buy appropriate fire and other peril coverage and see that the lender is named on the policy as a *loss payee*. Today it is now possible to buy hazard insurance on the structure, and even the contents, so that payment for losses is made on a replacement cost basis, thus eliminating any deduction for depreciation. You should talk to your insurance advisor about all this and not fail to obtain the best possible protection for your investment.

If you have employees you should learn if the law requires that you carry workers' compensation insurance. This pays for medical expenses and lost wages for employees injured on the job. It's entirely possible that a resident manager will be considered your employee, even though you believe he or she has the status of an independent contractor. You may also wish to ask your insurance advisor about insurance covering the possible loss of rent money and other property either through burglary, robbery, or through the dishonesty of an employee.

Summary. Start now to collect copies of lease contracts to learn about what they contain. You'll have to make many decisions in order to handle your property and it's important to know as much as you can about how others operate. You can get preprinted lease agreement forms in stationery stores and, if you expect to use a property management service, you can talk to them about the lease terms you should use. Although you can be agreeable to negotiating special terms, you really ought to be equipped in advance of talking to the first rental prospect with firm ideas of what you are offering.

Dealing with Tenants

One of the many challenges of owning and managing rental property is that created by tenant's requests. There's no end to the variety of things you can be asked for—and almost all will cost you money if you say yes. There's no universally applicable test or procedure. Your goal is to maximize your return from the investment. You will constantly be balancing the cost of taking care of a tenant's request against the potentially greater cost you'll have if a dissatisfied tenant moves out. Through experience you'll learn how to make good decisions. In general, a prompt response will produce by far the best results. Saying no quickly is better than dragging it out.

The lease or rental agreement should include a provision for assessing damages for failure to live up to the terms, thus making it easier to pursue defaulting tenants. Remember that when the lease is properly written, you will have a cause of action against the tenant for all unpaid rent even for the time after the premises have been vacated. On a month-to-month basis you will be limited to a maximum of one month's rent for failure to give notice and for unpaid rent. But what about evicting a business tenant? It is much less common to have to get an eviction and have the sheriff remove a business or professional tenant but it can be done. As a rule the regulations do not distinguish between residential and business tenancy. You will probably need legal counsel, however, to avoid forfeiting some rights. Know in advance to whom you can turn for timely assistance.

Summary

Assume you were a prospective tenant for office space in the building we've used for our example. What would you need to know to make a decision to rent? Include everything you can think of under such an assumption when, as a landlord, you prepare a rental agreement. That should take care of the provisions from the tenant's point of view. Now, as the owner, what do you need to know about the prospective tenant and what agreements do you want to have with a tenant? Include those either in the application for rent or the agreement and you'll have completed the task of getting ready to offer the property to prospective tenants.

Resolve to check out carefully a prospective tenant's references, both financial and those of prior landlords. When feasible, get a credit report. Don't hesitate to ask others for their judgment about people. And, finally, make use of professional counsel, both legal and property management, to protect your investment.

RECORD KEEPING

The only satisfactory way to measure your investment return and to judge what action, if any, you should take, is to maintain adequate records of financial transactions. As a minimum, of course, you must be able to file accurate tax returns. Records, therefore, are essential. Whether you are to incur the expense of a professional accounting or bookkeeping service is a decision to be made early. Except for very complex properties, you, as an individual private investor, can easily keep all the records needed by following the instructions below. As long as you have the basic information for each transaction, you can obtain professional assistance in interpreting it and preparing tax returns and financial statements.

You should establish a bank checking account for your property investment. All revenues are to be deposited to it and all expenses connected with the project are to be paid by check. Never mix your personal financial affairs with the business. If you decide to take some money from the investment, write yourself a check on the project bank account; don't just use some of the rent money.

Your basic record keeping will involve simply creating a record of all money received and from whom. Primarily through your checkbook entries you'll have a record of all payments made. Each is to be supported by invoices, statements, or any other document containing information relative to the expenditure. All rent and lease agreements, plus tenant applications, should be kept in a systematic fashion. Most landlords set up a file folder for each tenant.

At the end of each month you should prepare an operating statement for each property. At the end of the year you should pull together all the figures for an annual profit and loss statement. Then, because you need to be able to tell over time just how your investment is prospering, you'll want to keep a running summary. Here's how to do it.

EXAMPLE: Assume you bought a small office building for $300,000, paid half cash and borrowed $150,000 for twenty-five years at 12 percent interest. The monthly rents amount to $2,500 and during the year you receive additional income from storage space rentals.

Monthly Records

In the course of a single month you will not have a large number of transactions for a property. From either your receipt book or a simple listing made when rents are received, you can quickly total the revenue for the period. Next you must classify the expenditures; recall from the chapter on investment analysis that operating expenses are grouped by type. By listing the amount for each check, by type of expense, you will have all you need to compute the results for the month. As illustrated on the following page, by relating

MONTHLY RECORD OF INCOME/EXPENSE

Location: **879 Regal**   Year Ending **19XX**

Income	Jan	Feb	Mar	Apr	May	June	July	Aug	Sep	Oct	Nov	Dec	Totals
Rents	2,500 –												
Deposits													
Storage	50 –												
Total	2,550 –												
Expenses													
Property Taxes													
Utils.	210 –												
Insur.													
Maint.	285 –												
Mgmt.													
1st. Mtge. Pmt.	1,580 –												
2nd. Mtge. Pmt.													
Interest													
Total	2,075												
To Bank	475												
Beg. Bal	1,000												
End. Bal	1,475												

income and outgo, you can strike a balance to use in reconciling the bank account.

To set targets for yourself you can prepare an operating budget and cash forecast. You do this by estimating expected rents and anticipated expenses for the ensuing year. If you do that a month at a time, when you have your actual record of transactions you can compare and learn whether you are ahead or behind your financial plan. If you see things are getting out of hand, you may be able to take appropriate action to prevent a major problem.

Annual Operating Statement

Accountants have taught us to expect income and outgo to be presented in the form of an operating or profit and loss statement. You can prepare such a summary for each property by using the totals from the Monthly Record plus the results of a few computations for interest and depreciation expense. A typical statement is shown on pages 230–31.

For Section A, *Cash Flow Before Income Tax*, you simply enter the numbers from the "Totals" column of the Monthly Record. We are using what is termed the *cash basis* of accounting and, therefore, will show where the cash came from and where it went. The net change in the bank account from one period to the next should equal the difference between cash income and outgo for the same time. Of course, this may show a negative result. That is to say, when expenses exceed cash income, there may be a deficit. Don't be alarmed at such a result. On an after-tax basis you will likely have a positive result and that's what really counts. When you maximize leverage it is unlikely the cash income will be enough to cover all the cash expenses; this should lead to a tax shelter benefit. As long as the property is increasing in value and the tax shelter benefit is large enough, you will probably come out very well on your investment.

Refer now to Section B, *Income Tax Computation*. Here we find that taxable income is not just the difference between cash in and cash out. Under income tax rules, only specified expenses can be deducted from revenues. We need to compute the portion of the mortgage payment that is interest; usually some part of the total is applied to principal. In Section A we used the entire payment, here only interest expense. At the end of the year financial institutions typically provide borrowers with a breakdown of the payments so you would have just the numbers you need. If, however, you need to compute the interest expense and the amount by which the mortgages are reduced, you can use the tables in the Appendix if the loans are fully amortizing. For the illustrated example, here is the procedure followed.

1. From the table for a 25-year loan at 12%, the monthly payment for each $1,000 borrowed is $10.5322; for $150,000, the total monthly payment is 150 times 10.5322 = $1,580 rounded. For the year the total would be 12 times, hence $18,960.

2. To calculate the portion charged to interest in the first year, multiply the factor from the "Interest" column in the table by 150, hence 119.637 times 150 = $17,946 rounded.

3. To compute the unpaid mortgage balance, multiply the "Balance Due" factor by 150: 993.25 times 150 = $148,988 rounded.

4. Note that if you subtract the total interest expense from the total payments the result will be the amount credited to the principal. That amount should be the same as the difference between the beginning and ending mortgage loan balances; rounding will account for minor discrepancies in these two figures.

Depreciation expense here is computed on the basis of these assumptions: that the land value is $100,000 so that $200,000 is the total to be depreciated over the remaining useful life; here we use twenty-five years. On a straight-line basis, the annual depreciation charge is $200,000 divided by twenty-five years to give $8,000 a year.

In the example we see that the cash income for the year is just about equal to the cash outlays. We are more concerned, however, about the after-income-tax result. When there is a

ANNUAL OPERATING STATEMENT

For Property at ___879 REGAL___   For Year Ended ___19— —___

A. Cash Flow before Income Tax

Total Rental Income Received	$ 30,000	
Other Income	500	$ 30,500
Less: Property Taxes	$ 3,500	
Utilities	2,800	
Insurance	1,500	
Maintenance	3,600	
Total Operating Expenses	$ 11,400	
Mortgage Payments—First	18,960	
—Second		
—Third		
Total Cash Outlay		$ 30,360
Net Cash Inco		140

B. Income Tax Computation

Total Income .... $ 30,500

Less: Total Operating Expenses .... $ 11,400

    Total Mortgage Int. Exp. 17,946

    Depreciation—Building 8,000

         —Equipment ....

    Total Deductible Expense .... $ 37,346

Net Taxable Income .... $ <6,846>

Income Tax Liability: __40%__ × Net Tax. Inc. .... $ <2,738>
                Rate

(If net taxable inc. is negative, the tax liab. is
your tax shelter benefit.)

C. Mortgage Reduction

Total of Mortgage Balances at Beginning of Year .... $ 150,000

Less Ending Balances, All Mortgages, End of Year 148,988

Total Mortgage Reduction .... $ 1,012

D. Reconciliation of Cash Gain

Net Cash Income .... $ 140

Less Inc. Tax Liab. or Plus Tax Shelter Benefit 2,738

Total Spendable Cash after Income Tax .... $ 2,878

negative taxable income, there will be a tax shelter benefit. The amount is obtained by multiplying the tax rate against the taxable income as shown in the illustration. Because this means that total income taxes on all sources of income are reduced, it is considered a cash gain. When it is added to the net cash income the result is the total after-tax cash return from the investment; it is termed *net spendable*.

Depreciation Schedule

Each year you will need to check whether the depreciation charge is to be the same as for the preceding period. Under the straight-line method, the amount will be uniform unless you make improvements or remove a part of the property. As discussed previously, if you use an accelerated depreciation method, the amount must be computed each time. You need to maintain a record of how you have treated depreciation on your tax return. A suggested form is shown at right.

Summary of Investment Results

So far we've examined the accounting records for each property prepared at the end of each year. Especially because we are involved in a long-term investment, it is important to be able to see whether we are actually making good progress. We certainly must consider when it is desirable to sell and only if we have a cumulative record can we know. From the next illustration you can see how you would make entries each year to create the appropriate summary to date.

Income Tax Credits

Real estate investors must keep abreast of developments in tax regulation. This can be done by reading the *Wall Street Journal* and other financial publications, as well as by obtaining each year appropriate publications from the Internal Revenue Service. At present there are two income tax matters of

DEPRECIATION SCHEDULES

ENTER HERE THE FIGURES TO BE USED IN PREPARING INCOME TAX RETURNS

Building: Date Acquired _1-1-19--_ Total Purchase Price $ **290,000**

Rem. Useful Life _25 YEARS_ Costs Not Expensed $ **10,000**

Total $ **300,000**

Depreciation Method

STRAIGHT LINE Less Land Value $ **100,000**

200,000 ÷ 25 = $8,000 A YEAR Basis For Dep'n $ **200,000**

End of Year	Beginning Bk. Val.	Depreciation	Ending Bk. Val.	Total Dep'n
19 - -	$300,000	$ 8,000	$292,000	$ 8,000
19				
19				
19				
19				
19				
19				
19				
19				
19				

Equipment: Description _____ Date Acquired _____

Cost $_____ Estimated Useful Life _____

Salvage $_____

Amount to Be Depreciated $_____ Method _____

End of Year	Beginning Bk. Val.	Depreciation	Ending Bk. Val.	Total Dep'n
19				
19				
19				
19				
19				
19				
19				

SUMMARY OF INVESTMENT RESULTS

Property at **879 REGAL**

Purchased on **JAN. 1, 19XX** for $ **300,000**

Costs: Mortgage Points/Fees $ **7,500**

Title Ins./Escrow Fees **1,000**

Other One-Time Fees **1,500**

Total Costs $ **10,000**

Cash Down Payment $ **140,000**

Total Costs **10,000**

Total Cash Invested $ **150,000**

Year	Rental Income	Net Cash Income	Tax or Shelter Benefit	Total Cash Gain	% of Cash Invested	Cumul. Cash Recovery	Mort'ge. Redct'n.	Total Gain	% of Cash Invested	Addt'l. Capital Invested
19	$30,500	140	TSB $2,738	$2,878	1.9%	$2,878	$1,012	$3,890	2.6%	—
19										
19										
19										
19										
19										
19										
19										
19										
19										

NOTES: Enter data from the annual operating statement. Prepare a summary form for each separate property. This provides a year-by-year summary of investment returns and performance. The cumulative cash recovery column enables you to see when your total cash investment has been recovered. Total gain includes the reduction in the mortgages. This will be realized only if the property is ultimately sold for at least its original cost plus resale expense. Gain on resale may be subject to income tax.

Do not include the prorations part of the closing costs when computing the amount of cash invested.

special interest to owners of income property: tax credits for energy-saving devices and the special investment tax credit. The former is also of possible importance to you if you own your home.

For specific details concerning ways to reduce taxes through use of energy conservation devices, see IRS Publication 903, *Energy Credits*. Some states also allow tax credits for these so be certain you contact local authorities for information. There is a 10 percent tax credit granted to purchasers of personal property such as equipment that will be used over a specified period of years. Although this does not currently apply generally to residential income property, it can be important for other types of investment properties. To learn how you might be able to offset income taxes by 10 percent of the cost of eligible purchases, consult IRS Publication 572, *Investment Credit*. And while dealing with the IRS ask also for Publication 550, *Investment Income and Expenses*; it contains information needed by all investors.

Although it is essential that you take income tax regulations into account when making and evaluating an investment, you need not be intimidated by such a prospect. You can obtain assistance from the government tax offices and the publications generally are very easy to understand. There's no doubt that professional assistance can be important, of course. Check with friends and business associates for recommendations for accountants and lawyers so you can be prepared if you decide to seek help.

CLOSING THOUGHTS

It is not enough to drive the hardest bargain and buy at a rock-bottom price. Once you own property you can maximize both your enjoyment and financial returns by paying close attention to all that's involved in managing it. This is true even if your investment is limited to your own home. When you have income property and are handling revenues and expenditures, such matters may appear to be more relevant, of course.

As a landlord you have two basic choices: to do all the managing yourself or to employ a property management service. Even though you use a service, you will not be completely removed from decision-making, nor should you want to be; remember it's your money at risk. Regardless of how the managing is done, keep in mind that there are two separate functions: finding tenants and taking care of them and the property transactions once the tenants have moved in. Many investors choose to handle one of these functions and contract out the other.

Whether you own residential income property or buildings rented for business or professional use, you should maintain accurate and complete records. This is not hard to achieve. Resolve to deposit all revenues to a bank checking account and make all payments by check. Avoid using cash because of the lack of records of the transaction. With the basic record of deposits and checks you can easily prepare Annual Operating Statements and Investment Summaries as described in this chapter. From these you can know at all times where you stand and the progress, if any, you are making in building your future financial security.

Finally, don't operate your property in a vacuum. Keep informed about the market. What are your competitors charging? Can you anticipate a change in the demand (or the supply) of the type of property you own? Is it time to trade up? Trade down? Liquidate? Obtain more property? Refinance? As the owner of property you are in business—and, as you know, business people never rest!

9

Selling and Reinvesting

Sooner or later you will be faced with selling your home or income property. There will be many factors to consider and perhaps some tough decisions to make. Should you trade up, trade down, or cash out? And when is the best time? Have you maximized the gain? What about income tax considerations? And a really tough one: should you do it yourself or hire a real estate broker?

DECISIONS

Even though the home you bought was perfect at the time, later you may see the need to sell it. Perhaps you need more space or want to move to a different neighborhood. Maybe you'd like to live in a condominium or co-op where someone else can worry about maintenance, repairs, and decorating. Or, you may be prompted to think about selling in order to get your hands on your equity. You could refinance, of course, and often that would be a more prudent plan if all you want is some cash. If you do sell and buy another home, at least you may not have to worry about paying capital gains taxes at the time because the gain can be rolled over into the new property. Once you've reached fifty-five, you may be totally free of gains tax when you sell for the last time. You will need to check your income tax situation carefully once you've decided to sell, however. The terms of sale can be greatly influenced by income tax implications. In spite of the

237

apparent complexities of taxes, financing, and paperwork, it is quite practical for most people to handle the sale on a do-it-yourself basis. Some owners, however, based on their experience, would be quick to recommend having a competent real estate dealer to take care of the transaction.

In considering the sale of income property, timing can be the most important factor. Can you get a maximum price or is the market depressed because financing is not available? Have you held the property long enough to qualify for long-term capital gain treatment? Would a sale at this point help you to achieve your objectives? Of course, perhaps you've decided you don't want to be a landlord any longer and you want to convert your investment into a mortgage loan. That's what you can do by financing the sale yourself. On the other hand, you may want to further pyramid your holdings by moving your equity into more and larger properties. Here again, income taxes will play an important role in your decision-making process.

This chapter will provide you with a guide to the factors which will help you make good financial decisions.

SELLING YOUR HOME

Assume you own your home, have enjoyed it for a number of years, but now find there's a reason to consider making a change. It will be important to carefully look at a whole range of factors and alternatives, starting with a definition of your objectives. In making this change, consider what you want to accomplish. Then comes the "how," along with an appraisal of the potential consequences.

Objectives

Once you can state clearly your objective in leaving your present housing, what you need to do to achieve that objective will become clear. If your present home is too large for a reduced family, set down the specifications for a replacement home. On the other hand, maybe you need more space. If so, try to define in precise terms what is required. When you start seeking a replacement property, be certain you stick to your requirements to save time, effort, and to have the best chance to meet your objective.

Maybe you want to change neighborhoods. Try to identify what has led to your current dissatisfaction and work to avoid a repeat in another location. It's easy to jump from the frying pan into the fire.

There are financial aspects to almost every housing decision. At the outset most people will have to decide whether they need to sell their present home in order to purchase its replacement. When that is so, there can be some interesting challenges. Often you will find an ideal new home and will want to act quickly to secure it. But, until you can get a buyer for the old one, what can you do? The prospect of owning two houses at the same time, each complete with its own mortgage payment, is not a prospect to be savored. In some situations you may be able either to sell your property to a real estate dealer who is handling both deals or get an advance on the old house to provide the down payment on the new. When you want to borrow funds for a short time for this purpose, the loan is known as a *bridge* or *swing loan*. Some financial institutions will make these loans to good customers; otherwise you may be able to find a private investor. In any case, if you must maximize the amount of cash to be obtained through the sale of your present property, that will have a great bearing on how the sale is structured and on how you can finance the purchase of other property.

But what if you don't intend to buy again; instead, you plan to move to rental property. That could make it a lot easier to sell because you would not have to obtain maximum cash. Instead of selling, you may want to consider turning your current home into rental property. Either that rental income, or mortgage payments received if you finance the sale, should certainly help you to take care of your future housing costs. In exploring these options be certain to determine your position for both selling and investing the cash versus retaining it and generating rental income. Remember that as an owner of income property, you could charge depreciation expense which might serve to shelter other income, at least in part, from income taxes. Your tax situation at the time you make the change will influence some of your decisions.

Your current operating and living expenses must also be considered. You should have a well-defined family budget and know precisely what your current housing expense is. Then, taking each of the options that are attractive, you should calculate revised figures. Be careful; this may put a damper on all enthusiasm to make any change. That nice, new, larger home will undoubtedly be more expensive. Better to compute that in advance of making a commitment, however. Or, you may be all excited about the possibility of moving to a condominium to get rid of some of the chores of home ownership. Hold back a bit on the excitement until you have prepared your new budget and made allowance for the condo homeowners' association fee. There's no free lunch, as you'll quickly discover. For although you won't have to take care of the exterior painting, or the gardening, or shovelling the snow, someone will be doing it in your behalf—and they have to paid. None of this is designed to discourage condo living. It is, however, to alert you to how imperative it is to analyze the financial consequences first, not last.

Financing Alternatives

Once you've decided to sell your present home, how you can make a sale will be greatly influenced by how it can be financed. Financing will be governed by your objectives, the amount and nature of the current indebtedness on the property, and the needs of a buyer. You should assume that all buyers need a great deal of help and you should prearrange financing as far as you can. Here are the alternatives.

Cash Out.   You could offer the property on the basis that the buyer is to pay all cash if the property is clear or cash to the loan. In either case you would maximize the total number of dollars realized at the time the sale is closed. A buyer, to meet these terms, would have to come up with all cash, get a new loan, or qualify to take over your loan. In anticipation of the fact that most buyers do not know how to proceed, you should seriously consider refinancing the property prior to offering it for sale if your equity is substantial.

Refinancing.   If you have a mature loan—that is, you borrowed a few years ago at a lower than current interest rate, and your equity has been increasing—it is quite likely your present lender would be interested in granting you a new loan that would pay off the old and give you the difference in cash. In this manner you could tap your equity without waiting for a sale to take place. Note, of course, that until the sale is made, your monthly payments would be increased, so don't overlook the impact on the family budget. Once done, you might even change your mind about selling. But, on with the proposition that you've done this to make it easier for someone to buy your home. If you do get the maximum loan possible and have made sure it can be assumed by a buyer, all you need is someone with a large enough cash down payment to complete the purchase. Once you find such a person and all goes well, after the escrow is closed you should have realized all cash for your equity through a combination of the cash sprung through refinancing and the buyer's down payment. Don't overlook, however, that you incurred costs in obtaining the new loan for loan fees and title insurance. Be certain to reflect them when setting your sales price. As a rule you can get a higher sales price when the amount of cash required to buy is lower than otherwise.

An alternative to actually getting the new loan is to obtain a written commitment from your present lender or some other, to make a loan under stated terms to a qualified buyer. You will find it very important to be able to tell prospective buyers what financing is possible. Without such information, many people will simply not consider your property further. It is true you could advise them to approach a lender themselves but not many are willing to exert themselves to do so.

Land Contract.   So far we've looked at alternatives under which the seller passes title to the buyer through a deed and the lender takes a mortgage. It is possible instead for sellers to enter into a sales or land contract with a purchaser under which title does not pass at the time, only after the contract price has been paid in full. The contract purchaser agrees to an overall price, makes a cash down payment, and the periodic (usually monthly) payments of principal and interest. Once the principal is paid off, the seller is obligated to execute a deed in favor of the contract purchaser.

This device can be used when the property is free and clear or if it is encumbered. In the latter case, the contract seller retains the responsibility for paying off the existing loan; the payments on the contract should be more than ample for that purpose. Failure, however, to pay off the underlying debt in no way relieves the seller of an ultimate obligation to deliver free and clear title once the contract price has been paid. The purchaser must, to protect his or her interest, make certain that the contract is recorded. That is accomplished by delivering it to the county recorder or registrar of deeds where the property is located. If not recorded, the buyer runs the risk of other parties gaining a legally enforceable interest. How would you like to find that the seller sold the property two or three more times to others? Where would you stand?

By means of the land contract, the seller is, in effect, financing the sale to the extent of the difference between the sales price and the cash down payment. If this looks and sounds similar to a mortgage to you, that means you have been paying attention. The difference, however, is that under a mortgage, the buyer gets title and if there's a default, the seller must take legal action under the terms of the mortgage, to foreclose. When there's a default under a land contract, the seller would still be faced with some legal action, but some people feel it is easier to control the situation when you still have title to the property. Notwithstanding adverse features of a land contract, such as for the buyer who has trouble later getting title from an uncooperative seller, it is a very flexible financing device and is widely used throughout the country.

Mortgages.   Here we are concerned with mortgages taken back by the seller. They may be first, second, third, or what have you. As discussed previously, a very popular type of second or junior mortgage is the *wraparound*. The seller may be an enthusiastic mortgage lender or clearly be quite reluctant. If you are very anxious to make a sale and the buyer just can't come up with enough cash, you might reluctantly agree to take back a mortgage to make the sale possible. If your objective is to generate interest income, then taking mortgages on property you sell is a great way to go. A word of caution is in order, however.

First, the documentation must be handled properly and you will likely find it to your advantage to have a lawyer handle it. Your security interest will be in the form of a mortgage or deed of trust and if it's defective and there's a default, you might find yourself empty-handed. In addition to the amount of the mortgage principal, you must decide on an interest rate, amount *and* frequency of payments, late charge, prepayment penalty, and due date, if any. Because you have vowed to keep in touch with what's happening, you will know about the current mortgage market interest rates and other terms set by lenders and can set realistic conditions. Once you and the buyer-borrower have settled on the interest rate, next comes the basis for determining the monthly payment. If you choose to have the borrower make a payment that would fully amortize the loan over a stated time period, you can use the Tables in the Appendix to calculate the amount. Unless agreed to otherwise, the repayment would extend over the full term and it would be a long time before you were paid off. If you want your money sooner than that, you have two choices: shorten the amortization period, thus increasing the monthly payment, or set a due date on which the unpaid principal balance is payable in full. This is called a *balloon* payment. When a payment of principal and interest is made, the interest earned is deducted first and the balance of the payment applied to the principal. Over time the portion to interest reduces and that credited to principal increases. Due dates and balloon payment conditions are customary for junior mortgages, so you won't be breaking new ground if you propose them.

If your primary concern is to use a mortgage to generate interest income, you may wish to offer an interest-only loan. Some buyers would be attracted to such an alternative because the periodic payment would be smaller than otherwise. For this to function, however, you would want to set a due date within a few years at the most so the buyer would have to make plans to refinance, assuming you did in fact want the loan paid off at that time. From your point of view an interest-only loan has the advantage that all of the principal is earning interest. When a loan is being amortized you are getting some of your principal back but in small chunks. You then must find a way to reinvest it assuming you wish to preserve your capital. You could always find a way to spend it, of course.

Assume that you picked a mortgage term of twenty-five or thirty years to be amortized by monthly payments. The factor for the interest rate and term is found in the Tables. To estimate what the balloon payment would be, take the factor for the number of years the payments are to be made in the "Balance Due" column. Apply it to the original loan in thousands and you will have what you need. But there's another way to handle all this. Instead of using the payment needed to fully amortize the loan over an extended term, you may wish simply to specify a monthly payment—$500, $800, $1,000 or whatever. You still must have an interest rate to compute the part of the payment attributable to mortgage interest. Note, therefore, that the payment amount will have to be at least equal to the interest charge and that sets a minimum amount for the *stipulated* payment option. To calculate it, divide the interest rate by the number of times payments are to be made (twelve for monthly, for example) and apply the result to the original loan balance. If the contract rate is 12 percent, then the stipulated monthly payment would have to be at least 1 percent of the loan. But how do you compute the balloon payment? The Tables will not serve this purpose as they contain factors for amortizing the loan over a specified term. Instead, you would have to separately calculate the apportionment of interest and principal for each payment and carry a running reducing principal balance. The amount outstanding on the due date would be the balloon payment.

It would seem reasonable that all borrowers would be encouraged to pay off the debt as soon as possible. Not so if you wanted the principal to be working for you producing maximum interest income and you wished to avoid having to find another way to reinvest the money. Most loans are made to achieve these objectives so it is customary to include a prepayment penalty provision to be applied if the borrower pays more on the principal than called for by the repayment schedule. You should check around to see what the practice is in your area as it differs throughout the country. Even if you include a prepayment penalty, you don't have to enforce it if you want to remove a block to premature payoff. When the penalty is imposed the amount is simply added to the unpaid mortgage balance claimed at the time the borrower liquidates the debt.

Do you want to encourage the borrower to make the payments on time? If so, consider including a late charge to be levied if the payment is late more than a stated number of days. In some states there are controls on the amount that can be charged; check with local authorities. If you don't provide for a late charge in the mortgage contract there's not much you can do about a borrower who is late in making payments. There must be a basis in the mortgage on which default is declared, but you don't want to threaten default and foreclosure each time the payment is delayed. You do need, of course, to be alert to when an actual default is in progress. As a lender you will have to monitor carefully when payments are due and received and be prepared to take timely action. Making a concession can serve to set a precedent that would impair your rights to legal remedies associated with default.

So much for your financing all or part of the sale. Everything stated in the foregoing would apply whether you were making a first, second, or wraparound mortgage. In fact, much would also apply to a land contract. In general you can set your lending terms on the same basis as any institutional lender, making concessions where you thought it wise and profitable. When it comes time for you to decide on lending terms, check not only with savings and loan associations and commercial banks but also mortgage loan brokers and finance companies. Anything they can do, you can do, too.

Land Lease.   Now here's an old idea to be applied in a new way. In parts of Europe, Canada, and the United States (Hawaii is a good example), people buy structures but lease the land on which they have been built. As a buyer you will want a long, long lease, of course, with a renewal option. When the lease finally comes to an end, the structure will belong to the landowner. How can we make use of this financing device here?

Let's assume that when you want to sell, mortgage financing is tight and interest rates are very high. You own the property free and clear or, at most, have a small mortgage balance. To make a sale, therefore, you must find a buyer with a lot of cash; that's the hardest kind of buyer to locate. What can you do? Well, under certain conditions, and you'll want your lawyer to work this one out for you, you could sell the structure by financing the sale through taking back a mortgage on it and leasing the land to the buyer. The objective is to reduce the amount of the periodic payment to make it easier for the buyer to swing the deal, to reduce the down payment as needed, and to give you interest income on the mortgage and rental income on the land. This has been widely used in commercial and industrial property financing and we'll discuss it in more detail in a later section. There's no reason why, in selected situations, the plan could not be used to finance the sale or purchase of a home.

Exchanging.   There may be significant tax advantages to
trading your property for another when it involves rental income but this is not likely to be so for your home. On the
other hand, exchanging one home for another may solve
some financing problems so we should look at how it is done.
Here we are dealing only with the case where the property
you want to buy is owned by someone who wants yours and
that you actually trade or exchange deeds. If the equities are
not the same, one party would pay the difference in cash to
the other. In the rare cases where this can be done, new loans
are avoided, assuming the existing mortgages can, in fact, be
assumed. For analytical purposes it is best to view this as
separate buy-and-sell transactions and then find the net difference, if any, that one person owes the other. Probably the
greatest challenge will be reaching an agreement on the market price of each property. When brokers are involved it is
customary for each seller to pay a regular commission but
that is subject to negotiation, of course. Shortly, when we
discuss the income tax considerations in selling, we'll see
that because you can roll over gains into a replacement home,
there's no separate tax-deferral feature to exchanging your
home for another.

Installment Sale.   Financing and income tax regulations
are intertwined and shortly we will look carefully at how
gains from the sale of your home may or may not be taxable.
Because of the special concessions made with respect to sale
of property used as your principal residence, you may not
have any tax to pay regardless of how you finance its sale.
But, if you sell a home not used as your principal residence or
subject to other conditions under which the gain may be subject to income tax, you do need to know how the tax regulations could affect the sale and financing terms. That's what
we'll explore here.

If a buyer is short of cash or cannot obtain a new loan or
assume yours, you may be influenced to provide the financing yourself, using one of the plans we've been discussing. In
one way or another, the buyer would put up a cash down

payment and enter into an agreement to pay off the balance of the purchase price. The lower the cash down payment the easier it will be for the buyer to make the deal. But if the balance is due you, you will want to minimize the risk of default by getting as large a down payment as possible. The more the buyer has at risk, the less likely there will be a default. So there you stand, in between conflicting objectives. But another factor may govern the amount of the down payment you will require. When this is not your principal home, you will want to minimize income tax payable on the gain (if there is one) by qualifying for *installment sale* treatment. You can do this by ensuring that you do not receive from the buyer, in the year of sale, more than 30 percent of the purchase price in cash. Perhaps you've noticed property offered at "29 percent down"; that indicates someone anxious to qualify for favorable tax treatment.

Because the installment sale device is of much greater importance when dealing in rental income property, we'll examine it in more detail below. Meanwhile, when thinking of how you might structure the financing for the sale of property, keep the 29 percent down payment limit in mind.

Summary. How the financing plan for the sale of your home is put together is directly associated with the reasons you have to sell. It is also affected by the supply of mortgage money and prospective purchasers' ability to come up with cash and to qualify for a loan. And, then, there are income taxes.

Income Tax Factors

Thanks to a beneficial Congress, homeowners have little to worry about with respect to income taxes on the capital gain realized from selling the family home. If within eighteen months of selling you buy another property for use as your principal residence, for an amount not less than the sale price of the former home, capital gains are rolled over into the new home and are not subject to tax until you do all this for the last time. If you don't take this last step until you are at least fifty-five, then the first $100,000 of gain accumulated from all prior principal residence sales is exempt from taxation. The balance, if any, would be subject to long-term preference, assuming the gain over the exemption came after owning property for at least one year. For complete details of this special tax sheltering for homeowners, see IRS Publication 523, *Tax Information on Selling or Buying Your Home.* You should also check with your state income tax office to obtain those regulations—they are not likely the same as for federal income tax.

Computing Gain.   Because you cannot know in advance whether you will be eligible to postpone taxes through buying a replacement home, or how the $100,000 exemption might apply, you must keep good records. For each home purchase you will want to retain the purchase agreement and escrow documents to establish original cost. As you make improvements to the property, be sure to keep a record of all the expenditures. For tax purposes, you must use your records to determine the property's *basis.* It will be the original cost plus the cost of any improvements. If you've had an uninsured loss and did not make the repairs, you would deduct the value of the damage. You can charge the uninsured loss against current income if you itemize deductions. The sales price less any cost of selling, minus the basis at the time of sale, gives the amount of the realized gain. The gain is computed here quite independently of how the sale has been financed.

Assuming you follow a typical pattern, you will have a series of home purchase and sale transactions in your lifetime. Here's an example of how you would compute the gain for income tax purposes.

Purchase price of first home, all costs	$ 35,000
Cost of improvements while owned	5,000
Basis at time of sale	$ 40,000
Sale price less costs	$125,000
Long-term capital gain	$ 85,000

If you do not buy a replacement home (it can be any type of

housing including a condo unit or co-op apartment or even an apartment property in which you make your home), for at least $125,000 within eighteen months, you will be subject to income tax on the gain of $85,000. The amount of the tax will depend on how the sale was financed; if you received 30 percent of the price or more, in cash, the entire gain would be taxable as it would not qualify as an installment sale. If you were at least fifty-five, you would be able to take the $100,000 exemption; it can be used once only.

Assume instead that you bought another home and paid $150,000 for it; ignore how it was financed. Your beginning basis would be $150,000 less the postponed gain of $85,000 from the prior transaction and hence would amount to $65,000. Later, when you sell the second property, the gain will be based on the difference between the sales price and $65,000, adjusted as needed for improvements. By this time you might well have accumulated at least $100,000 in gain and would welcome the exemption, if you were able to use it. In addition to the age requirement, you must also have lived in the property as your principal home for at least three of the previous five years. When you think you may be eligible, contact the IRS for instructions. Note that you would not want to take the exemption until you were certain you had accumulated all the gains from the sale of homes and could no longer rollover a gain because you didn't act within the required eighteen months.

All told, homeowners are greatly favored when it comes to income taxes. Current taxes can be reduced through itemizing mortgage interest and property tax expenses and most if not all capital gains may be exempted from taxes. How can you afford *not* to own your own home?

SALES STRATEGY

We come now to the plan of action to be formulated to obtain a buyer and close the escrow all in the shortest time possible. Through setting your objectives you will know how you want the sale to be financed. You will have to decide on a minimum sales price and the other terms. But also: what could you do to fix up the place to enhance the sale? And, a very important question: who, if anyone, is to help you complete the deal?

Setting the Price and Terms

Before offering the property you will have to decide on an asking price. This means you must learn what comparable properties are selling for and how they are financed. You will be unable to judge offers that may come along if you don't know values. A major service provided by real estate brokers is that of advising owners about current market prices and conditions. If you don't use a broker, you'll be on your own in this critical area. You can check out similar properties that are for sale, read the classified advertising, and talk with lenders. You may be well-advised to talk with one or more brokers before making a decision whether to list the property. In some areas competition is so brisk that brokers offer to provide a free appraisal in the hopes of getting the listing. This is certainly one way to get some idea of what your home might be worth. If you do sign a listing agreement (this will be discussed fully below) it is likely the listing broker will invite other brokers to visit the property not only to obtain their cooperation in finding a buyer but also in advising you on the price. It is customary for a group of dealers, once having toured the property, to offer individual estimates of market price. When averaged, the result can often be a very reliable guide to a realistic sales price.

Now for the terms. Earlier we discussed many of the considerations in setting up the financing. Before offering the property you should make up your mind about most of them. If you are going to carry all or part of the financing, decide exactly on the terms—you need to be very specific about such matters when dealing with a prospective buyer. If there's a chance the purchaser will be using FHA or VA financing you will probably have to pay some or all of the mortgage points and loan fees imposed by the lender. Discuss these factors with local financial institutions that are making government-insured loans so you can be prepared when the subject arises. Have at least a tentative idea of the rock-bottom, minimum amount of cash you must get out of the deal and thus be able to intelligently respond to offers and compromises.

In an earlier section we reviewed a number of potential contingencies. Likely the most difficult one you may have to face is that requested by a prospective buyer who has to sell another house to buy yours. Before agreeing to such a contingent purchase, inspect the other property and evaluate the chances of the owner being able to sell it. And what about the proposed time frame? Depending on your plans, you may not be able to wait for the time needed by the buyer. If you did accept and the deal ultimately fell through, where would you stand? At this point in real-life transaction, before committing yourself, you would do well to review all the angles treated in Chapter 7, *Negotiating the Deal.* You're on the other side now.

If you are not hard-pressed to realize all cash from the sale, or even if you are but it's not easy to find a buyer with cash or one who is able to get a mortgage loan, you may wish to consider a lease option. Perhaps a prospective buyer is anxious to have your home but cannot or does not want to complete the purchase now. You might be asked to consider, or you may wish to initiate a proposal that the potential buyer lease the property instead, with an option to buy it at a stated price at an agreed time. Some, all, or none of the rent payments may be applied to the purchase price. In doing this you must allow for the possibility that the option to buy is not taken up so that at the end of the lease period you must start all over again to find a buyer. This has been a successful device for many people and you should keep it in mind for an appropriate situation. Never presume that when you own property, to sell it all you need do is tell the world it's for sale. Qualified buyers are never easy to come by and you may have to do handstands to persuade someone to take the property off your hands. Be prepared to be ingenious.

Properties are bought either in a fully repaired condition or on what is termed "as is." Some buyers are looking for property to fix up, especially when they are in a position to do most or all of the work themselves. If your property is in need of significant repair, you will have to decide whether to sell under conditions where all repairs will be at your expense or sell at a price that reflects the potential cost to repair it. Entering into this matter will usually be the requirement that there be a pest control (termite) inspection report made on the property. Buyers should never fail to require this if there is any possibility of termite or dry-rot damage. Ordinarily it cannot be seen and experienced inspectors are required to determine the extent of the destruction. It is customary in many areas for the cost of this report to be paid by the buyer and the cost of making the repairs indicated by the report to be assessed against the seller. These arrangements are negotiable, however. The decision whether to have the repairs made—that is, can the property be sold "as is"?—may be influenced by the lender, if it is an institutional one. As a rule such lenders will require that the repairs be made so that the security for the loan is complete. If you believe you have a termite or dry-rot problem, you may want to get an inspection report before you put the house on the market. In that way you'll have a good idea what you should do about having the repairs made or selling "as is." Incidentally, in some states copies of all inspection reports for pest control are to be filed and open to the public so you may not be able to keep it a secret if a report on your property shows a serious problem—if you were disposed to such a tactic.

All told, there can be a virtue to selling (and buying) on an "as is" basis. The seller is gambling that the repairs would cost more than was allowed in the price reduction; the buyer, especially if planning to do the work himself or herself, is expecting to incur a cost that is smaller than the adjustment in the price. Can they both win? It's quite possible.

Preparation for Sale

When you bought the property, what were the features that attracted you? What could you do to the house now that would increase its appeal to others? Consider first the paint—inside and outside. Be careful; you can make a big mistake here deciding to redecorate. Unless the place is in horrible condition, you are probably better off drawing a prospect's attention to the fact that the property could stand painting, that he or she could pick out the colors and perhaps even do the work, and that you've made a generous allowance in the price. The alternative is to incur the expense yourself and hope you can get enough more for the property so you don't lose by doing so; you also incur the risk that you will drive prospects away because you chose a color that you liked but was offensive to others.

There can be no question about the need for the house to be neat and tidy when prospective buyers inspect it. This can be a traumatic time for family members, when they must remember to put things away and, most important, stay out of the way when buyers are around. Every effort should be made to control prospects by requiring appointments to tour the property, but you do have to be prepared to show your home at the prospects' convenience even though inconvenient for you. Once you offer your home for sale, you must have it ready to show at all times.

Even if you have not been paying much attention to the garden, now is the time to realize its importance. As applicable, consider hiring someone to clean it up to allow the landscaping, no matter how modest, to favorably influence buyers. Don't make any major changes, however. As before, you could make a change that would not appeal to buyers. If you make certain that what you have is spick-and-span, the rubbish removed, and a pleasing appearance is maximized, that's as far as you need to go in getting the place ready for sale. If you have decided to make repairs, it usually is best to have all the work completed before putting the property on the market. Plan ahead.

Do-It-Yourself Selling

A decision on whether to use a real estate broker should be made only after a careful examination of all that is involved; it's not one to be taken lightly. Here we'll look at what you would do if selling you home was completely a do-it-yourself project.

To make a sale you must set a realistic price, be able to arrange financing (because must buyers don't know how), introduce the property to qualified and interested prospective buyers, and handle the purchase agreement and escrow instructions. Are you ready to do all this?

To learn market prices you should visit properties similar to yours in your area that are being offered for sale. It's in order to pose as a prospective buyer and learn all you can about prices, financing, and other terms. All this will take substantial time and energy but is a vital activity. You should go one step further, however, in connection with financing. If there already is a loan on the property, visit your current lender and determine whether a new loan could be obtained by a qualified buyer. If possible, get a written commitment from the lender so you can show it to prospective buyers. If the house is free and clear you could pursue several different lenders and ask for loan commitments. Not all lenders will go this far in the absence of a firm sales contract but you should do your best to get this very important information. It also will be useful to have a lender state what the borrower's qualifications as to income, for example, would have to be for the loan to buy your house. If you can get this information, you'll be able to screen out those prospective buyers who would have no chance of being able to borrow enough to buy.

Once you have set the terms, lined up financing, and, perhaps, obtained an inspection report, you must prepare a fact sheet on which you set forth all the pertinent information needed by a prospective buyer. Have a supply on hand when you first offer the property and give a copy to those who indicate an interest. In preparing this very important sales tool, just think of all the things you'd like to know if you were thinking about buying a specific piece of property and then be certain your handout gives all that's needed.

But how do you communicate with people who are looking for property to buy? It needs to be advertised in newspapers. In many areas a *For Sale* sign on the property itself is very effective in prompting prospects to inquire. When advertising, you need to give a price indication, size of the property (such as the number of bedrooms), and location. Some sellers try to be cagey about price. This is a mistake. You want to spend your time only on people who know in advance at least the general price range, so never hesitate to include a price indication in your advertising. It acts as a screening device.

Once you place the property on the market and provide a convenient way for interested persons to contact you, be certain they can, in fact, do so. If you advertise and give a phone number, realize that you, or someone else, must stay by the phone to respond to calls. With a sign on the house, you must be prepared to talk to people who come to the door. To deter less serious buyers you may wish to put a telephone number on the *For Sale* sign, thus implying that the owner is elsewhere. You should not tell the world your home is for sale without considering first the possible security problems arising from such an invitation to the public to visit you. This consideration should not be allowed to totally inhibit you but should prompt you to be prudent and thoughtful. We'll treat below the important matter of holding an *open house*. There's nothing to prevent you from doing this yourself, but because it is an important sales tool used by real estate brokers, we'll discuss it in that context. For security reasons some sellers would not choose to throw their homes open to the public unless a broker was handling the deal.

Advance preparations are needed so that if a prospect indicates he wishes to buy, you can quickly and efficiently get him to sign on the dotted line and put his check into an escrow account. This means having a supply of purchase agreements (recall we reviewed that contract in detail in a prior chapter) and a good idea of how to complete them. Other advance preparations include having either an inspection report in hand or suggestions on where a buyer could order one. You also should have opened an escrow or know exactly how to do it once you have a deposit from a buyer. The buyer's deposit should be made payable to an escrow agent, not to you personally, if you are to avoid damaging your credibility. Many buyers are nervous and if they get the idea you might leave town with their deposit, they will run, not walk, away from you. All told, before you show the house to the very first prospect, you should rehearse in your mind all the things you will need to do if the prospect suddenly turns into a buyer. Be calm, cool, and collected and give the impression you've done it all many times before even when it is your very first time. It's not hard to do, really.

The objective in embarking on this do-it-yourself project is presumably to save money. You know that a broker is paid a commission and, after you've done a little arithmetic, you may have felt that it was a big price to pay for something you might be able to handle yourself. As stated before, when a buyer deals directly with an owner-seller, the buyer expects to save the commission—that is, will demand a lower price on the basis that the seller will not be paying a real estate broker. If you sell literally at a price you could have obtained through a broker, reduced only by the commission amount, then you've gone through all the agonies (and the ecstasy) of completing the deal on your own with no cash gain whatever for your efforts. Now isn't that a discouraging realization? Probably most do-it-yourselfers here expect to find a buyer who doesn't insist on a lower price so that, in fact, the net proceeds to the seller are higher than if a broker handled the transaction. When it comes time for you to make this decision, you'll have to judge how likely this latter result can be achieved. Let's examine now what you might get for your money if you ask a real estate dealer to find a buyer and see the deal through to conclusion.

Using a Real Estate Broker

There's nothing quite like the experience of doing all this by yourself to gain an understanding of how the real estate business operates. Without actually doing it, however, let's see what would be involved if you did have a broker handle your affairs. There's nothing much to prevent you from at least trying to get a sale on your own first. Then, if you don't make it, you could call for help. You will have to be aware of a potential disadvantage to this course of action, however. If a broker knows you've tried to sell the property on your own first, he or she may be a little hard to get along with when you ask for assistance. Of course, there's usually a lot of competition amongst brokers to get listings so this does not have to be a big problem. Nonetheless, it's a factor to keep in mind. After all, asking for help is an admission of failure and they may have a human reaction and want to rub it in. Brokers never like to think nonbrokers can do their job successfully.

Selecting a real estate broker can be likened to the process of choosing a lawyer, doctor, dentist, accountant, or other professional. You want someone who is competent and with whom you will feel comfortable. You want someone with integrity. Some real estate practitioners are more skilled than others. Some have talents and facilities of more use to you than those of others. Locating the right broker will ordinarily involve checking with friends and acquaintances for their recommendations. If you have confidence in the judgment of someone who states that he has had satisfactory dealings with a particular broker, that would provide you with a good lead. Once you've selected a broker to consider, you probably would find it a useful exercise to approach him or her posing as a potential buyer. Although the person who makes a good impression on buyers is what you want, you will also have to judge how well he will represent you as the seller. That may be a tougher part of the assignment.

If you put a *For Sale* sign on your property, more than likely the first callers will be real estate salespeople seeking to list the property. This, then, is an easy way to meet practitioners and from such callers you could indeed find someone who meets your specifications. Another way to make contact with a broker is to check local newspaper advertising to see which real estate offices appear to handle property similar to yours. All things considered, a broker with a real estate office in your immediate area will probably serve you best, assuming competence of course. Remember how buyers select a broker: they go to the neighborhood in which they want to buy and call on real estate offices. Location is by far the single most important factor when looking for a home to buy. So, given that you now, in one way or another, have found a broker, what's next?

Through prior research you should have some idea of what your property is worth. The broker, however, when performing as he or she should, will be able to tell you the price at which it should be offered, given current market conditions. This is one of the most important services a real estate broker can and should offer. Next comes financing. Unless the broker can tell you what can be arranged to finance the sale to achieve your objectives, don't waste any more time with that person. You're dealing with the wrong one and should go to another office. You will be paying the broker a commission if a sale is arranged. Getting a buyer is one thing, but knowing how to get the maximum price and the most favorable terms for you, the seller, is another. These are the services you are paying for, so be certain you receive them.

The broker is expected to have some prospects for your property and should be able to introduce them to your house immediately as it is listed. If a real estate office can't do a better job of finding prospects than you could on your own, there's not much justification in employing a broker. In a well-run real estate firm, records are kept of prospective buyers in a form that enables the broker to match new listings with them. As a result, there should be a flurry of activity right after the listing is taken. Because it may take time to find a buyer, however, the listing agreement will cover a stipulated time period, such as sixty or ninety days. If during this time you see little activity on the part of your broker, you probably have picked the wrong one. You do have to judge the overall market, of course. If financing is very tight or there is a surplus of properties, or if your home is overpriced, the lack of activity may not be entirely the fault of your broker. He or she, of course, is expected to advise you if terms ought to be modified to facilitate a sale.

Just who does a real estate salesperson represent? First, realize that all persons who engage in selling, buying, or managing property for others must be licensed by the state. Typically those who start out will be licensed as a *salesperson* and will operate under the direction of a licensed real estate *broker*. In many states, experience gained as a licensed salesperson is required before being eligible to take an examination for a broker's license; there may be other educational requirements as well. Except in the case of small, one-person offices, the majority of those dealing with the public will hold a salesperson's license. Technically, they operate under the broker's guidance and the broker is responsible for their actions. In some cases, all documents, even though prepared by a sales associate, must be checked and signed by the broker. But, from the buyer's and seller's point of view, who is representing whom?

When you list your property you expect the salesperson or the broker to have your best interest at heart and to act as your agent. But what is the situation when that person undertakes to represent a prospective buyer of your property? The buyer expects that same person to act as his agent, get him the best deal, and so on. Can one person fairly represent both parties? In practice, most of the time, the answer is "yes." The role played is typically that of an intermediary, seeking to satisfy both parties. The vast majority of real estate deals involve compromise. Don't think for a minute that if you are handling the sale yourself you won't be faced with making compromises. In fact, due to lack of knowledge, you are more likely to make compromises resulting in less favorable results than if a real estate person is conducting the negotiations in behalf of both buyer and seller. Certainly when the commission is a function of the sales price, a usual condition, the larger the price, the greater will be the payment to the real estate office. The buyer, of course, is not forced to buy and must be prepared to make suitable judgments on price and terms. If you, as buyer or seller, are concerned about this possible dual-interest conflict, settle it by engaging a broker who will represent only your side of the transaction. You will be expected to pay for the services independently of what the other party pays someone else.

Listing.   To employ a real estate broker when you are the seller, you must enter into a listing agreement. (Prospective buyers, unless engaging a broker to serve them exclusively, sign nothing and are not obligated to pay for the services.) There are several kinds of listing agreements so we need to look at the options.

You can say to one or more brokers that you'll permit them to bring prospects to your house and if they can get someone to make an offer you'll consider it. If a deal is made you'll pay a commission. This is often called an *open* listing. Under this arrangement you would be free to arrange a sale yourself and pay no one a commission. While you may think this would give you the best of all worlds, you'd be making a mistake in so believing. No broker is going to make much effort to find a buyer knowing that you and others are also working on the property and that it might be sold out from under him. It's rare that deals are made on this type of listing.

At the other end of the spectrum is the *exclusive authoriza-*

tion to sell listing. In such an agreement you bind yourself to pay a commission to the broker for simply bringing a buyer who offers to buy on your terms, even if you reject the offer or the deal falls through otherwise. Further, if you did, in fact, arrange a sale on your own, you'd still owe the listing broker a commission. Under this listing the broker has the most incentive to apply all his or her talents to finding a buyer and closing the deal. The risk you take, however, is that it doesn't work out and during the listing period you have had to rely solely on the listing office. In between the two extremes we have the *Multiple Listing Service* (MLS). In most areas, the local association of real estate dealers has established a system whereby owners can give an exclusive listing to a member broker and, in turn, the information is sent to all other members of the service. They are given the right to show your property and arrange its sale. The commission you pay will be split between the listing office, the selling office, and the MLS. The seller will be charged a regular commission and pays nothing extra for this type of service. Outside of the MLS arrangement, there's nothing to prevent a broker from permitting other brokers to work on properties for which he or she has an exclusive listing. In that way there should be more activity than if only the listing office was involved.

So, sellers can choose to offer an open listing, an exclusive listing, or sign an exclusive listing under a Multiple Listing Service. You will want a broker to explain the pros and cons of these so you can decide wisely. In most communities brokers work quite closely and when one gets a listing it is commonplace for word to be passed on to others. Many brokers would rather have a share of the commission earned through the sale of a listed property by a competing broker than wait in vain to earn a full commission, something that could happen only if he or she made the sale himself or herself.

Commissions.   It is important to understand that commission rates or fees for services are negotiable. It is against the law for two or more brokers to agree to set a price for their work. You will probably find, however, that most real estate brokers, just by coincidence, tend to charge the same rate. Full-service real estate offices will ask owners to pay between 6 percent and 8 percent of the sales price of homes. In some markets there is substantial competition and some brokers offer all or part services at much reduced percentages or even a flat fee regardless of price. In the latter case, typically, the seller does some of the work such as show the property, perhaps pay the cost and arrange for the advertising, and otherwise carry some of the burden. The flat-fee broker then will take care of the paperwork when a buyer is ready.

In general, a seller is prepared to pay a full commission when a broker takes care of all the details and a sale is made for the asking price. What might happen, however, when a buyer is located but makes an offer at a price below the listing amount? In such a case it behooves a seller to suggest to the broker that they share the reduction. The seller could offer to agree to the lower price provided the sales commission was reduced below the previously agreed rate. Brokers frequently agree to this arrangement inasmuch as part of a commission is better than none at all, given that the seller might not agree to accept the lower offer unless the broker did, in fact, participate through a reduced commission. When a seller must realize a particular minimum amount of cash and a prospective buyer's offer involves less than needed, some brokers are agreeable to taking a note or even a second mortgage in place of cash for the commission in order for a deal to be closed. There is a great deal of room for negotiation in most real estate transactions.

Listing Agreement.   To avoid misunderstanding you should have a written contract with the person who is to handle the property in your behalf. A widely used exclusive authorization listing form is illustrated below. You will see that the seller must make decisions concerning a number of matters in order for the agreement to be filled in and executed. The basis for the commission must be determined and so must the duration of the agreement. To justify the expenditure of time and effort to find a buyer, the listing broker will probably want at least ninety days, or even longer. Once you sign this agreement you will not be able to enter into other contracts or deals except under the agreement with brokers or buyers, without incurring liability to pay the listing broker. Consequently, as you run the risk of having your property tied to an inactive practitioner, you will want to judge the situation carefully before signing a listing agreement.

Open House. Brokers have found that holding an open house serves to attract not only prospects for that property but also for other listings. It is likely you will be asked to cooperate by making your home available for this activity. It is assumed that the property is occupied during the selling effort. Here are some rules to follow when the public is to have access to the house, whether you are handling the showing yourself or when arranged by a listing real estate broker.

1. See that all family members have made themselves scarce for the time the house is to be open. Weekends usually are the best time and Saturday and Sunday afternoons are popular. There should be only one knowledgeable person (the owner or the broker if listed) available to greet visitors and discuss the property. To protect personal property, the owner may want one or two other adults stationed in the home who will direct questioners to the person in charge but otherwise simply provide a physical presence as a deterrent. Don't overlook the risks involved when you open your home to the public.

2. In getting the house ready for "Open House," put moveable valuables out of sight and safeguard breakables. Anticipate that children will not be well-supervised when accompanying prospects.

3. Make certain that blinds and drapes are open to provide lots of light. Use lamps to supplement. Maximize a homey, comfortable appearance.

4. Make certain radios, hi-fi's, and TV's are *silent*. If you are on duty and bored between visitors, read a nice quiet book!

EXCLUSIVE AUTHORIZATION AND RIGHT TO SELL

THIS IS INTENDED TO BE A LEGALLY BINDING AGREEMENT — READ IT CAREFULLY.
CALIFORNIA ASSOCIATION OF REALTORS® STANDARD FORM

1. **Right to Sell.** I hereby employ and grant _____
hereinafter called "Agent," the exclusive and irrevocable right commencing on _____ , 19 _____ , and expiring at
midnight on _____ , 19 _____ , to sell or exchange the real property situated in _____ ,
County of _____ , California described as follows:

_____
_____
_____
_____

2. **Terms of Sale.** The purchase price shall be $ _____ , to be paid in the following terms:

_____
_____

   (a) The following items of personal property are to be included in the above-stated price:

_____
_____
_____

   (b) Agent is hereby authorized to accept and hold on my behalf a deposit upon the purchase price.
   (c) Evidence of title to the property shall be in the form of a California Land Title Association Standard Coverage
Policy of Title Insurance in the amount of the selling price to be paid for by_____ .
   (d) I warrant that I am the owner of the property or have the authority to execute this agreement. I hereby authorize
a FOR SALE sign to be placed on my property by Agent.
3. **Compensation to Agent.** I hereby agree to compensate Agent as follows:
   (a)_____ % of the selling price if the property is sold during the term hereof, or any extension thereof, by Agent,
on the terms herein set forth or any other price and terms I may accept, or through any other person, or by me, or_____ %
of the price shown in 2, if said property is withdrawn from sale, transferred, conveyed, leased without the consent of Agent, or
made unmarketable by my voluntary act during the term hereof or any extension thereof.
   (b) the compensation provided for in subparagraph (a) above if property is sold, conveyed or otherwise transferred
within _____days after the termination of this authority or any extension thereof to anyone with whom Agent has had
negotiations prior to final termination, provided I have received notice in writing, including the names of the prospective
purchasers, before or upon termination of this agreement or any extension thereof. However, I shall not be obligated to pay
the compensation provided for in subparagraph (a) if a valid listing agreement is entered into during the term of said protection
period with another licensed real estate broker and a sale, lease or exchange of the property is made during the term of said
valid listing agreement.
4. If action be instituted to enforce this agreement, the prevailing party shall receive reasonable attorney's fees and costs
as fixed by the Court.
5. I authorize the Agent named herein to cooperate with sub-agents.
6. This property is offered in compliance with state and federal anti-discrimination laws.
7. In the event of an exchange, permission is hereby given Agent to represent all parties and collect compensation or
commissions from them, provided there is full disclosure to all principals of such agency. Agent is authorized to divide with
other agents such compensation or commissions in any manner acceptable to them.
8. I agree to save and hold Agent harmless from all claims, disputes, litigation, and/or judgments arising from any
incorrect information supplied by me, or from any material fact known by me concerning the property which I fail to disclose.
9. Other provisions:

_____
_____

10. I acknowledge that I have read and understand this Agreement, and that I have received a copy hereof.
Dated _____ , 19 _____   _____ , California

       OWNER   OWNER

      ADDRESS   CITY—STATE—PHONE

11. In consideration of the above, Agent agrees to use diligence in procuring a purchaser.

       AGENT   ADDRESS—CITY
By_____
                                     PHONE   DATE

For these forms address California Association of Realtors®
505 Shatto Place, Los Angeles 90020. All rights reserved.
Copyright 1978 by California Association of Realtors.®   FORM A-11   (Rev. 4-78)

Music and noise can be extremely offensive and can drive prospects away.

5. Cooperate with the listing broker as to time and frequency of holding open house. He or she ought to know what is best. If not you'll want to look elsewhere when the listing period is up and an extension is being considered.

Completing the Deal

The first step requires an evaluation of the offer and a decision whether to accept. If you are doing-it-yourself you won't have any help with this. If you have a broker, he or she has a responsibility to advise you and should help to explore all the options. Whenever the offer is not on exactly the terms you set, which is almost all of the time, a counteroffer will be needed if a deal is to come about. You should maintain control and take appropriate action. Realize that once you accept the offer by signing the purchase agreement, it's too late to change the terms without penalty. By the same token you have a right to expect the buyer to perform according to the contract, too.

If you are handling the sale yourself you will probably have to guide the buyer through the financing and escrow processing. This can be a "sweaty palms" experience. If you are using a broker, you may be able to sit back, relax, and have everything taken care of. Don't be too complacent, however, because it can be important to check on the broker to make sure everything is, in fact, going smoothly.

Summary

In devising your sales strategy you will be faced with many decisions. One of the more important is whether to handle the transaction on your own. No one can make that choice for you; there are risks associated with both alternatives. Regardless, prepare an outline of your plan, establish a timetable, and do what is needed, when it is needed. Through careful planning you probably can avoid making poor decisions when there is pressure.

INCOME PROPERTY

The factors that must enter into your decision to sell or retain your income property include your investment objectives, a review of the operating results, future prospects for income and expenses, availability of financing, and income tax considerations. Recall that an investment in real estate should be made in full recognition of the long-term aspects. Further, except in rare instances, you should not allow yourself to be in the position where you have to sell in a hurry. As a consequence, once you acquire property you must be certain to monitor the results on a continuing basis and take all appropriate steps to maximize returns. By so doing you should easily become aware of when it may be desirable to sell. You will also be able to evaluate offers and know which to accept.

Assuming that you wish to continue to have an investment in real estate and want to build your holdings, you will constantly be challenged to judge your property's performance against your objectives and to decide what action, if any, to take. As a general rule you should always have a sound plan for the proceeds of a sale if you liquidate a property. If you can't find another piece of real estate in which to invest maybe it's premature to sell.

Objectives

You will own income property in order to generate current income, to provide living expenses, or to achieve tax sheltering accompanied by long-term capital appreciation. Obviously, you want to maximize your returns, whichever goal you are pursuing. Each property should be evaluated regularly to compare the actual results against what you were counting on or hoped for. But there's another consideration. Is it possible you can't afford to keep the property? No, we're not referring to expenses outstripping income. Instead, consider how the current return measures up to what you could realize from the property, not just what you have invested. In an inflationary period it is important to estimate what a property might sell for and then estimate the return from employing the funds obtained from liquidation. It's that return you need to compare with what you are now earning.

EXAMPLE: Assume you have $50,000 invested in income property and the net spendable, including tax shelter benefit, is $6,000 a year. This means you are earning an annual after-tax rate of 12 percent. Not bad. But suppose you could sell the property and get out of the sale, in cash, $80,000. You owned it long enough to achieve some capital appreciation and a modest equity build. What could you do with the $80,000? Could it be employed to earn more than $6,000 after tax? Chances are, yes. So, this situation ought to prompt you to explore alternatives to sitting still.

Some investors judge how well their properties are doing and whether they are meeting their objectives by comparing a possible sale price against what they would be willing to pay if they were buying. Assume you have owned an apartment property for a number of years and receive an offer to sell it for a substantial increase over your cost. Pretend that you are seeking properties and are looking at this apartment for the first time. After a thorough evaluation, including estimating future capital appreciation, how much would you pay for it? If that figure is much below what you are now being offered, you ought to seriously consider selling. As a rule, whenever you can sell an asset for at least a decent amount above what you'd pay yourself, sell. This strategy, however, requires that you have a suitable place, as stated previously, to invest the proceeds.

So, let's look at the options you have whether you are prompted by an offer or as a result of checking performance against your goals. Here's a list of choices:

1. Trade up
2. Trade down
3. Cash out

Trading Up.   Let's say you now own a small residential income property such as a pair of flats, a fourplex, or similar units. After you examine the economics of larger properties you might conclude you could increase your return by getting rid of what you have and buying a larger property. Many private investors have successfully used a series of sales and purchases to build a substantial estate. The secret lies in developing your equity, selling, and putting the proceeds— along with more borrowed funds—to work in a larger project. One highly successful way to increase your equity is to increase the income level of the property through remodeling and increasing the number of rental units on the lot. You can increase your total holdings through either separate buy-and-sell transactions or actually exchanging property with another owner. We'll examine later the income tax aspects and how to make a tax-deferred exchange, but for now, realize that trading up is not dependent upon actual trading. It is totally practical to pyramid a rather modest beginning equity into significant wealth. Why not you?

Trading Down.   As you increase the size and number of your holdings, your managerial activity and responsibilities will also increase. For many people that's fine and the way they want it. But what about when you reach the point where you want to start reducing your obligations? That's when you look for ways to sell what you own and perhaps invest the cash in smaller properties. If this coincides with retirement, how better could it be? The market is so large and diverse that after you have developed significant holdings, you will likely find it easy to sell off your properties to those who are starting out to do what you did.

Getting Out.   There will come a day when you no longer wish to be a landlord. When that feeling overtakes you, that will be the time to develop a plan to liquidate and invest the cash elsewhere. You could continue to receive the benefits from real estate investing by employing the funds in a non-participative place such as a REIT or syndicate and thus escape landlording. You could, of course, move to Tahiti. So that the liquidation and retirement from landlording is done under the most advantageous conditions, it will be most important for you to keep your investment objectives in mind at all times and be prepared to take appropriate action when conditions change.

Terms and Financing

What you want to accomplish will determine how you should structure the sale of your income property. If you are going to reinvest in other real estate, you will likely want a maximum amount of cash. If an actual exchange is to take place, the terms you may offer on yours will be affected by how the other property is financed. If you are anxious to move from ownership to being a mortgagee-lender, you must set the terms of the mortgage to meet your needs. All the financing methods discussed in an earlier chapter can be considered here—you are simply on the other side of the transaction now. There are many different potential situations here but let's explore two in some detail.

Maximizing Cash Gain. Not every sale is made to maximize the cash realization, strange though that may seem. To have the greatest interest income from taking back a mortgage from the buyer, you would want the loan amount to be large and the cash down payment small. On the other hand, it often makes more sense to get as much cash as possible. Yes, by requiring a buyer to cash you out through a combination of cash down and loans from others, you could obtain all cash. But it's the total that counts.

Recall from the material on property valuation that a basic determinant of value and, hence, sales price is the level of rental income. The greater the total income, the greater the amount you can ask a buyer to pay. But, even though you keep rents as high as the market will bear, the potential selling price will not likely be as high as the total you could get if you sold the property in pieces. But how on earth can you sell income property in parts? You condominiumize, that's how!

In recent years not only has there been a boom in the construction of property to be sold under condominium ownership, but the amount of property of all kinds converted has been substantial. Be sure you realize that virtually any type of property can be owned on a shared basis; the concept is not restricted to large apartments, for example. You could even divide a duplex into two condo units although the expense and effort might not be worth it. Many business and professional offices, industrial parks, and even shopping centers are in condominium form. Either they were built that way originally or they were converted. Let's see how you might use this device to maximize your cash gain on liquidation.

Assume you own a small income property which ought to bring $300,000 based on its rental income from six apartment units. Once you have explored single-family homes offering comparable space currently for sale you conclude you should be able to get at least $70,000 for each of your apartment units as condos. This would give you $420,000 gross, more than one-third more than if you sold the building as a whole. There would be conversion and sales costs, of course, and you'd have to find six buyers instead of one. In many areas, because of the relatively high cost of single-family homes, condo conversions go like hotcakes. They can be priced somewhat below detached single-family dwellings and are especially attractive to first-time buyers and to retirees. Note that buyers can get condo-unit financing just like single-family housing, so with each sale producing all cash to you, you will maximize the cash proceeds from your property. You need no longer wonder why so many existing buildings are being converted to condominium ownership.

Maximizing Total Gain. Assume you don't need to maximize cash from the sale but you do want to get the largest total price without going the condo route. As long as you are willing to help finance the sale, you should be able to sell for more than otherwise. Here's how. Assume you have a property for sale where your equity is substantial. If a buyer is to cash you out either he or she will have to have a lot of cash (not a usual condition) or refinancing will be required. Even then, a buyer may be short of cash to meet the down payment. As long as you don't need maximum cash you can consider financing the sale yourself. This is where the wraparound mortgage can be used to great advantage not only to provide above average interest income but make possible a larger sales price.

EXAMPLE: Let's say that to get a new loan, your buyer finds that an institutional lender would lend two-thirds of $300,000. The buyer would need $100,000 in cash plus funds for mortgage points and other settlement costs. If you can take back a wraparound, you could offer to sell the property for $400,000 with $60,000 down and a wrap for $340,000 on terms that would require periodic payments about equal to those required for the alternative bank loan. From the buyer's point of view, the cash flow from operations would be unchanged but the cash down payment would be reduced by $40,000 and there could be a saving of the mortgage points. These benefits would justify the buyer agreeing to the higher total purchase price.[1]

From your point of view as the seller, you have increased the overall consideration by $100,000 and taken a cash down payment presumably large enough to protect yourself against potential default. The periodic loan payments must be large enough to cover the underlying existing loan, assuming there is one, as well as to give you interest income and even some amortization of your equity. As values increase, the buyer's equity will increase and, hence, so will your protection. None of this is without risk, however, and the seller must not throw caution to the wind in evaluating a potential buyer. Nonetheless, it is through this type of seller financing that sales prices

[1]This is known as "The Gospel According to St. Levin" in California.

can be maximized and the seller's ultimate realization be the greatest. Some sellers, in doing this, consider they are locking in some future, not-yet-realized capital appreciation. Not a bad way of looking at it.

But what if you get tired waiting for the wraparound to be paid off? Find an investor who is looking for high yield mortgages and sell the wraparound note. This will call for a discount so you'll have to forego some of your gain, but if it was large to begin with don't feel you've lost. Through computing the present value of the outstanding wraparound mortgage to produce a yield required by the prospective buyer of the note you can determine what it's worth. Once the sale is made, you'll have more cash than if you had sold property initially for cash. (Ask your banker or a mortgage loan broker to help you with the computation if needed.)

Prepayment Penalties. When structuring the terms of sale you must be alert to the possibility that a premature payoff of the loan on the property will trigger the imposition of a prepayment penalty, something you agreed to when you borrowed the money. To avoid this when it makes sense to do so, you can use the *land* or *installment* sales contract. As an alternative you should consider arranging for the buyer to assume your loan. It would not likely ever be wise to risk losing a sale through setting terms to avoid a prepayment penalty, but you should be aware in advance if the penalty might be applied. There's no need to be surprised when reviewing the escrow statement. Check the terms of all loans on your property and know where you stand.

Income Tax Considerations

The decision to sell income property must take fully into account the prospective income tax consequences. If you sell too soon you could find that all the gain is taxed as current income. Under federal rules capital assets must be held for at least a year to qualify for long-term preferential treatment. Your state rules may be quite different so you should determine what they are if you don't already know.

You can minimize the amount of tax on gain through the installment sale contract if you limit the buyer's cash payment in the year of sale. You may be able to defer taxes through a properly arranged exchange of your property for another's. Regardless of using these options, you should choose the best depreciation method for your situation and, as always in investing, you must maintain adequate and accurate records.

Don't confuse the special benefits for homeowners with owning income property. There's no rollover of gains to newly acquired property nor the $100,000 capital gains exemption. In spite of that, there are substantial tax concessions available—make the most of them.

Depreciation.   Recall from our earlier discussion that you can charge depreciation against current rental income and thus reduce income taxes. This benefit is partially offset, of course, when the amount of capital gain is increased by the accumulated depreciation expense. There are choices to make in how you calculate depreciation and we'll examine them here. Your choice during the time you hold the property should be made in light of the possible impact on the proceeds of a sale. So, plan ahead.

Depreciation can be charged on buildings but not on the value of the lot. You need to apportion the purchase price between the land and improvements. This can be done, for example, by using the assessor's percentages shown on the tax bill if you don't have any other basis. Next you must decide on the estimated remaining useful life of the property. Because your goal is to minimize taxes, you will quickly see that the greatest benefit is realized when you use the largest depreciation charge. A short life and a large total amount to be depreciated will give you the largest depreciation expense base. So, what limits are imposed on you? They are spelled out in the IRS Publication 534, *Tax Information on Depreciation.* Every property owner should have a copy of this, and since the regulations change, you should get a new one each year.

The IRS recognizes forty years as the useful life for most

new buildings. For used buildings you may be able just to subtract the number of years it's been used to get the value needed. For older buildings you will be required to use a reasonable useful life regardless of how they relate to the forty-year measure. All depreciation is an estimate and subject not only to challenge by the IRS but also to adjustment at the time you sell. So much for buildings. How about equipment?

Appliances, furnishings, carpeting, and any other items of personal property used in the business of rental real estate is also subject to depreciation. Typically, the useful life is much shorter for these items than for buildings, and the computation of the charge differs slightly. We do not consider salvage value when depreciating a building but do so for personal property. Although depreciation on equipment can be important, we'll limit our examples to buildings and leave it to you to read the IRS material for things not covered here.

EXAMPLE: Assume you buy an apartment for $250,000; the land is worth $50,000 and the building is estimated to have 25 years remaining. Let's see how you would compute depreciation first on the *straight-line* method and then by using one of the optional accelerated forms.

Under straight line the total amount to be depreciated over the useful life is $250,000 less $50,000 = $200,000. Annual depreciation charge:

$200,000 divided by 25 years = $8,000 each year

Note that the annual straight-line *rate* is 100% divided by 25 years = 4%. If you adopted straight line you would include a charge of $8,000 each year when computing taxable income. But, when would you not use straight line?

Have you noticed that some assets seem to drop in value through depreciation at a faster rate during their early life rather than later? This is certainly true of automobiles and equipment, for example. Is it true for real estate? Probably not, but the IRS doesn't seem to mind that that is the case. As a consequence, the owner of income real estate can elect to compute depreciation as though the value was actually reducing and at a faster rate at the outset. There are two methods recognized by the IRS to provide accelerated depreciation: *sum-of-the-year's digits* and *declining balance*. The first is used for both buildings and equipment; it is described fully in the IRS publications. The second is an important option for real estate investors, especially those buying new residential income property. Let's see how the calculations are made.

You can always adopt the straight-line method. It produces the smallest charge and hence provides the lowest tax benefit. The declining balance method can be used instead, provided the property qualifies. Use and age are the determining factors.

Residential property: If at least 80 percent of the rental income is from residential use, the declining balance method can be used. If the property is brand new, the first user can use the 200 percent method; if not new, the 125 percent method can be applied. The 200% form is called "double-declining balance." Nonresidential property: If new, the first user can apply the 150 percent declining balance rate; otherwise, only straight line can be applied.

Returning to our example, let's assume we want to maximize tax savings so we'll use accelerated depreciation. Because we are not the first user, we can only use the 125% form. The percentages apply to the straight-line rate. Therefore, we will use 125% of 4% = 5%.

First year's depreciation: $200,000 times 5% = $10,000

Note that you take the total amount to be depreciated and multiply it by the adjusted straight-line rate. If this property had been eligible for first user 200 percent, we would use 200% of 4% = 8% in the computation.

But how about the second year? This method is called *declining balance* because after the first year you must subtract the previous year's charge before applying the percentage.

Second year: $200,000 less $10,000 = $190,000
$190,000 times 5% = $ 9,500

You can see that, for each computation, the percentage multiplier remains the same but is applied to a balance reduced by the depreciation charged previously.

It might occur to you that if you owned the property long enough the accelerated depreciation charge might ultimately be less than if you had used straight line. That is indeed the case but when it happens the IRS lets you change over to straight line. To show a comparison, here's a chart of the annual depreciation expense using the two methods.

Year	Straight Line	125% Declining Balance
1	$ 8,000	$10,000
2	8,000	9,500
3	8,000	9,025
4	8,000	8,574
5	8,000	8,145
Totals	$40,000	$45,244

It is clear that when depreciation is charged as an expense against rental income, your taxable income is less and so will be your income tax. Let's see now what effect this has on your long-term tax picture. Assume that you sell the property you paid $250,000 for to an all-cash buyer after five years. What is the taxable gain?

	Straight Line	125% Declining
Net sales proceeds	$400,000	$400,000
Less adjusted basis:		
$250,000 less $40,000	210,000	
or		
$250,000 less $45,244		204,756
Long-term capital gain	$190,000	$195,244

You should now see that by taking the larger depreciation each year during the holding period, you will have a larger capital gain and hence will be subject to greater capital gains taxes. At first you might say this is fine because only 40 percent of such gains are taxable. To convert current income to long-term capital gain is desirable, therefore. But, there's a catch. When you use accelerated depreciation and thus increase the long-term capital gain as illustrated, when you sell the property, Uncle Sam requires that the excess depreciation be treated as current income at that time. Thus we say that the difference between what you would have taken under straight line and what you charged, using an accelerated method, is "recaptured." Is this all bad? Not necessarily. It all depends on whether your income tax rate changes. The greatest advantage is obtained by the person who is subject to high rates during the time the property is owned and a lower rate at the time of the sale. This would be so, for example, for the investor who retired, thus reducing current income from a salary, and then sold the property after owning it long enough to qualify for long-term capital gain treatment, and during the ownership period, charged the maximum allowable depreciation on the building. Because the IRS rules are somewhat complex in this area, if you consider using accelerated depreciation you may wish to develop your tax plan in consultation with a qualified professional advisor.[2]

So, what conclusions can we draw? If you use straight-line depreciation on buildings, no adjustment will be needed. Always take the maximum amount you can, using straight line, to maximize conversion of current income to long-term capital gain. Timing the sale to match changes in your personal tax rate is always important but even more so if you have used accelerated depreciation.

Regardless of what decisions you made during the time you owned the property, is there anything that can be done to

---

[2]You may be liable for the minimum tax on tax preference items, such as accelerated depreciation, during the time you own the property; see IRS form 4625. Excess depreciation is to be reported on form 4797 when sale is made.

minimize payment of taxes on gains realized through sale? Well, there's the installment sale device.

Installment Sale.   When you sell real property under conditions where there is a long-term gain, you will have to pay the capital gains income taxes in full when you next file a tax return, regardless of whether you, in fact, received enough cash from the sale to cover the taxes. That will be your situation unless you make certain you structure the sale to qualify for the benefits that flow from an *installment* sale. The key lies in the amount of cash down payment the seller receives in the tax year in which the sale occurs. Here's how all this operates.

You could be in one or the other of these two positions:

A. Because the gain is large and your current tax bracket is also large, the total tax in dollars is large;
B. You are prepared to sell on a small down payment basis but discover that the cash obtained won't be enough to cover the income tax on the gain. You might be prepared to live with the first condition but not with the second. If there's a chance that your tax bracket is about to be reduced, you can see the opportunity to save on taxes in the first position if you could only postpone taking some of the gain. Either way, then, you can benefit from knowing how to use the installment sale method.

EXAMPLE: Assume you sell property for $400,000 and through a combination of refinancing by the buyer and a cash down payment you cash out and realize a long-term taxable capital gain of $200,000. Given that you are in a current tax bracket of 45%, your tax bill will be 45% times 40% of $200,000 = $36,000. (Recall that 60% of long-term gains under the federal rules are excluded.) Of course, by cashing out you'd have enough money to pay the taxes but $36,000 is a big bite all at one time. To avoid this, let's make the sale on the basis that you receive in cash not more than 30% of the purchase price. If done, it would qualify as an installment sale and thus make it possible to spread the payment of income taxes on the gain into the future.

If the property is clear, you would sell for a cash down payment of not more than 29% (29% of $400,000 = $116,000) and take back a mortgage for the balance. The buyer would then make periodic payments of interest and principal in the conventional manner. Assume that your adjusted cost basis was $200,000 so your gain on the sale would be $200,000. From this you calculate the percentage of gain on the sale. Here that would be:

$$\frac{\$\ 200{,}000}{\$\ 400{,}000} \times 100\% = 50\%$$

To determine the amount of taxable gain each year you apply this percentage to the total amount received in the year by way of payments on the purchase, excluding interest; interest is to be reported as current income and is fully taxable at current rates.

To qualify as an installment sale, the seller must not receive more than 30% of the sale price in cash in the first year. By restricting the amount to 29%, you can be certain of meeting this requirement. But be careful. If you took, as in our example, a cash down of the full 29%, you would need to postpone any further payments on the principal until the following tax year. The IRS, incidentally, allows for an unrestricted payment, including the balance in full in the second year, without disqualifying the transaction as an installment sale.

To illustrate, assume here that you received $116,000 in cash in the year of the sale (or a cash down payment plus subsequent payments on the principal which in the aggregate did not exceed 30% of the sale price), your income tax would then be:

50% of 40% of $116,000 = $23,200 times 45% = $10,440

If in the following tax year you received total payments to the principal amounting to $15,000, the income tax computation, assuming you were still in the 45% tax bracket, would be:

50% of 40% of $15,000 = $3,000 times 45% = $1,350

You can see if you timed the sale to coincide with a lowered tax rate, your tax savings could be important. If, of course, you remained in the same tax bracket until the mortgage was paid off, your total taxes would be the same as if you'd made the sale on a noninstallment basis and paid all the tax at one time.

While the potential benefits from making an installment sale are apparent, what are the possible disadvantages? If you are anxious to raise as much cash as possible or avoid the risks involved in financing the sale, you would instead cash out and pay the taxes. Having to wait for a mortgagor to pay you over an extended future period may be hazardous.

Note that in this example we assumed the property was clear. Will this work if there is a mortgage already in place? Yes. You would use either a land contract or a wraparound mortgage. To qualify, however, regardless of the underlying financing, the seller's cash proceeds in the year of sale must not exceed 30 percent.

EXAMPLE: Assume that you sold the same property instead for 10% down with the buyer assuming an existing loan and giving you a second mortgage for the balance of your equity. Once again the percentage of gain is 50% and your current tax rate is 45%. Cash from sale is $40,000 and cash paid on principal in the year of sale is $500.
Taxable gain in year of sale:

50% of 40% of $40,500 = $8,100
taxes at 45% of $8,100 = $3,645.

No problem, of course, in paying a $3,645 tax bill out of the cash from the sale. Note that if you sold for 10% down and did not claim it as an installment sale, you would have had to pay the full tax bill of $36,000 (as computed above) and thereby used up almost all the cash. When accumulated long-term gains are even more than as used in this example, it is clear that selling on a low down payment basis could place you in the position of owing more in taxes than you received in cash. Hooray for the installment sale!

Alternative Minimum Tax.   Uncle Sam seems to be unduly concerned that someone is going to make too much through capital gains. When the excluded amount (60 percent of long-term gains), together with some other tax preference items, gets too high, in the government's opinion, the taxpayer may have to pay more income taxes. To determine how this might affect you, check with the IRS and complete a Form 6251. You'll see that whenever capital gains are minimized, such as through the installment sale method, you may avoid this extra tax. Making a tax-deferred exchange may also help here. Let's see what that's all about.

Tax-Deferred Exchange.   When your objective is to increase your holdings, you can achieve it either through a series of sales and purchases to pyramid your position, or to trade a smaller property for a larger, for example. This may also work on the way down—exchange a larger property for a smaller as you want to reduce your landlording activities. When there are gains exposed to taxation, you will want to minimize the tax liability. Here we'll look at the way the IRS provides for deferring gains so that you can legally avoid paying taxes until some future time, presumably long after the exchange took place. If you are in a more advantageous tax position then, so much the better for you. Meanwhile you have conserved your cash by not having to pay taxes. Keeping all your funds at work should produce greater returns.

Stated simply, when you structure a qualifying tax-deferred exchange you can, in effect, rollover capital gains into the newly acquired property so that taxes will not be payable on the gains until you make an outright sale. Once again you may be aiming at the timing of a sale to come when you have reached a lower tax bracket. How do you do all this? Having decided to get rid of property, you must find someone who owns property of like kind, and persuade that person to trade. To illustrate, let's take an example outside of real estate investment.

EXAMPLE: Assume that many years ago you bought 100 shares of Xerox common stock. You now find it has greatly appreciated but you judge it won't continue to grow. In talking with a friend you learn that he owns 100 shares of another stock that has the same market value as your Xerox shares and he too has achieved substantial capital appreciation. By some strange coincidence, he too believes his stock has stopped appreciating. You each believe, however, that the other is mistaken: you would like to own his stock and he yours. You each could sell and buy, but in doing so you both will have to pay income tax on the gain. Instead, you trade holdings and avoid paying any tax.

Now that tax deferred exchanging is crystal clear, substitute income property, vacant land, or any other type of real estate for the shares in the foregoing example. But, be careful. The exchange must involve like-kind. That is, real estate held for investment can be traded for any other kind of real estate to likewise be held for investment. Perhaps you own an apartment and want to trade it for a commercial building; that would qualify. But, for example, you couldn't have the tax-deferral benefit if you traded securities for real estate.

The next vital matter is that of actually making a trade. The cleanest deal is where two property owners in fact give each other a deed and thus exchange. When one property has a greater value than the other, or there is a difference in the cash and loans, the tax consequences can be complex. You'll find needed instructions in IRS Publication 544, *Sales and Other Dispositions of Assets*. But let's pursue the actual trade requirement further. Why not just sell one property and buy another? That transaction does not meet the IRS regulation nor does, technically, the so-called three-way exchange, unless great care is used to make certain deeds are in fact exchanged. Sometimes an owner is invited to participate in an ostensible tax-deferred exchange when in reality what is proposed is a series of sales and purchases.

What are the real-life chances of finding a property you'd like to own with an owner who wants your property? Not great. Are there many tax-deferred exchange transactions? Yes, because through ingenuity, some real estate practitioners are able to set them up so that all the IRS requirements are met. There also has been some assistance from the courts. In a ruling in 1979, a court held that the exchange did not have to take place at exactly the same time and that the promise to turn over like-kind property at a future point in time qualified. So, unless changed, it would appear that the rules would allow for you to trade your property to someone who promises to give you property that you would prescribe. That someone would proceed to acquire the property you wanted and then complete the exchange. He gets yours and you get what you want even though shortly before, it was owned by someone outside the trade.

It would seem obvious that if, through a tax-deferred exchange, you could delay paying taxes, your advantage would come from keeping all of your invested funds at work. There may be some disadvantages, however, and you would want to discuss them with your tax advisor. To make a match you might find it necessary to accept a smaller price for your property than that available through an outright sale. The negotiations could be much more time-consuming and more expenses might be incurred for professional services for an exchange than for a sale. Finally, because your tax basis for the newly acquired property will be reduced by the impact of the value of the property traded, you may, in fact, have smaller current tax benefits accruing from depreciation. Through a careful analysis of all your choices, you should be able to make the right one at the right time for your particular position.

Summary

If you invest in real estate and fail to take into account the potential impact of income tax regulations on your activities, it is unlikely you will maximize your returns. You could inadvertently increase your tax liability or, through ignorance, fail to make the most of the benefits legally available. Your silent partner in real estate is the IRS. Don't overlook your state tax collector, either, but don't assume his or her rules are the same as Uncle Sam's; find out and act accordingly.

Congress intends that income tax regulations serve to provide incentives to those who would construct and own residential housing. Favorable provisions are indeed NOT tax loopholes. Our lawmakers deliberately established them to provide the motivation and financial incentives needed to increase housing. This is the basis for your opportunity to invest in real estate. When you buy and operate, keep in mind what you must do to maximize your investment return when you sell and make certain your decisions are tax-sensitive. This is important.

SALES STRATEGY

Much of what we discussed in the preceding section dealing with selling your home is applicable to developing the sales strategy needed to sell income property, but it is worthwhile to take another look. Prior to offering the property there are a number of things you can do that should improve the financial returns. After checking the property's performance and considering your investment objectives, you'll be able to make decisions concerning how you would like to structure the sale. You may be able to prepare the property to improve both its physical and financial appeal. Once again you will have to decide whether to use the services of a real estate office. And regardless, you'll want to put together pertinent information, especially with regard to financing, to make it easy for prospective buyers to become actual purchasers.

Setting the Price and Terms

We've stressed how important it is for you to keep in touch

with the market, particularly with respect to similar properties. You should always know, for example, what a current gross rent multiplier is and a capitalization rate used by investors in your area. Keeping up to date with these items is not necessarily easy unless you are dealing in real estate all the time, but it is possible, Of course, working with a real estate broker can make the task easier. Some investors have benefited greatly through accepting advice and counsel from professionals in the income property field.

An inescapable fact is that the potential sales price of income property is greatly affected by the amount of rental income. No matter how valuable you may think your property is, unless there is income to justify your asking price, it is unlikely you'll find someone to pay it. This means that you should establish and maintain a policy of maximizing rent schedules, thus being able to ask a maximum price when you want to sell. Some owners prefer to defer raising rents, especially when there are long-time tenants in the property, believing that they can persuade a potential buyer to purchase on the assumption he or she can raise the rents. Sometimes, of course, this will work. The safest plan, to obtain the maximum price, is to keep rents up to market levels and thus fully support a market level sales price.

Financing is the key to virtually every sale. We've shown that, as a general rule, when the seller can provide the financing, the greatest total price can be obtained. Here, of course, your need for cash will affect what you might be able to do about taking back a second mortgage or using wraparound financing. When you wish to cash out do what you can, in advance of offering the property, to obtain a loan commitment from a commercial lender. When a prospective buyer can see a firm financing plan, it is much easier to make a decision. It may also eliminate the need for you to accept a contingent purchase offer.

Once you've decided on the price and terms, prepare a fact or data sheet showing clearly all the details a prospective purchaser must have. Put yourself in the prospect's shoes and judge whether your information sheet is complete and informative. Do this even if you plan to use a real estate broker; it will be useful to the broker, too.

Using a Broker

Unless you are an active investor, dealing in property frequently, it is likely you would find the services of a competent real estate professional to be essential here. The challenge may be in locating a real estate dealer who is qualified to handle business and commercial income property. The vast majority of real estate brokers handle only home sales and often lack the expertise required to maximize an investor's returns from other types. Those who specialize advertise their specialty so you should look for appropriate indications in newspaper and telephone directory advertising. Some REALTORS® hold the *CCIM* professional designation which indicates that they have met educational and experience requirements entitling them to be called a *Certified Commercial-Investment Member* of the Marketing Institute of the NATIONAL ASSOCIATION OF REALTORS®. This is not to infer that someone who does not have the CCIM designation is less skilled, of course. When you are considering selling your income property and need to discuss your plans with a real estate broker, contact several candidates before making your decision.

You will be faced with many decisions once you conclude you want to dispose of your present property. When using a broker, probably the most important consideration is the listing option. In many areas it's possible to have use of the *Multiple Listing Service*. A broker may suggest this to you or may tell you he or she would rather have an exclusive listing. You must decide which offers the best deal for you. When you can be satisfied that you would be dealing with an active, successful office where the sales staff is competent in handling income properties, you are probably better off granting an exclusive listing, but recognize the risks. You will be tying up the property for probably a number of months and if that office is unable to produce a buyer, you will be faced with starting all over again when the listing expires.

Before making the final decision concerning whether to list with a broker, make an outline of all the things you would have to do to handle the sale yourself. Don't overlook the cost of the advertising and your time in showing the property and dealing with prospects. Balance that against both your appraisal of the likely success a broker will have and the commission cost. After that you will be in a position to make a good decision.

Preparing the Property

Most potential buyers will condition an offer on making a physical inspection of the property and your accounting records, so be prepared. If you have followed a policy of deferring maintenance, be ready to have to make a concession in the price. Savvy buyers will require a bigger discount than what it would cost to do the work. Unlike the usual situation for houses, you may well be better off to have the property repaired if it is needed, before putting it on the market. It would only be for smaller income properties that you are likely to bump into a buyer who wanted to have a fixer-upper and would be able to do the work himself or herself.

Do you alert tenants that you are planning to sell? There is not a satisfactory answer to this question; situations differ. Until you have an interested and qualified prospect who is really serious about buying, you will not have to show all the units in the building. For this reason you need to arrange, probably, with only one tenant to permit prospects to prowl around and, if so, you may be able to keep your intentions relatively quiet—but don't count on it. Some owners have found it is better practice to formally advise each tenant of the intent to sell and, in so doing, reassure them as to their continued tenancy. As a rule, disclosure of full and accurate information will serve everyone better than trying to keep things a secret. The lack of information can lead to misunderstanding.

And speaking of tenants, be prepared to show a potential buyer copies of lease and rental agreements and other rent roll data. Because advance rent and damage deposits are to be transferred, you should be prepared to calculate the amount and advise the buyer. Ordinarily this is an offset to the cash to be put up by the purchaser and can be important in helping a cash-short buyer to see how a purchase can be made.

Completing the Deal

Once you have a signed offer in hand, take time to study it carefully and contemplate all the implications, especially if there are contingencies. As applicable, seek legal counsel and advice. Prudent buyers will insist on title insurance and both buyer and seller should insist on the transaction being handled by an escrow agent. If the buyer is to make future payments to you, such as on an installment contract or mortgage, you may wish to arrange with a bank or savings and loan association to handle the collections. Finally, you'll want to have your plans finalized as to what to do with the proceeds of the deal. If you are reinvesting, return to the beginning of this book and start over; that's what reinvesting will mean.

CLOSING THOUGHTS

Investing in real estate is not, to use the language of the stock market, a "one decision" proposition. You don't buy real estate, set it away, and forget it. No, whether it's your home or income property, vacant land, or a city lot, you must constantly attend to it. It's presumed you set your investment objectives carefully, found property best suited to achieving them, and then continually checked the performance against what you expected. Once an investment fails to achieve your goals, or has so met the goals it is time to make a change, you then need to sell. Most of your decisions will require careful attention to what you want to do next, how financing can be arranged, and what the tax consequences will be. As you ponder these matters and reach tentative conclusions, you can prepare an action plan. You can build financial security through real estate investing, but better than average results are achieved by those who go about both buying and selling in a systematic way. This chapter has given you all the material you will need to do it in that manner.

10

Lending on Real Estate

You don't have to be an owner to make a profit from real estate. Millions of people borrow and give mortgages as security. If you are looking for a steady, relatively secure income from high interest rates, become a mortgage lender.

MORTGAGE LENDING

Perhaps you were raised to believe that you should never borrow money and that it was foolish to lend money to others. By now you've learned, of course, the world has changed and, fortunately, not everyone believes these old-fashioned platitudes. When a borrower has a reliable income, does not live beyond his or her means, and has a sense of responsibility, there's no reason why he shouldn't borrow nor why you shouldn't lend to such a person. This is especially so if the borrowing is done to provide a home or make an investment in real estate. These are highly respectable reasons to borrow and at the same time provide great security against potential loss for the lender. Let's see how you can participate in all this as a lender. If and when your investment objective, now or in the future, is to generate maximum current income, you should look to mortgage lending as a highly satisfactory way to achieve such a goal.

The Borrowers

Your first chance to be a mortgagee (the lender) may come when you try to sell your property to someone who is short of cash and asks you, as the seller, to help out with the financing. If you own the property free and clear, you might consider making a first mortgage loan and thus carry all the debt after the down payment. Alternatively, you may be asked to make up a cash shortage by taking back a second mortgage or, if in Los Angeles, third, fourth, or fifth mortgage. Although as a seller you perhaps expected to cash out, you may through necessity wind up becoming a lender. Note carefully that by taking back a mortgage from the buyer, you are not required to put up any cash. You are simply taking a part of the purchase price in the form of a piece of paper, the promissory note, in place of cash.

Apart from being a seller-lender, if you are attracted to the idea of obtaining interest income through lending, you could take advantage of the many opportunities there are to advance your surplus cash to people who are buying real estate or who already own it and wish to give a security interest in property to support a loan. Here are some of the situations which give rise to such opportunities.

Refinancing. The owner wants to tap an equity by borrowing enough to repay an existing loan and have cash left over to use for other purposes. If the existing loan has favorable terms, the owner may wish instead to leave it in place and borrow only on the remaining equity.

Purchase. When the seller does not wish to participate as a lender, the buyer may want to borrow from a private lender, such as you. This could involve a first mortgage, or a second mortgage to supplement the buyer's cash down payment, or could be in the form of a wraparound or all-inclusive mortgage where the existing mortgage remains. A second mortgage is sometimes called a *piggyback* loan because it is riding on top of the first.

Because so many purchase transactions involve the sale of other property, an important contingency, there often is a need for short-term financing. Assume an owner puts property on the market and at the same time sets out to find a replacement. Frequently the replacement is found before cash can be realized from a sale either because the buyer can't close soon enough or, sometimes, a buyer has not yet been found. To make certain the replacement property can be secured, a commitment must be made to buy it, but that will take cash. If you were in this position, what could you do? Here you would look for a private lender to make what is termed a *bridge* loan. This is a short-term loan usually by way of a mortgage taken on the borrower's present property, to be repaid out of the sales proceeds. This cash makes it possible to go ahead with the purchase. Those who make bridge loans, of course, must satisfy themselves that the borrower can, in fact, ultimately sell the property and satisfy the short-term loan. Because there is substantial risk here, the interest rate on bridge loans is typically quite high and thus, when successful, provides an excellent return for those who are not faint-hearted. You should look for deals where there is a firm purchase contract in force on the borrower's current property, from a responsible buyer for whom there is little or no risk of failure to complete the purchase. Whenever possible you should obtain not only the protection of a recorded mortgage but an assignment of whatever other assets the borrower might have. Realize that if the sale falls through you might have to force a foreclosure to recover your loan. Because this financing spans two transactions—a purchase and sale—it is termed *bridge*.

Loan Term.   A private lender will have opportunities to make both short- and long-term loans and hence can tailor the activity to suit investment needs. Although we generally associate mortgage loans with extended repayment periods running into even twenty-five or thirty years, borrowers and lenders are totally free to negotiate whatever is required. As a rule, private lenders are more interested in short-term lending, such as up to five to seven years, thus reducing the risk. We'll explore this aspect in more detail shortly.

The Risk

A lender runs the risk that the loan will not be repaid as agreed. Unless there is loan security, a lender may be faced with an absolute loss. Lending on real estate, however, is attractive because of the relative security provided by the collateral. If you make certain that the documentation is in order and that your security interest (the mortgage loan agreement) is recorded, and you take timely action when default is indicated, you will have minimized the chance of incurring a loss.

When the borrower encounters difficulties and is unable or unwilling to make loan payments, a lender must decide whether to declare default, proceed to assert rights to foreclose, and have the property seized and sold to satisfy the debt. The end result of foreclosure will not necessarily be payment in full of the unpaid balance, of course. Unless the proceeds from the foreclosure sale are enough, the lender may lose at least part of the loan. Whether you can sue the borrower for the remaining unpaid debt may depend on the type of loan and local laws. In some states when a loan is made to purchase a home, hence is called a *purchase-money* mortgage, no deficiency judgments are permitted; the property is the sole source of recovery, adequate or not.

Whenever making a junior loan—any loan that is not secured by a first mortgage—you stand a chance of being wiped out if there is a default. If the proceeds of a foreclosure sale are not more than enough to pay off the loans standing ahead of yours, you lose. It is this risk that all junior loans such as second, wrap, piggy-back, and bridge, face. For that reason, interest rates must be higher and repayment periods shorter than for first loans.

Private lenders generally can charge high interest rates because they are willing to do things other lenders are unable or unwilling to do. But, no matter whether you are receiving an above-market rate or not, you face what is termed an interest-rate risk. Some feel, however, that this risk is hedged against because you can, in fact, lend at above average rates. Here's the problem.

When you lend money at a fixed interest rate for a stated time period, your yield is set with no opportunity for it to change. If rates payable on other investments increase, and you have your cash locked up in mortgages, you will have to forego such other opportunities to earn more. If you try to liquidate your mortgage loans to get cash to invest elsewhere, you'll have to sell at a discount. Once again we see that almost everything associated with real estate has a relatively long-term and somewhat illiquid characteristic. That is not necessarily a bad feature but it certainly must be recognized by all who would make mortgage loans. On the other hand, if market rates go down, it is possible you could sell your mortgages at a premium. You would do this, of course, if you had other equally profitable places to employ the funds.

There are a number of things a lender can do to reduce some or all of the risks outlined above. Let's look at them.

Loan Underwriting. There are several steps to take before making a loan. You need to check out the credit-worthiness of the borrower and look into the value of the collateral. There is a tendency for private mortgage lenders to overlook the need to know how well the borrower is likely to meet his or her obligation. This probably occurs because of the feeling that if there is a default there will always be the chance to take the collateral and sell it for enough to pay off what is owed. Problems can easily be avoided by checking into the bill-paying record, employment, and financial position of the borrower and making loans only to those who meet your standards. Next you must have a way to measure the collateral and the borrower's equity. Unless there is enough at stake, there's limited motivation for the borrower to avoid default.

The measure used by lenders to control this aspect of risk is known as the *loan-to-value* ratio. The smaller this ratio is, the more protection the lender has. The critical starting point is the actual market value of the property to be used to secure the loan. You will need to either make an appraisal yourself or obtain one from a professional appraiser. In addition you must set a ratio standard to apply. Commercial lenders, for example, may require a borrower to have a 20 percent equity. This translates into an 80 percent loan-to-value ratio. This would mean, for example, if a property has a market value of $100,000, the mortgage loans should not exceed $80,000. The ratio is applied to the market value to obtain the maximum borrowing. Let's assume you decided to limit your lending to an 80 percent ratio and were asked to make a second mortgage for $20,000 over an existing first loan of $50,000 on the property appraised at $100,000. The total of $70,000 is less than 80 percent so, all other things being equal, you could agree to making the second loan; the borrower's equity would be 30 percent. When mortgage money becomes scarce and/or interest rates increase, lenders often reduce their loan-to-value ratios. You too will have to keep informed about the market to know what's happening and to set loan terms that offer you optimum protection.

Some private lenders take comfort in how inflation serves to increase market values and hence, borrowers' equities. When this actually occurs, then lenders do benefit. If the borrower gets into difficulty, it is probable he or she could sell the property for more than enough to pay off the loans and get cash as well. With that prospect a lender is likely protected against a default. Instead the borrower will take action to sell and thus pay off the lender. Notice, of course, what can happen if values start to decline and the owner's equity is modest. (If you use a 90 percent loan-to-value ratio, the beginning equity will be only 10 percent.) It can be wiped out quickly and all motivation to make the loan payments may disappear. By watching carefully that your lending is done on a conservative basis, you may be able to avoid these difficulties.

Loan Agreement.   In addition to evaluating the borrower and the collateral, you must also protect yourself against loss through appropriate language in the mortgage instrument. Here are the typical provisions.

A. If you wish to insure that your loan funds will be fully invested for the entire term of the loan, you then provide that premature payment of the principal is prohibited. This is known as a *lock-in clause*. Here the borrower would be stuck with having the loan in place unless you were agreeable to removing the restriction when requested. If you thought interest rates were likely to substantially decline, you might want this condition.

B. If you don't wish to prohibit premature payoff but would like to collect something extra if the borrower does liquidate the debt, you can include a *prepayment penalty* provision. Such a penalty may give you enough to offset the costs of finding a new loan to make.

C. To encourage prompt payment you will want to include a *late payment* charge in the agreement, large enough to really motivate.

D. It's presumed that you will lend funds only after you've satisfied yourself that the borrower and the collateral are satisfactory. What will your position be, however, if a change occurs? The borrower may sell the property or may further encumber it. Either of these actions could result in damaging your position. To protect yourself you will want to have a *due-on* clause in the loan agreement, written to take care of the situations you may be concerned about. This condition will enable you to require repayment of the loan balance if the property is sold or is used as collateral for more borrowing.

All told, then, through prudent analysis and careful drafting of the loan agreement, a lender can minimize risk. We'll treat some of these matters in more detail below but first, let's look more closely at the legal nature of the collateral supporting a mortgage loan.

Security Interest

As a lender, you need legally acceptable evidence of the

debt in order to enforce your rights and a legally efficient way to convert the collateral into cash in the event of default. For the first you must have the borrowers execute a promissory note which satisfies the legal requirements for negotiability. For the second you may have a choice between a mortgage and a deed of trust. This choice may have already been made for you, however. In some states, only the mortgage is acceptable and in others, through custom, the deed of trust is the document in widespread use. In this and other matters connected with mortgage lending, you may wish to rely on legal counsel. In many areas, title insurance companies are very helpful in providing guidance. You may even be able to obtain satisfactory forms and documents from this source. This is not to imply that professional legal services are not desirable nor needed. It is to assert, however, that through experience you may well be able to handle the drafting of acceptable and sufficient notes and loan agreements yourself; it is not difficult to obtain samples from commercial lenders. Obviously you are assuming some risks when you do things for yourself which may be better done by a lawyer.

Mortgage.   Without going into all the intricate details of a real estate mortgage contract, we can examine the major feature: the provisions relating to granting the power to sell the security in the event of default and to apply the proceeds to satisfy the debt. This will then be compared with the deed of trust. The alternative to a mortgage or deed of trust is to leave the lender in the position of having to obtain a judicial foreclosure through bringing a lawsuit against the borrower. If you took only a promissory note, for example, without an accompanying mortgage, that would be your position. A judicial foreclosure is a much more time-consuming and expensive procedure than to pursue rights granted to the lender by the borrower by signing the mortgage agreement. The borrower is still protected against unlawful actions of a lender, under the terms of a mortgage however, and the lender is still required to follow rigidly outlined procedures to effect recovery.

The borrower still retains an opportunity to redeem the property by settling the debt before the foreclosure sale and must be granted specified time periods in which to act. In sum, however, through the mortgage contract device, a lender has sufficient rights to timely repayment so that those with money to loan are quite willing to do so. As a security interest, the mortgage is far more attractive than many alternatives open to lenders and investors.

Trust Deed.   As stressed throughout this chapter, the risk inherent in lending lies in potential failure to repay. If the borrower pledges something of value that can readily be converted to cash, the lender has hedged against possible loss. Historically, lenders have been discouraged by restrictions on converting collateral. The mortgage was developed to simplify the process, but there is an even more efficient way to restore a lender following default. It is provided by a contract known as the *deed of trust*, used in place of the mortgage. You may find it referred to instead as a *trust deed*. This is used in a number of states for all types of real estate lending, not only for first loans but juniors as well.

Stated simply, through the deed of trust the borrower executes a deed to the property in which the security interest is granted in favor of the lender. This deed is held by an independent trustee such as a bank, title insurance company, or entity established specifically for this service. If there is a default, the lender notifies the trustee and, allowing for time periods set by law, the trustee holds a sale of the property and can pass acceptable title to a buyer. Defaulting borrowers have rights of redemption prior to such a sale but not afterwards. Most agree that because the process is streamlined, the deed of trust is preferred to the mortgage. Both are far superior to a judicial foreclosure because it takes a much longer period of time before the property can be sold and the proceeds applied to the loan balance. Realize that once there is a default, the lender's funds are tied up without income being received. Although accrued interest is added to the claim against the borrower, the lender receives nothing until the property is sold. Time then is an important factor; it is minimized in the case of the trust deed mechanism.

Installment Contract. When a property owner sells on an installment contract, he or she is, in effect, making a loan in the amount of the contract balance. By retaining title to the property, however, the lender needs only the evidence of the debt and does not need, nor could legally obtain, a mortgage or trust deed contract from the buyer-borrower. From the buyer's point of view, the installment contract provides evidence of an equitable interest in the property as well, of course, as evidence of the debt. If you are lending money on the security of real estate and are not also the seller, you will not have anything to do with an installment contract.

Promissory Note. The promissory note is a valuable document and is to be kept secure. Once the obligation is repaid, the note is to be marked paid and returned to the borrower. Where a mortgage has been used, the lender will execute a *satisfaction*. If a trust deed has been used, the lender is required to execute a *reconveyance* which is a document that serves to cancel the transfer of the title at the time the loan was made. All documents, except the note, are to be recorded, including the satisfaction or reconveyance after the debt is paid. In that way, official title to the property as it appears in the public record will be cleared of the encumbrance.

LOAN TERMS

Although you, as a lender, are committing your cash, you are not totally free to set any terms you wish. First, you must be concerned about your state's *usury* law. And you must be competitive. You will be competing with many other private lenders as well as commercial sources. Borrowers have a wide range of prospective sources for funds although this changes frequently. In some situations, if you are prepared to act quickly, you can make loans to the exclusion of others. Frequently, borrowers need or want to complete financing in a hurry. You can be prepared by learning all you can about this activity, and by having a supply of forms ready, not to mention the money. While waiting for a lending opportunity, you should have your funds employed at as high a yield as possible yet be readily available. Money-market mutual funds that offer immediate withdrawal without penalty are popular places for keeping cash while waiting for a more permanent place for it.

Before making a loan you must decide on a number of items. Let's consider each of the major things to be covered in a loan agreement.

Interest Rates

The charge for the use of borrowed money is based on an interest rate to be applied to the amount of money for the time used. Mortgage interest generally is charged in arrears, that is, computed at the end of specified periods and payable at that time. Typically, rates are used on an annual, or *per annum*, basis. The rate level is affected by the measure of risk which takes into account the time for repayment, the credit-worthiness of the borrower, and the nature of the collateral. In general, mortgage loans carry lower interest rates than other types of loans primarily because of the relative safety of the collateral. Rates, including mortgage rates, are affected by inflationary expectation. The essential problem with making a long-term loan at fixed repayment amounts and level interest rates is the likely drop in purchasing value of payment dollars received in the future. Lenders try to offset this through higher interest rates when inflation is anticipated.

Because there is a potential for abuse in lending money, our lawmakers have set maximum rates that can be charged, especially by private lenders. These limits are contained, state by state, in usury statutes. The penalties for violating these laws can be substantial. Check with your state department of finance or secretary of state to get a copy of the law that would apply to what you plan to do. In most states, maximum usury rates are not the same for individuals as for financial institutions, so don't assume you are free to charge what banks, for example, can charge. Further, under a law passed in 1980, usury laws applicable to loans for housing have been suspended under federal regulation but may be reimposed by state action later. In short, this area is undergoing a change and you should become informed if you are going to make loans. With the lifting of some very unrealistic low limits in some states, lending opportunities will be much more attractive.

For many years the typical mortgage loan was made at a fixed rate and level payments. Because of the volatility in interest rates and the erosion due to inflation, several alternative lending terms have been devised, which can be used by private lenders as well as institutions. The alternatives include variable interest rates, mortgage points, and participation clauses.

Variable Rates. In place of a fixed interest rate to be applied to the unpaid loan balance, you and a borrower could agree that, according to movements in an independent measure, the rate will not be fixed but instead will vary from time to time. At the time the loan is made, the current market rate is usually used although some financial institutions offer a beginning rate slightly below the level rate level. The loan agreement then will provide the basis on which the rate is to vary. Note that changes can be either up or down. This device may be of less value to a private lender than a bank, for example. Inasmuch as you are simply employing funds you already have, and are not subject to a change in the cost of your funds as is a financial firm, you don't face the same difficulties. While it might be nice to think that the interest rate on the loans you made could go up under a variable plan, you also run the risk of a lower return. To learn how to word the language for your loan agreement to have a variable rate mortgage, check with a savings and loan association or savings bank.

Rollover Mortgages. Although some financial institutions have promoted the variable rate plan, it has met some resistance. Some people do not want to be faced with frequent changes in the interest rate. To overcome this feature, the industry has developed the rollover plan; you as a private lender may wish to make your loans on this basis. Here the rate is subject to change at the end of three or five years, subject to limits such as no more than half of 1 percent a year nor a total of 5 percent during the term of the loan. While these are rules imposed by the Federal Home Loan Bank Board on federally chartered savings institutions and would not be enforceable on private lenders, you would probably find it necessary to be no more restrictive as a matter of being competitive. Under this plan the loan is made for a typical period such as thirty years and the periodic payment computed as for the fixed-rate mortgage. At the end of the initial three- or five-year period, the borrower is free to shop around for another loan and will not be subject to a penalty if the original mortgage is paid off. On the other hand, the original lender is obligated to continue the loan if the borrower requests and agrees to pay the new rate. This plan has been used in Canada for many years.

Mortgage Points.   Lenders assess a point charge to offset a loan contract interest rate that is deemed inadequate to reflect the current market value of money. Instead of charging points, lenders could simply increase the interest rate. There is, however, some appeal to charging points instead. This amounts to a lump sum source of income to some lenders and, in the final analysis, serves to increase the yield for all mortgagees. In addition to points, commercial lenders often impose a loan origination fee to cover other costs. Don't confuse these two items.

A mortgage point is 1 percent of the amount of the loan. For most situations, one point is equivalent to one-eighth of 1 percent increase in the contract interest rate. The custom is to deduct the point charge from the loan proceeds. If you made a thirty year $50,000 mortgage loan at say 14 percent plus four points, the cash to be disbursed would be:

$$\$50,000 \text{ less } 4\% = \$48,000$$
$$\text{The point charge is } \$2,000.$$

Note that the borrower would have to come up with an extra $2,000 in cash if the purchase required a full $50,000 loan. Depending on the circumstances, the transaction may be subject to the federal Truth-in-Lending law. It requires that lenders making loans to consumers must state the equivalent annual simple interest rate, called the *Annual Percentage Rate* or *APR*. This requires relating the periodic payments needed to pay the amount borrowed, here $50,000, to the funds actually advanced, $48,000. In this example the APR would be approximately 14½ percent. As a lender, you would have current interest income of $2,000 from the points plus the interest the borrower paid on $50,000 at 14 percent. The borrower can treat the point charge as interest expense and, hence, tax-deductible, only if the loan involved the purchase of a principal residence. Otherwise, the point charge is to be added to the cost of the property.

Participation.   In an earlier section we discussed how landlords may share in the success of business tenants by charging rents consisting of a base rate plus a share of the sales revenues. Lenders can accomplish much the same through including a *participation* provision in the loan agreement. In that case, the lender may be able to increase the yield from the loan if the specified events occur. You may link the extra payment, over and above the usual amortization of the principal and interest charge, to either net profits, gross revenues, or proceeds of the sale. The borrower may, for example, have obtained the loan in order to convert the property to a condominium. In order to be able to sell the units, a partial release from all lenders will be required. A lender may stipulate that, as a loan condition, a fixed amount be paid in order for the partial release to be made. In most areas, loan conditions calling for extra payments are often referred to as *kickers* or *sweeteners*. There is lots of room to use your imagination here in devising a basis.

Well, so much for variations on the fixed rate, level payment mortgage loan. Once you've made any kind of loan, how do you get your money back and the interest due?

Repayment

The basic provisions of the loan contract relating to repaying the loan in the regular way are found in the promissory note. This agreement will state the total amount borrowed, the interest rate, the amount of the periodic payment, and the loan term. If the note recites the obligation to pay a stated amount "or more," there is no prohibition to paying the loan off prematurely. Not all loans are made on the basis that repayment is to be made in equal payments; some loans may require only payment of interest with no partial repayment of principal. All loan terms should be stated clearly.

Amortization. This term refers to a process of repaying or paying off an obligation. A mortgage loan may be fully amortizing or not. When a fixed payment is to be made for a specified number of periods and it is sufficient to fully repay the principal as well as pay the interest, we describe the loan as fully *amortizing*. There are several variations on this standard, and private lenders need to know about them. We'll start with the typical situation.

EXAMPLE: You make a second mortgage loan for $15,000 at 14 percent annual interest, repayable in monthly amounts over twenty years. (You are free to call for payments other than monthly if you wish.) To find the monthly payment amount exactly right to pay accrued interest and pay off the principal, we can turn to the Tables in the Appendix; note this is a fully amortizing loan.

Monthly payment is $12.4352 times 15 = $186.53

When you receive the first payment you would apportion it first to interest and the balance to principal, thus:

From I = Prt, I = $15,000 times .14 times 1/12 = $175.00

(Note that because the rate and time remain constant, you can simply multiply the loan balance by .14/12, simplified to the decimal equivalent of .0167.) The credit to the principal would then be:

$186.53 less $175 = $11.53

Each month thereafter, although the payment remains the same at $186.53, the amount charged to interest will go down and the portion to principal will increase; the unpaid balance is reduced each time. For this reason we describe a fully amortizing loan as one for which interest is charged on the declining unpaid principal balance. This is the least expensive way for mortgage loan interest to be computed, from a borrower's point of view. Because the total amounts charged to interest and credited to principal from monthly payments are often needed annually, the tables show such accumulations. If payments were made other than monthly, the numbers would be different.

As implied in the fully amortizing loan definition, the lender will receive full repayment of the original loan by the end of the loan term; here that is twenty years. Are there some alternatives to having to wait this long? Yes.

Balloon Payment.   You and the borrower might agree to a lump sum settlement on a date stipulated. You could offer this loan, for example, on the same basis described except that you stipulate that the principal balance due at the end of say five years (or any other term) will be payable in full. During the five years the borrower will make the regular monthly payment of $186.53 but will have to come up with $14,764.64 on the due date. (From the table the balance due: $984.309 times 15 = $14,764.64.)

Instead of using the fully amortizing loan payment for the rate and term, you may instead simply require an arbitrarily selected periodic payment and then ask the borrower to settle the unpaid balance on the due date. This is then termed a *stipulated payment* mortgage. To allocate principal and interest and hence to compute the balloon payment due on the due date, you would apply the I = Prt formula as above.

Income Taxes.   As a lender you will report all interest payments received during the tax year as taxable income. Any repayment of principal is a return of your capital and is not taxable. Payments made under participation agreements will ordinarily be treated as interest income. In general, earnings from lending are taxed as current income and are not subject to capital gains treatment.

Prepayment Penalty. Those who make loans as a business view premature payoff differently than you would if you loaned your neighbor or a relative $100 and they paid it back sooner than you expected. Mortgage lenders, except when interest rates increase dramatically in a short time, are not anxious to have loans repaid too soon. When it does occur, they must go to the expense of finding another place to put the money to work. To discourage both premature repayment of principal as well as offset the cost to make the loan, commercial lenders typically include a prepayment penalty in the loan agreement. As a private lender you can do so, too; whether you choose to enforce it remains an option. Where the expectation is great that the loan will be paid off in advance, lenders are encouraged to apply this penalty because it is an important source of additional income from the loan.

Lenders are limited in the terms of this penalty by competition and, in some states, by law or regulation. There is a wide variety of ways in which the penalty is imposed. It may be stated as a fixed percentage of the original loan or a percentage applied to the balance of the loan when it is liquidated. It may be effective regardless of the time between the date the loan was made and paid off, or it may be waived after a period of time, five years, for example. Partial repayments of principal up to stated lump sum amounts may be allowed without penalty. By checking the terms used by local financial institutions, you can get an idea of what you should do.

Due-On Clauses

You can include in your loan agreement conditions whereby you could accelerate the payment of the loan balance if a borrower either passed title (due-on sale) or gave an additional security interest in the property to support further borrowing (due-on encumbrance). These conditions are sometimes referred to as *acceleration* clauses. Provided the language incorporated in the loan agreement was legally sufficient, and the lender followed the necessary procedure for giving notice, once the lender learned of a condition that would apply, the demand could be made for payment of the unpaid principal balance in full. The amount would be determined according to the repayment terms of the loan. The borrower's failure to pay would constitute default and foreclosure proceedings could then follow.

The due-on sale clause is designed to protect the lender against a noncredit-worthy borrower replacing the entity to which the loan was made. This clause can, of course, serve to prevent an owner from making a sale under conditions where it is important for the buyer to be able to assume the existing loan. When mortgage money is scarce or market rates far exceed the rate on the loan, a seller may be adversely affected by the lender invoking this restrictive provision. In some states, the courts have refused to enforce this clause unless the lender can show its position, and security would be significantly impaired if ownership is transferred and the loan assumed. Many private lenders, presuming there is no local legal restriction against it, customarily include a due-on sale clause but intend to agree to an assumption as long as the proposed substitute owner-borrower meets reasonable standards. When there is a large difference in interest rates, a lender has substantial incentive to force a repayment of the loan which, of course, would occur if the buyer gets a new loan. Alternatively, the lender could agree to a substitution at an increase in the loan interest rate.

It may not be easy to learn when a borrower has obtained additional loan money and has thus reduced his or her equity in the property. Short of searching the public record from time to time you may not learn of this unless the borrower tells you. As stated previously, part of the protection a mortgage lender has against default is the extent of the borrower's equity and if it is reduced you should take such development seriously. In order to enforce your rights you may have to declare default and force a sale of the property.

LOAN PROCEDURE

Once you have decided to make mortgage loans, either as a seller taking back a mortgage or as a private lender, you should follow certain procedures to protect your interests and to serve the borrower efficiently. If you are granting a mortgage on property you are selling, it is customary for the broker handling the sale to take care of the paperwork; otherwise, it will be up to you. If you are using the services of a mortgage loan broker, again all the details will be handled for you. As a private lender pursuing this on a do-it-yourself basis, you will have to find ways to contact prospective borrowers and develop a procedure for evaluating those who have a serious interest in using your money. We'll assume you are going to make second mortgage loans either to buyers or to owners who wish to tap their equities and will review the things you must be prepared to do.

Borrower Evaluation

You should use a loan application form to obtain all the necessary data from the person who wants to borrow your money. You probably can readily adapt a form used by a commercial lender to your individual use. You should arrange to obtain a credit report—contact local credit reporting services—to verify information stated on the application. In the absence of a report you can, on your own, verify employment and bill-paying record. If you find that false information has been given, you should reject the opportunity. If the applicant has stable employment and has demonstrated a sense of responsibility by paying debts as agreed, your chances for avoiding a loss are much better than otherwise. Next, you need a valuation of the security to apply a loan-to-value ratio you believe is appropriate. Be certain to relate the total of all borrowing—the existing loan balances plus the new loan—to the overall valuation of the property. Prudent lenders prefer that this not exceed 80 percent, thus leaving the borrower with at least a 20 percent stake.

Documentation

You will need a promissory note form and a mortgage loan agreement containing all the appropriate provisions discussed above. The names of the borrowers should match exactly the way in which title to the property stands; be certain everyone who has an interest signs. The description of the property must be that used in the official record, not just the street address, for example. Obviously, you would expect your lawyer to take care of all these details. If doing it yourself you may be able to obtain substantial help from the title insurance company or escrow agency. A reminder: be certain that executed documents, except the note, are sent for official recording to become a part of the public record. In some areas you can request the official recorder to send you notice of any default filed against the property. This is especially important for lenders making junior loans.

Insurance

The security for the mortgage loan is an interest in real property and, if the improvements are damaged or destroyed, the security would be impaired. Therefore, it is customary to require borrowers to obtain suitable fire and other hazard insurance to protect the lender's interest. The most satisfactory way for this to be accomplished is to ask the borrower to see that all policies in his or her name on the property are endorsed to show your interest as a lender. You are to be given copies of the policies. When all this is done correctly, the insurance company is obligated to give you notice of any change in the coverage and, in particular, notice of cancellation. You should assume the responsibility of keeping track of whether your borrower renews the policies. You should also make a diary record of the expiration date and check in advance. It is usual to include in the loan agreement a provision giving you the right to obtain insurance for your interest at the borrower's expense if he or she fails to provide you with acceptable protection.

You should also protect yourself through title insurance. In most areas the cost for this is imposed on the borrower. In this way, if subsequently the title to the collateral is not clear and your right to levy on the property to collect what is due is impaired, such loss may be covered by title insurance.

Disbursement and Collection

Once the loan papers are properly executed and the other requirements, such as hazard insurance, have been met, you will then pass over the loan funds to the borrower. When money is being advanced in a purchase transaction, it is customary for the private lender to send the loan proceeds directly to the seller, probably in care of an escrow agent.

You should make it clear to the borrower where to send the loan payments. It is usual to record them, by hand, in a loan payment book which is returned to the borrower. Blank books can be obtained at stationery stores; some title insurers make them available to private lenders as a part of their service. In addition to the receipt you give the borrower, such as by entries in the payment book, you should keep an accurate record yourself. You must always be able to determine exactly what has been paid on the debt and what balance is remaining. If appropriate, safeguard your accounting records to avoid problems that would result if your record was destroyed. Some lenders keep a duplicate of the entries in a secondary location.

If you do not wish to handle the collection process yourself, you may find that a local savings institution will do it for a fee. Some give this service on a complimentary basis because it serves to increase deposits. But what happens if the borrower doesn't pay on time? If you are handling collections yourself, you must know precisely when the borrower is late and take timely action. If a late payment provision is included in the loan agreement, you should impose it to motivate the borrower. If a savings association is handling the collection, it is not likely they will also pursue delinquencies, so you must be prepared to do this yourself.

Now that we have discussed all the things to do to put your

excess funds to work earning interest, it's time to review how to locate the borrowers.

HOW TO FIND BORROWERS

When you offer to help finance the sale of your own property, borrowers will come to you quite readily. Here, however, we are concerned with how you find qualified people to borrow your cash and give you a security interest such as a second mortgage to support the loan. There are several things you can do to spread the word that you have money to lend on real estate.

Loan Brokers

In most states there are individuals and firms that operate to bring private lenders and borrowers together. They are usually identified as *mortgage loan brokers*. They may or may not operate also as real estate brokers. It is their function to attract borrowers and arrange for the loan to be funded by private lenders like you. The borrower pays all the costs of getting the loan, including the fee to the broker. As a rule, the lender simply puts up the face amount of the loan. In some cases you may also be able to charge loan fees or points. The loan broker will arrange for all the paperwork and, optionally, make collections and remit to the lender. If you prefer, you could have the borrower make the payments directly to you. While loan brokers can arrange any type of financing borrowers and lenders agree to, most loans are of the short term (three to five years), second mortgage, or trust deed type. The cash is needed either to complete the purchase of a home or to spring the equity in property already owned. Although the majority of this loan activity involves homes, all other types of real estate are eligible and could be used as collateral.

You can expect the mortgage loan broker to know not only the maximum rate that can be charged under the state's usury law, but also the current market rate. You should be able to maximize your returns, particularly if you can require a prepayment penalty provision. If the broker needs to put together a larger loan, you may be asked to join with others and take a share. In short, loan brokers may be able to give you lending opportunities not otherwise available while acting on your own.

Before handing over your cash, you should check around to determine the reputation of the broker and obtain information concerning his or her expertise. Ask for names of both borrowers and lenders and check with them. It's possible that the local office of the *Better Business Bureau* can give you information on whether there have been complaints against a firm. You are not lending the money to the broker, of course, but at least momentarily the broker will have your money; thus there is a risk. Further, if the broker is not skilled in handling the paperwork or in evaluating borrowers, you could face a default or inability for other reasons to collect on the loan. There are many skilled and responsible mortgage loan brokers around. All you have to do is find one in your area. Start your research by looking in the phone book and the newspaper.

Real Estate Brokers

The person most likely to know when mortgage loan money is needed is the real estate broker working to put a deal together. If you make contact with brokers in whom you have confidence and let them know you want to make loans secured by real estate, you should have no trouble putting out all the cash you have. In most states a real estate broker does not charge a fee for this type of loan arranging, so it is less costly for the borrower. The best arrangement from the lender's point of view is simply to send the cash to an escrow agency with instructions to have the appropriate loan documents executed and recorded before disbursing the funds. You may also be able to use the real estate firm for collecting the loan payments.

Group Lending

As an alternative to making individual loans, you may be

attracted to putting your cash with others' funds; you can do this by becoming a limited partner in a mortgage loan syndicate. These are typically organized by real estate brokers and investment dealers. This technique gives you a way to spread the risk, because your money will usually be invested in many different loans. Further, you can be involved in loans larger than you would want to or be able to make on your own. There often are participation benefits associated with larger mortgages arranged in this manner. If you aren't able to locate a syndicate already in operation, why not organize one yourself?

Advertising

Once you feel comfortable in handling the details of mortgage loans on your own, you may be able to reach qualified borrowers simply by advertising in the local newspaper or the *Wall Street Journal.* Look at these sources and you'll see how others use them. Realize that when you act for yourself, you must be prepared to do all the work. This requires sufficient know-how to minimize your risk. You would be foolish to lend your money if you are unable to check the credit-worthiness of the prospective borrower or couldn't handle the documentation adequately.

LIQUIDATION

The goal of a private lender typically is to lend money for a short time, such as three to five years, and to be repaid in monthly installments without any hassle or loss. That, of course, is the way it works—most of the time. What if you get tired of waiting for repayment, have better opportunities to employ the money, or develop some anxiety about the borrower? Or, what do you do if you can't collect what is owing? Here are some suggestions.

Default

Either you or a mortgage servicing firm must keep close

track of the borrower and the collateral. Even if the payments are being made on time, it could be important to visit the property occasionally to see if there are any developments that might lead to a default. Has the owner changed the use? Any construction activity? Is the place falling apart? What's happening in the neighborhood? If an adverse condition is developing, you will either need to increase your vigilance with respect to monitoring the payments or develop a plan to sell the mortgage. If it becomes apparent the borrower is not living up to the loan agreement, you must be prepared to file notice of default in order to protect your rights. In many cities there are foreclosure service firms that will handle this procedure in your behalf. Most lawyers, of course, will be familiar with the process. Unless you turn everything over to a mortgage loan servicing firm that will take care of collections, delinquencies, and foreclosures, you will have to handle these matters yourself. This may be far less onerous than landlording, but don't underestimate the importance of shepherding your loans until they are paid off.

Sale

The holding of a promissory note and mortgage loan agreement is like the ownership of other property—it can be sold. The documents represent a legal right to receive money and that right can be transferred, presuming the paperwork is in order. If you want to get rid of a mortgage loan, how can you find someone to buy it and how do you set the price?

Mortgage loan brokers and some real estate brokers deal in buying and selling mortgage loans. Once a price is agreed on, the papers can be exchanged for the money and an assignment recorded. The borrower should be notified of the change and be instructed where to send the periodic payments. Note the importance of safeguarding the note. It is the primary evidence of the debt and may be needed to prove the right to the unpaid mortgage balance. If you use the services of a broker to find a buyer, the paperwork will be done for you. Otherwise you'll need to be ready to do what is necessary yourself. Assistance is available from your banker, lawyers, or a title insurance company.

Most sales of existing mortgages are made at a discount. The seller usually is prompted to offer the note because he or she didn't want to be a lender originally. When you want to get rid of something you ordinarily are prepared to sacrifice part of the value. That is certainly true here in practice. There is always some risk in holding a mortgage and the purchaser of your note will want a concession to offset the risk. Finally, if interest rates have increased over the rate applicable to the loan, the cash price for it will be less than the unpaid principal balance. To better understand why all these things are at work, let's see how prices are set.

EXAMPLE: Assume you sold some property and, in order to make it possible, you reluctantly took back a mortgage for $10,000 with interest at 12%, monthly payments of $110.11 and a five-year due date. (Even though you have set a near-term due date, you used the monthly payment for a twenty-year term; see the Tables for the appropriate factor.)

Because you would prefer cash you search for a way to liquidate the note, perhaps even before the first payment is due. Through a broker or by contacting a buyer who advertised in the newspaper, you locate someone who offers to give you $7,500 cash. This, of course, represents a 25 percent discount from the $10,000 unpaid balance. Whether you should accept it will depend on your desire for the cash and degree of enthusiasm for being a mortgagee. What's the going rate for discounting? This will vary from one community to another and depends on market conditions. It is not at all unusual for junior mortgage loans to be discounted as high as 50 percent. You will want to bargain, of course. The buyer is obviously out to earn a maximum return, so let's see how the yield is determined.

The sale of the note will not affect the borrower, so he or she will continue to make the $110.11 payments to the note-holder. If a buyer pays $7,500 then the yield will be in excess of the contract rate of 12 percent. The interest component of the monthly payment is to be related to the purchaser's investment to get the yield. Using the first payment, we find that $100 is attributable to interest. This return on $7,500 for one month gives an annualized yield of 16 percent. But there's more. The unpaid balance payable on the due date will greatly exceed the $7,500, so the note-holder will get back a substantial gain over the original amount invested. When the gain from the payoff is included, the annualized yield to maturity in this example will be approximately 21 percent.[1] Tables available in public libraries, real estate and stock brokerage offices, and banks can be used to make this computation.

Now that you've seen how discounting works, perhaps you'd just as soon look for lenders who want to liquidate rather than make new loans yourself. Just remember the relationship between risk and rate of return; they go hand in hand. As a rule, the higher the yield, the greater the risk. Sometimes a lender wants to unload a mortgage loan because there is trouble brewing. Beware! But also be prepared to seize opportunities.

Taxes. You need to consider the income tax considerations here. First, what will your position be if you take back a mortgage when you sell property, then immediately sell the note at a discount? In effect you just reduced the price you received for the property, so be sure to mark your records. When computing the gain (or loss) on the property deal, make the appropriate adjustment. Next, what are the tax consequences of buying a loan on a discount basis?

Under current tax regulations, all receipts from holding a note bought at a discount over the amount invested are to be treated as interest income and, therefore, not subject to capital gains treatment. If, on the other hand, you ultimately sell the note before its due date for an amount greater than the ad-

---

[1]The yield will be the interest rate required so that the present value of the remaining monthly payments of $110.11 plus the present value of the unpaid balance due on the due date, $9,174.43, equals $7,500. Recall that you can obtain balloon payments from the Tables in the Appendix.

justed basis of the note, the difference can be reported as a capital gain. Because there are many options and the tax rules may be complex, you would be well-advised to consult a tax specialist to maximize your after-tax returns from dealing in mortgages. Here again, you need to have a copy of IRS Publication 544, *Sales and Other Dispositions of Assets.*

CLOSING THOUGHTS

Landlording has many potential money-making features. Some of the related features, however, are unattractive to some people. In this chapter we've discussed how you might obtain a highly satisfactory return from a real estate investment without the possible adverse aspects of ownership. Yes, lending on real estate can give you many of the advantages possible from this investment vehicle. It is important, however, to realize that basically this return is in the form of interest which must be treated as current income for tax purposes. Lending does not provide tax sheltering nor, except in rare instances, does it give you any capital appreciation that would be taxed on a preferred basis. When your investment objective is to maximize current income from funds invested, try making mortgage loans. That just might be the best step you ever took.

At first blush it may appear that to protect yourself you should avoid mortgage lending as a do-it-yourself project. Certainly through the use of professional services of attorneys and loan brokers, you may minimize your risks. But through experience, education, and applying common sense, you should be able to put your money to work with a minimum of outside assistance and the expense that goes with it. Try it; you might like it!

Appendix

TABLE 1 PAYMENT AMORTIZES LOAN
Term: 5 to 30 years in 5-year intervals
Rates: 8% to 16% at 1/2% intervals

Mortgage of $1000.00 for 5 Years at 8.00 Percent
Monthly Payment: $20.2765

End of Year	Balance Due	Interest	Mtge. Reduct.
1	830.559	73.8767	169.441
2	647.055	59.8132	183.504
3	448.319	44.5824	198.735
4	233.089	28.0875	215.23
5	–0–	10.2234	233.089

Mortgage of $1000.00 for 5 Years at 8.50 Percent
Monthly Payment: $20.5165

End of Year	Balance Due	Interest	Mtge. Reduct.
1	832.372	78.5693	167.628
2	649.927	63.7524	182.445
3	451.355	47.626	198.572
4	235.231	30.0741	216.124
5	–0–	10.9708	235.231

Mortgage of $1000.00 for 5 Years at 9.00 Percent
Monthly Payment: $20.7584

End of Year	Balance Due	Interest	Mtge. Reduct.
1	834.169	83.2704	165.831
2	652.782	67.714	181.387
3	454.379	50.6986	198.403
4	237.366	32.0873	217.014
5	—0—	11.7299	237.366

Mortgage of $1000.00 for 5 Years at 9.50 Percent
Monthly Payment: $21.0018

End of Year	Balance Due	Interest	Mtge. Reduct.
1	835.958	87.9793	164.042
2	655.636	71.6985	180.323
3	457.417	53.802	198.219
4	239.525	34.1293	217.892
5	—0—	12.5041	239.525

Mortgage of $1000.00 for 5 Years at 10.00 Percent
Monthly Payment: $21.2469

End of Year	Balance Due	Interest	Mtge. Reduct.
1	837.734	92.6964	162.266
2	658.476	75.7052	179.257
3	460.448	56.9346	198.028
4	241.684	36.1985	218.764
5	—0—	13.2909	241.684

Mortgage of $1000.00 for 5 Years at 10.50 Percent
Monthly Payment: $21.4939

End of Year	Balance Due	Interest	Mtge. Reduct.
1	839.494	97.4213	160.506
2	661.299	79.7328	178.195
3	463.467	60.0953	197.832
4	243.834	38.2937	219.634
5	—0—	14.0893	243.834

Mortgage of $1000.00 for 5 Years at 11.00 Percent
Monthly Payment: $21.7424

End of Year	Balance Due	Interest	Mtge. Reduct.
1	841.245	102.154	158.755
2	664.12	83.7834	177.125
3	466.498	63.2867	197.622
4	246.007	40.418	220.491
5	—0—	14.9032	246.007

Mortgage of $1000.00 for 5 Years at 11.50 Percent
Monthly Payment: $21.9928

End of Year	Balance Due	Interest	Mtge. Reduct.
1	842.982	106.895	157.018
2	666.923	87.8547	176.058
3	469.516	66.5061	197.407
4	248.172	42.5688	221.344
5	—0—	15.7287	248.172

Mortgage of $1000.00 for 5 Years at 12.00 Percent
Monthly Payment: $22.2445

End of Year	Balance Due	Interest	Mtge. Reduct.
1	844.709	111.643	155.291
2	669.724	91.9482	174.986
3	472.545	69.7557	197.178
4	250.36	44.7487	222.185
5	—0—	16.57	250.36

Mortgage of $1000.00 for 5 Years at 12.50 Percent
Monthly Payment: $22.4979

End of Year	Balance Due	Interest	Mtge. Reduct.
1	846.425	116.399	153.575
2	672.513	96.0632	173.911
3	475.573	73.0344	196.94
4	252.555	46.9563	223.018
5	—0—	17.4252	252.555

Mortgage of $1000.00 for 5 Years at 13.00 Percent
Monthly Payment: $22.7532

End of Year	Balance Due	Interest	Mtge. Reduct.
1	848.123	121.162	151.877
2	675.282	100.198	172.841
3	478.584	76.3406	196.698
4	254.735	49.1897	223.849
5	—0—	18.2911	254.735

Mortgage of $1000.00 for 5 Years at 13.50 Percent
Monthly Payment: $23.0098

End of Year	Balance Due	Interest	Mtge. Reduct.
1	849.815	125.932	150.185
2	678.052	104.355	171.763
3	481.611	79.6767	196.441
4	256.947	51.4533	224.664
5	—0—	19.1747	256.947

Mortgage of $1000.00 for 5 Years at 14.00 Percent
Monthly Payment: $23.2681

End of Year	Balance Due	Interest	Mtge. Reduct.
1	851.493	130.71	148.507
2	680.807	108.532	170.686
3	484.631	83.0413	196.176
4	259.157	53.744	225.473
5	—0—	20.0712	259.157

Mortgage of $1000.00 for 5 Years at 14.50 Percent
Monthly Payment: $23.5284

End of Year	Balance Due	Interest	Mtge. Reduct.
1	853.154	135.495	146.846
2	683.542	112.728	169.612
3	487.634	86.4327	195.908
4	261.353	56.0598	226.281
5	—0—	20.9783	261.353

Mortgage of $1000.00 for 5 Years at 15.00 Percent
Monthly Payment: $23.7899

End of Year	Balance Due	Interest	Mtge. Reduct.
1	854.807	140.286	145.193
2	686.274	116.946	168.533
3	490.649	89.8538	195.625
4	263.576	58.4061	227.073
5	—0—	21.903	263.576

Mortgage of $1000.00 for 5 Years at 15.50 Percent
Monthly Payment: $24.0533

End of Year	Balance Due	Interest	Mtge. Reduct.
1	856.445	145.085	143.555
2	688.989	121.183	167.456
3	493.652	93.3022	195.338
4	265.79	60.7783	227.861
5	—0—	22.8395	265.79

Mortgage of $1000.00 for 5 Years at 16.00 Percent
Monthly Payment: $24.318

End of Year	Balance Due	Interest	Mtge. Reduct.
1	858.075	149.891	141.925
2	691.7	125.441	166.375
3	496.664	96.7796	195.036
4	268.029	63.1805	228.635
5	—0—	23.7935	268.029

Mortgage of $1000.00 for 10 Years at 8.00 Percent
Monthly Payment: $12.1328

End of Year	Balance Due	Interest	Mtge. Reduct.
1	931.947	77.5406	68.053
2	858.246	71.8923	73.7013
3	778.427	65.7751	79.8185
4	691.984	59.1502	86.4434
5	598.366	51.9758	93.6178
6	496.978	44.2052	101.388
7	387.174	35.79	109.804
8	268.257	26.6763	118.917
9	139.47	16.8063	128.787
10	—0—	6.11703	139.47

Mortgage of $1000.00 for 10 Years at 8.50 Percent
Monthly Payment: $12.3985

End of Year	Balance Due	Interest	Mtge. Reduct.
1	933.673	82.4553	66.3271
2	861.483	76.5928	72.1897
3	782.913	70.2119	78.5706
4	697.397	63.267	85.5155
5	604.323	55.7081	93.0743
6	503.022	47.4814	101.301
7	392.766	38.5272	110.255
8	272.765	28.7815	120.001
9	142.158	18.1747	130.608
10	–0–	6.6300	142.158

Mortgage of $1000.00 for 10 Years at 9.00 Percent
Monthly Payment: $12.6676

End of Year	Balance Due	Interest	Mtge. Reduct.
1	935.366	87.377	64.6344
2	864.668	81.314	70.6974
3	787.339	74.682	77.3293
4	702.755	67.4279	84.5835
5	610.238	59.4935	92.5178
6	509.041	50.8146	101.197
7	398.351	41.3217	110.69
8	277.278	30.9382	121.073
9	144.847	19.5807	132.431
10	–0–	7.15775	144.847

Mortgage of $1000.00 for 10 Years at 9.50 Percent
Monthly Payment: $12.9397

End of Year	Balance Due	Interest	Mtge. Reduct.
1	937.028	92.3049	62.9716
2	867.807	86.0552	69.2213
3	791.716	79.1852	76.0913
4	708.073	71.6333	83.6432
5	616.128	63.3322	91.9443
6	515.058	54.2065	101.07
7	403.958	44.1757	111.101
8	281.83	33.1492	122.127
9	147.582	21.0283	134.248
10	–0–	7.70453	147.582

Mortgage of $1000.00 for 10 Years at 10.00 Percent
Monthly Payment: $13.215

End of Year	Balance Due	Interest	Mtge. Reduct.
1	938.659	97.239	61.3411
2	870.895	90.8157	67.7643
3	796.035	83.7202	74.8599
4	713.336	75.8812	82.6989
5	621.977	67.2214	91.3586
6	521.052	57.6552	100.925
7	409.559	47.0869	111.493
8	286.392	35.4122	123.168
9	150.327	22.5149	136.065
10	—0—	8.26718	150.327

Mortgage of $1000.00 for 10 Years at 10.50 Percent
Monthly Payment: $13.4935

End of Year	Balance Due	Interest	Mtge. Reduct.
1	940.257	102.179	59.743
2	873.93	95.5953	66.3269
3	800.294	88.2858	73.6365
4	718.542	80.1708	81.7515
5	627.781	71.1616	90.7606
6	527.018	61.1592	100.763
7	415.151	50.0549	111.867
8	290.956	37.7268	124.195
9	153.074	24.0401	137.882
10	—0—	8.84494	153.074

Mortgage of $1000.00 for 10 Years at 11.00 Percent
Monthly Payment: $13.775

End of Year	Balance Due	Interest	Mtge. Reduct.
1	941.825	107.125	58.1748
2	876.918	100.393	64.9069
3	804.5	92.8819	72.418
4	723.702	84.5019	80.798
5	633.554	75.1519	90.1479
6	532.975	64.7206	100.579
7	420.757	53.0815	112.218
8	295.552	40.0956	125.204
9	155.86	25.6071	139.693
10	—0—	9.44205	155.86

Mortgage of $1000.00 for 10 Years at 11.50 Percent
Monthly Payment: $14.0596

End of Year	Balance Due	Interest	Mtge. Reduct.
1	943.361	112.076	56.639
2	879.854	105.208	63.5071
3	808.646	97.5074	71.208
4	728.803	88.8728	79.8425
5	639.279	79.1912	89.5242
6	538.899	68.3355	100.38
7	426.347	56.1634	112.552
8	300.147	42.5155	126.2
9	158.645	27.2127	141.503
10	—0—	10.0542	158.645

Mortgage of $1000.00 for 10 Years at 12.00 Percent
Monthly Payment: $14.3471

End of Year	Balance Due	Interest	Mtge. Reduct.
1	944.868	117.033	55.1323
2	882.743	110.041	62.1245
3	812.74	102.162	70.0032
4	733.859	93.2838	78.8815
5	644.973	83.2794	88.8859
6	544.814	72.0069	100.158
7	431.953	59.3042	112.861
8	304.778	44.9905	127.175
9	161.475	28.8616	143.304
10	—0—	10.6871	161.475

Mortgage of $1000.00 for 10 Years at 12.50 Percent
Monthly Payment: $14.6376

End of Year	Balance Due	Interest	Mtge. Reduct.
1	946.344	121.995	53.6562
2	885.583	114.89	60.7609
3	816.776	106.844	68.8066
4	738.859	97.7333	77.9177
5	650.623	87.4156	88.2354
6	550.704	75.7317	99.9193
7	437.554	62.5009	113.15
8	309.421	47.518	128.133
9	164.321	30.5512	145.1
10	—0—	11.3377	164.321

Mortgage of $1000.00 for 10 Years at 13.00 Percent
Monthly Payment: $14.9311

End of Year	Balance Due	Interest	Mtge. Reduct.
1	947.788	126.962	52.2119
2	888.369	119.755	59.4189
3	820.749	111.553	67.6206
4	743.794	102.219	76.9545
5	656.217	91.5967	87.577
6	556.552	79.5084	99.6653
7	443.129	65.7512	113.422
8	314.051	50.0953	129.078
9	167.156	32.2784	146.895
10	—0—	12.0021	167.156

Mortgage of $1000.00 for 10 Years at 13.50 Percent
Monthly Payment: $15.2274

End of Year	Balance Due	Interest	Mtge. Reduct.
1	949.204	131.933	50.7955
2	891.111	124.635	58.0936
3	824.67	116.288	66.4404
4	748.684	106.743	75.9861
5	661.781	95.8256	86.9032
6	562.392	83.3398	99.389
7	448.723	69.06	113.669
8	318.723	52.7288	130.000
9	170.046	34.0511	148.678
10	—0—	12.6899	170.046

Mortgage of $1000.00 for 10 Years at 14.00 Percent
Monthly Payment: $15.5266

End of Year	Balance Due	Interest	Mtge. Reduct.
1	950.59	136.909	49.4098
2	893.801	129.53	56.7892
3	828.531	121.049	65.2698
4	753.514	111.302	75.0172
5	667.293	100.098	86.2207
6	568.196	87.2221	99.0969
7	454.3	72.4227	113.896
8	323.394	55.4132	130.906
9	172.939	35.8635	150.456
10	—0—	13.3942	172.939

Mortgage of $1000.00 for 10 Years at 14.50 Percent
Monthly Payment: $15.8287

End of Year	Balance Due	Interest	Mtge. Reduct.
1	951.945	141.89	48.0552
2	896.439	134.439	55.5056
3	832.328	125.834	64.1108
4	758.278	115.894	74.0505
5	672.747	104.414	85.5308
6	573.956	91.1539	98.7908
7	459.849	75.8376	114.107
8	328.051	58.1469	131.798
9	175.82	37.7136	152.231
10	—0—	14.1125	175.82

Mortgage of $1000.00 for 10 Years at 15.00 Percent
Monthly Payment: $16.1335

End of Year	Balance Due	Interest	Mtge. Reduct.
1	953.272	146.874	46.7283
2	899.031	139.362	54.2402
3	836.072	130.643	62.9592
4	762.992	120.522	73.0802
5	678.164	108.774	84.8282
6	579.699	95.1372	98.4647
7	465.406	79.3088	114.293
8	332.739	60.9355	132.667
9	178.746	39.6089	153.993
10	—0—	14.8537	178.746

Mortgage of $1000.00 for 10 Years at 15.50 Percent
Monthly Payment: $16.4411

End of Year	Balance Due	Interest	Mtge. Reduct.
1	954.569	151.862	45.4309
2	901.574	144.298	52.9949
3	839.755	135.474	61.8188
4	767.644	125.182	72.1116
5	683.526	113.175	84.1182
6	585.402	99.1693	98.1239
7	470.94	82.8319	114.461
8	337.421	63.7741	133.519
9	181.671	41.5431	155.75
10	—0—	15.6108	181.671

Mortgage of $1000.00 for 10 Years at 16.00 Percent
Monthly Payment: $16.7513

End of Year	Balance Due	Interest	Mtge. Reduct.
1	955.839	156.854	44.161
2	904.07	149.247	51.7686
3	843.384	140.329	60.6868
4	772.242	129.874	71.1414
5	688.845	117.618	83.3968
6	591.082	103.252	97.7637
7	476.476	86.4099	114.605
8	342.128	66.6666	134.349
9	184.634	43.5222	157.493
10	−0−	16.3908	184.634

Mortgage of $1000.00 for 15 Years at 8.00 Percent
Monthly Payment: $9.55655

End of Year	Balance Due	Interest	Mtge. Reduct.
1	964.021	78.6995	35.979
2	925.056	75.7135	38.9651
3	882.857	72.4794	42.1991
4	837.155	68.977	45.7015
5	787.661	65.1838	49.4948
6	734.058	61.0756	53.6029
7	676.006	56.6267	58.0519
8	613.135	51.8083	62.8702
9	545.047	46.59	68.0885
10	471.307	40.939	73.7396

Mortgage of $1000.00 for 15 Years at 8.50 Percent
Monthly Payment: $9.84738

End of Year	Balance Due	Interest	Mtge. Reduct.
1	965.508	83.6769	34.4916
2	927.968	80.628	37.5405
3	887.109	77.31	40.8585
4	842.639	73.6983	44.4702
5	794.238	69.7675	48.401
6	741.559	65.4892	52.6793
7	684.223	60.8329	57.3356
8	621.82	55.765	62.4036
9	553.901	50.2493	67.9192
10	479.978	44.2457	73.9228

Mortgage of $1000.00 for 15 Years at 9.00 Percent
Monthly Payment: $10.1427

End of Year	Balance Due	Interest	Mtge. Reduct.
1	966.946	88.6586	33.0536
2	930.792	85.5582	36.1541
3	891.247	82.1664	39.5458
4	847.991	78.4567	43.2555
5	800.678	74.3992	47.313
6	748.927	69.9609	51.7513
7	692.321	65.106	56.6062
8	630.404	59.7961	61.9161
9	562.68	53.9879	67.7244
10	488.603	47.6349	74.0773

Mortgage of $1000.00 for 15 Years at 9.50 Percent
Monthly Payment: $10.4422

End of Year	Balance Due	Interest	Mtge. Reduct.
1	968.338	93.645	31.6616
2	933.534	90.5026	34.804
3	895.276	87.0483	38.2583
4	853.221	83.2513	42.0553
5	806.992	79.0775	46.2291
6	756.175	74.4894	50.8171
7	700.314	69.4459	55.8607
8	638.909	63.9017	61.4049
9	571.41	57.8078	67.4988
10	497.212	51.1085	74.1981

Mortgage of $1000.00 for 15 Years at 10.00 Percent
Monthly Payment: $10.746

End of Year	Balance Due	Interest	Mtge. Reduct.
1	969.683	98.6354	30.3167
2	936.192	95.461	33.4911
3	899.194	91.9539	36.9982
4	858.322	88.0799	40.8722
5	813.17	83.7999	45.1522
6	763.289	79.0717	49.8804
7	708.186	73.8487	55.1034
8	647.313	68.0788	60.8733
9	580.065	61.7044	67.2477
10	505.776	54.6627	74.2894

Mortgage of $1000.00 for 15 Years at 10.50 Percent
Monthly Payment: $11.054

End of Year	Balance Due	Interest	Mtge. Reduc
1	970.982	103.63	29.0182
2	938.766	100.432	32.2161
3	902.999	96.8815	35.7665
4	863.292	92.9404	39.7076
5	819.208	88.5641	44.0839
6	770.266	83.706	48.942
7	715.93	78.3123	54.3357
8	655.606	72.3242	60.3239
9	588.635	65.6763	66.9717
10	514.282	58.296	74.3521

Mortgage of $1000.00 for 15 Years at 11.00 Percent
Monthly Payment: $11.366

End of Year	Balance Due	Interest	Mtge. Reduct.
1	972.236	108.628	27.7638
2	941.26	105.415	30.9766
3	906.699	101.831	34.561
4	868.138	97.8313	38.5603
5	825.116	93.369	43.0226
6	777.115	88.3907	48.0009
7	723.559	82.836	53.5555
8	663.806	76.6383	59.7533
9	597.139	69.7241	66.6675
10	522.756	62.0094	74.3822

Mortgage of $1000.00 for 15 Years at 11.50 Percent
Monthly Payment: $11.6819

End of Year	Balance Due	Interest	Mtge. Reduct.
1	973.446	113.629	26.554
2	943.672	110.409	29.7738
3	910.288	106.799	33.3843
4	872.856	102.751	37.4323
5	830.884	98.2118	41.9714
6	783.824	93.1226	47.0607
7	731.056	87.4158	52.7675
8	671.89	81.0172	59.166
9	605.55	73.8429	66.3403
10	531.165	65.7985	74.3848

Mortgage of $1000.00 for 15 Years at 12.00 Percent
Monthly Payment: $12.0017

End of Year	Balance Due	Interest	Mtge. Reduct.
1	974.613	118.634	25.3866
2	946.007	115.414	28.6062
3	913.773	111.786	32.234
4	877.451	107.698	36.322
5	836.523	103.092	40.9286
6	790.403	97.9004	46.1199
7	738.434	92.0518	51.9685
8	679.875	85.4607	58.5596
9	613.888	78.0337	65.9866
10	539.533	69.6653	74.355

Mortgage of $1000.00 for 15 Years at 12.50 Percent
Monthly Payment: $12.3252

End of Year	Balance Due	Interest	Mtge. Reduct.
1	975.739	123.641	24.2611
2	948.265	120.429	27.4738
3	917.153	116.791	31.1117
4	881.922	112.671	35.2314
5	842.025	108.006	39.8967
6	796.846	102.723	45.1797
7	745.683	96.7401	51.1624
8	687.747	89.9658	57.9366
9	622.138	82.2939	65.6085
10	547.842	73.6063	74.2961

Mortgage of $1000.00 for 15 Years at 13.00 Percent
Monthly Payment: $12.6525

End of Year	Balance Due	Interest	Mtge. Reduct.
1	976.821	128.651	23.1786
2	950.444	125.452	26.3776
3	920.425	121.811	30.0187
4	886.263	117.667	34.1622
5	847.385	112.952	38.8777
6	803.141	107.585	44.244
7	752.79	101.478	50.3513
8	695.489	94.5281	57.3014
9	630.278	86.6187	65.2108
10	556.066	77.6176	74.2119

Mortgage of $1000.00 for 15 Years at 13.50 Percent
Monthly Payment: $12.9832

End of Year	Balance Due	Interest	Mtge. Reduct.
1	977.866	133.664	22.1344
2	952.551	130.484	25.3143
3	923.6	126.846	28.9515
4	890.489	122.687	33.1111
5	852.62	117.93	37.8684
6	809.311	112.489	43.3092
7	759.779	106.266	49.5316
8	703.131	99.1499	56.6481
9	638.344	91.011	64.787
10	564.249	81.703	74.095

Mortgage of $1000.00 for 15 Years at 14.00 Percent
Monthly Payment: $13.3174

End of Year	Balance Due	Interest	Mtge. Reduct.
1	978.87	138.678	21.1304
2	954.584	135.523	24.2858
3	926.671	131.896	27.913
4	894.589	127.727	32.0814
5	857.717	122.936	36.8727
6	815.338	117.429	42.3793
7	766.63	111.101	48.708
8	710.647	103.826	55.9824
9	646.304	95.4657	64.3429
10	572.352	85.8567	73.9519

Mortgage of $1000.00 for 15 Years at 14.50 Percent
Monthly Payment: $13.655

End of Year	Balance Due	Interest	Mtge. Reduct.
1	979.834	143.695	20.1656
2	956.542	140.568	23.292
3	929.639	136.957	26.9031
4	898.565	132.786	31.0741
5	862.674	127.969	35.8916
6	821.218	122.404	41.4561
7	773.334	115.977	47.8834
8	718.027	108.553	55.307
9	654.146	99.979	63.8813
10	580.36	90.075	73.7854

Mortgage of $1000.00 for 15 Years at 15.00 Percent
Monthly Payment: $13.9959

End of Year	Balance Due	Interest	Mtge. Reduct.
1	980.763	148.713	19.2371
2	958.433	145.62	22.33
3	932.513	142.031	25.9198
4	902.427	137.864	30.0863
5	867.504	133.028	34.9227
6	826.967	127.414	40.5367
7	779.914	120.897	47.0531
8	725.297	113.333	54.6171
9	661.9	104.553	63.3973
10	588.311	94.3617	73.5887

Mortgage of $1000.00 for 15 Years at 15.50 Percent
Monthly Payment: $14.3399

End of Year	Balance Due	Interest	Mtge. Reduct.
1	981.654	153.733	18.3463
2	960.253	150.678	21.4009
3	935.288	147.115	24.9644
4	906.168	142.958	29.1208
5	872.199	138.11	33.969
6	832.573	132.454	39.6251
7	786.351	125.856	46.2228
8	732.432	118.161	53.9186
9	669.536	109.183	62.8964
10	596.167	98.7106	73.3685

Mortgage of $1000.00 for 15 Years at 16.00 Percent
Monthly Payment: $14.687

End of Year	Balance Due	Interest	Mtge. Reduct.
1	982.51	158.754	17.4896
2	962.008	155.741	20.5026
3	937.973	152.209	24.0344
4	909.798	148.069	28.175
5	876.77	143.215	33.0287
6	838.051	137.525	38.7186
7	792.662	130.855	45.3888
8	739.454	123.036	53.2079
9	677.08	113.87	62.3741
10	603.961	103.124	73.1194

Mortgage of $1000.00 for 20 Years at 8.00 Percent
Monthly Payment: $8.36442

End of Year	Balance Due	Interest	Mtge. Reduct.
1	978.863	79.236	21.137
2	955.972	77.4818	22.8912
3	931.181	75.5819	24.7911
4	904.332	73.5242	26.8488
5	875.255	71.2957	29.0773
6	843.764	68.8823	31.4907
7	809.66	66.2686	34.1044
8	772.724	63.4379	36.9351
9	732.724	60.3726	40.0004
10	689.403	57.0523	43.3207

Mortgage of $1000.00 for 20 Years at 8.50 Percent
Monthly Payment: $8.67822

End of Year	Balance Due	Interest	Mtge. Reduct.
1	980.098	84.2365	19.9021
2	958.437	82.4776	21.661
3	934.861	80.5627	23.5759
4	909.201	78.4788	25.6598
5	881.273	76.2106	27.928
6	850.877	73.7421	30.3965
7	817.794	71.0555	33.0831
8	781.786	68.1312	36.0074
9	742.596	64.9483	39.1903
10	699.942	61.4845	42.6542

Mortgage of $1000.00 for 20 Years at 9.00 Percent
Monthly Payment: $8.99727

End of Year	Balance Due	Interest	Mtge. Reduct.
1	981.273	89.24	18.7273
2	960.789	87.4834	20.4839
3	938.383	85.5616	22.4056
4	913.876	83.4602	24.5071
5	887.07	81.1611	26.8062
6	857.749	78.6465	29.3208
7	825.678	75.8958	32.0714
8	790.598	72.8873	35.08
9	752.227	69.5966	38.3706
10	710.257	65.9972	41.9701

Mortgage of $1000.00 for 20 Years at 9.50 Percent
Monthly Payment: $9.32129

End of Year	Balance Due	Interest	Mtge. Reduct.
1	982.391	94.2464	17.6091
2	963.034	92.4984	19.3571
3	941.756	90.5775	21.278
4	918.366	88.4657	23.3898
5	892.655	86.1444	25.7111
6	864.392	83.5927	28.2628
7	833.324	80.7877	31.0677
8	799.173	77.7044	34.1511
9	761.633	74.315	37.5405
10	720.366	70.589	41.2665

Mortgage of $1000.00 for 20 Years at 10.00 Percent
Monthly Payment: $9.65018

End of Year	Balance Due	Interest	Mtge. Reduct.
1	983.453	99.2551	16.5471
2	965.173	97.5226	18.2797
3	944.979	95.6084	20.1938
4	922.671	93.4937	22.3085
5	898.026	91.1576	24.6447
6	870.801	88.5772	27.225
7	840.725	85.7264	30.0758
8	807.5	82.5771	33.2251
9	770.796	79.0979	36.7043
10	730.248	75.2545	40.5477

Mortgage of $1000.00 for 20 Years at 10.50 Percent
Monthly Payment: $9.9838

End of Year	Balance Due	Interest	Mtge. Reduct.
1	984.461	104.266	15.5394
2	967.209	102.554	17.2517
3	948.056	100.652	19.1532
4	926.792	98.5417	21.2639
5	903.185	96.1985	23.6072
6	876.976	93.5968	26.2089
7	847.879	90.7087	29.0969
8	815.575	87.502	32.3037
9	779.711	83.9419	35.8638
10	739.895	79.9897	39.8159

Mortgage of $1000.00 for 20 Years at 11.00 Percent
Monthly Payment: $10.3219

End of Year	Balance Due	Interest	Mtge. Reduct.
1	985.417	109.279	14.5833
2	969.146	107.592	16.2708
3	950.993	105.709	18.1533
4	930.738	103.608	20.2543
5	908.14	101.264	22.5984
6	882.927	98.6492	25.2134
7	854.796	95.7318	28.1307
8	823.41	92.4763	31.3862
9	788.392	88.8445	35.0181
10	749.321	84.7922	39.0703

Mortgage of $1000.00 for 20 Years at 11.50 Percent
Monthly Payment: $10.6643

End of Year	Balance Due	Interest	Mtge. Reduct.
1	986.322	114.294	13.6779
2	970.986	112.636	15.3363
3	953.79	110.776	17.196
4	934.508	108.69	19.2814
5	912.889	106.352	21.6194
6	888.648	103.731	24.2412
7	861.467	100.791	27.1804
8	830.991	97.4957	30.4762
9	796.819	93.8	34.1719
10	758.504	89.6567	38.3152

Mortgage of $1000.00 for 20 Years at 12.00 Percent
Monthly Payment: $11.0109

End of Year	Balance Due	Interest	Mtge. Reduct.
1	987.18	119.31	12.8201
2	972.734	117.684	14.446
3	956.455	115.852	16.2786
4	938.112	113.787	18.3429
5	917.443	111.461	20.6692
6	894.153	108.84	23.2905
7	867.908	105.886	26.2446
8	838.335	102.557	29.5729
9	805.012	98.8068	33.3236
10	767.462	94.5807	37.5497

Mortgage of $1000.00 for 20 Years at 12.50 Percent
Monthly Payment: $11.3614

End of Year	Balance Due	Interest	Mtge. Reduct.
1	987.991	124.327	12.0094
2	974.391	122.737	13.5996
3	958.991	120.936	15.4004
4	941.551	118.897	17.4397
5	921.802	116.588	19.7489
6	899.438	113.973	22.364
7	874.113	111.011	25.3253
8	845.434	107.658	28.6788
9	812.957	103.86	32.4764
10	776.18	99.5598	36.777

Mortgage of $1000.00 for 20 Years at 13.00 Percent
Monthly Payment: $11.7158

End of Year	Balance Due	Interest	Mtge. Reduct.
1	988.756	129.346	11.2435
2	975.961	127.794	12.7955
3	961.399	126.027	14.562
4	944.827	124.017	16.5719
5	925.968	121.73	18.8593
6	904.505	119.127	21.4625
7	880.08	116.164	24.4253
8	852.283	112.793	27.7966
9	820.65	108.956	31.6334
10	784.65	104.59	35.9998

Mortgage of $1000.00 for 20 Years at 13.50 Percent
Monthly Payment: $12.0737

End of Year	Balance Due	Interest	Mtge. Reduct.
1	989.48	134.365	10.5201
2	977.448	132.853	12.0314
3	963.689	131.125	13.7599
4	947.952	129.148	15.7369
5	929.954	126.887	17.998
6	909.37	124.301	20.5839
7	885.828	121.344	23.5413
8	858.905	117.961	26.9235
9	828.113	114.093	30.7917
10	792.898	109.669	35.2156

Mortgage of $1000.00 for 20 Years at 14.00 Percent
Monthly Payment: $12.4352

End of Year	Balance Due	Interest	Mtge. Reduct.
1	990.162	139.385	9.83765
2	978.855	137.915	11.3069
3	965.86	136.227	12.9955
4	950.924	134.286	14.9362
5	933.757	132.056	17.1666
6	914.027	129.492	19.7306
7	891.35	126.545	22.6769
8	865.286	123.159	26.0637
9	835.33	119.266	29.9562
10	800.9	114.793	34.4297

Mortgage of $1000.00 for 20 Years at 14.50 Percent
Monthly Payment: $12.8

End of Year	Balance Due	Interest	Mtge. Reduct.
1	990.805	144.405	9.19519
2	980.184	142.979	10.6207
3	967.917	141.333	12.2673
4	953.748	139.431	14.1692
5	937.382	137.234	16.366
6	918.479	134.697	18.9031
7	896.645	131.766	21.8336
8	871.426	128.381	25.2189
9	842.297	124.471	29.1285
10	808.653	119.955	33.6447

Mortgage of $1000.00 for 20 Years at 15.00 Percent
Monthly Payment: $13.1679

End of Year	Balance Due	Interest	Mtge. Reduct.
1	991.411	149.425	8.58936
2	981.44	148.044	9.97021
3	969.868	146.442	11.5728
4	956.434	144.581	13.4332
5	940.842	142.422	15.5928
6	922.742	139.915	18.0992
7	901.734	137.006	21.0089
8	877.347	133.629	24.3861
9	849.041	129.708	28.3063
10	816.185	125.158	32.8566

Mortgage of $1000.00 for 20 Years at 15.50 Percent
Monthly Payment: $13.5388

End of Year	Balance Due	Interest	Mtge. Reduct.
1	991.98	154.446	8.0199
2	982.625	153.111	9.35486
3	971.713	151.553	10.9125
4	958.983	149.736	12.7294
5	944.134	147.617	14.849
6	926.813	145.144	17.3213
7	906.608	142.26	20.2054
8	883.038	138.896	23.5696
9	855.544	134.972	27.4939
10	823.473	130.394	32.0717

Mortgage of $1000.00 for 20 Years at 16.00 Percent
Monthly Payment: $13.9125

End of Year	Balance Due	Interest	Mtge. Reduct.
1	992.516	159.467	7.48352
2	983.744	158.178	8.77283
3	973.459	156.666	10.2842
4	961.404	154.895	12.0558
5	947.271	152.818	14.1326
6	930.704	150.383	16.5671
7	911.283	147.529	19.4211
8	888.516	144.183	22.7672
9	861.826	140.261	26.6893
10	830.539	135.663	31.2871

Mortgage of $1000.00 for 25 Years at 8.00 Percent
Monthly Payment: $7.71817

End of Year	Balance Due	Interest	Mtge. Reduct.
1	986.909	79.527	13.0911
2	972.731	78.4404	14.1777
3	957.377	77.2637	15.3544
4	940.748	75.9893	16.6288
5	922.739	74.6092	18.0089
6	903.235	73.1144	19.5037
7	882.113	71.4957	21.1224
8	859.237	69.7422	22.8759
9	834.463	67.8437	24.7744
10	807.632	65.7875	26.8306

Mortgage of $1000.00 for 25 Years at 8.50 Percent
Monthly Payment: $8.05226

End of Year	Balance Due	Interest	Mtge. Reduct.
1	987.909	84.5362	12.0909
2	974.749	83.4673	13.1598
3	960.427	82.3044	14.3228
4	944.838	81.0384	15.5887
5	927.871	79.6605	16.9667
6	909.405	78.1607	18.4664
7	889.306	76.5284	20.0988
8	867.43	74.7516	21.8755
9	843.621	72.8182	23.809
10	817.708	70.7136	25.9136

Mortgage of $1000.00 for 25 Years at 9.00 Percent
Monthly Payment: $8.39197

End of Year	Balance Due	Interest	Mtge. Reduct.
1	988.844	89.5473	11.1564
2	976.641	88.5007	12.203
3	963.293	87.3562	13.3475
4	948.694	86.1042	14.5995
5	932.724	84.7343	15.9694
6	915.257	83.2363	17.4674
7	896.151	81.5977	19.106
8	875.252	79.8053	20.8984
9	852.394	77.845	22.8586
10	827.391	75.7008	25.0029

Mortgage of $1000.00 for 25 Years at 9.50 Percent
Monthly Payment: $8.73695

End of Year	Balance Due	Interest	Mtge. Reduct.
1	989.716	94.5598	10.2836
2	978.412	93.5391	11.3043
3	965.986	92.4173	12.4261
4	952.327	91.1841	13.6593
5	937.312	89.8284	15.015
6	920.806	88.338	16.5054
7	902.663	86.6997	18.1437
8	882.718	84.8993	19.9441
9	860.795	82.9198	21.9236
10	836.696	80.744	24.0994

Mortgage of $1000.00 for 25 Years at 10.00 Percent
Monthly Payment: $9.08699

End of Year	Balance Due	Interest	Mtge. Reduct.
1	990.53	99.5737	9.47009
2	980.068	98.5822	10.4617
3	968.511	97.4865	11.5574
4	955.743	96.2764	12.7675
5	941.639	94.9395	14.1044
6	926.058	93.4625	15.5813
7	908.845	91.8309	17.2129
8	889.83	90.0287	19.0151
9	868.823	88.0375	21.0063
10	845.617	85.8379	23.2059

Mortgage of $1000.00 for 25 Years at 10.50 Percent
Monthly Payment: $9.44182

End of Year	Balance Due	Interest	Mtge. Reduct.
1	991.287	104.589	8.71313
2	981.613	103.628	9.67371
3	970.874	102.562	10.7394
4	958.951	101.379	11.923
5	945.714	100.065	13.2371
6	931.018	98.6058	14.696
7	914.702	96.9864	16.3154
8	896.589	95.1884	18.1134
9	876.479	93.1924	20.1095
10	854.154	90.9762	22.3257

Mortgage of $1000.00 for 25 Years at 11.00 Percent
Monthly Payment: $9.80113

End of Year	Balance Due	Interest	Mtge. Reduct.
1	991.991	109.604	8.00928
2	983.055	108.677	8.93616
3	973.084	107.643	9.97034
4	961.96	106.489	11.1241
5	949.549	105.202	12.4111
6	935.701	103.766	13.8477
7	920.251	102.163	15.4501
8	903.013	100.376	17.2379
9	883.781	98.3809	19.2327
10	862.323	96.1556	21.4579

Mortgage of $1000.00 for 25 Years at 11.50 Percent
Monthly Payment: $10.1647

End of Year	Balance Due	Interest	Mtge. Reduct.
1	992.644	114.62	7.35596
2	984.396	113.728	8.24841
3	975.147	112.728	9.24817
4	964.778	111.607	10.3699
5	953.15	110.349	11.6274
6	940.113	108.939	13.0372
7	925.495	107.358	14.618
8	909.104	105.586	16.3906
9	890.726	103.598	18.3783
10	870.119	101.37	20.6064

Mortgage of $1000.00 for 25 Years at 12.00 Percent
Monthly Payment: $10.5322

End of Year	Balance Due	Interest	Mtge. Reduct.
1	993.25	119.637	6.75012
2	985.644	118.781	7.6062
3	977.073	117.816	8.57117
4	967.415	116.729	9.65796
5	956.531	115.504	10.8831
6	944.269	114.124	12.2628
7	930.45	112.568	13.8185
8	914.879	110.816	15.5708
9	897.334	108.841	17.5455
10	877.563	106.616	19.771

Mortgage of $1000.00 for 25 Years at 12.50 Percent
Monthly Payment: $10.9035

End of Year	Balance Due	Interest	Mtge. Reduct.
1	993.811	124.654	6.18884
2	986.802	123.834	7.00867
3	978.866	122.906	7.93677
4	969.878	121.855	8.98743
5	959.701	120.665	10.1777
6	948.175	119.317	11.5253
7	935.124	117.791	13.0514
8	920.344	116.062	14.7799
9	903.607	114.106	16.7367
10	884.654	111.889	18.9531

Mortgage of $1000.00 for 25 Years at 13.00 Percent
Monthly Payment: $11.2784

End of Year	Balance Due	Interest	Mtge. Reduct.
1	994.33	129.67	5.67017
2	987.877	128.887	6.453
3	980.533	127.996	7.34399
4	972.175	126.983	8.35754
5	962.664	125.829	9.51111
6	951.84	124.516	10.8241
7	939.522	123.022	12.3181
8	925.504	121.322	14.0183
9	909.55	119.387	15.9534
10	891.395	117.185	18.1553

Mortgage of $1000.00 for 25 Years at 13.50 Percent
Monthly Payment: $11.6564

End of Year	Balance Due	Interest	Mtge. Reduct.
1	994.809	134.686	5.1908
2	988.873	133.941	5.9364
3	982.083	133.088	6.78943
4	974.318	132.112	7.76489
5	965.438	130.997	8.88037
6	955.282	129.721	10.1564
7	943.666	128.262	11.6156
8	930.382	126.593	13.2843
9	915.189	124.684	15.193
10	897.813	122.501	17.3759

Mortgage of $1000.00 for 25 Years at 14.00 Percent
Monthly Payment: $12.0376

End of Year	Balance Due	Interest	Mtge. Reduct.
1	995.252	139.703	4.74817
2	989.795	138.994	5.45715
3	983.522	138.179	6.27234
4	976.313	137.242	7.20898
5	968.028	136.166	8.28552
6	958.505	134.928	9.52295
7	947.56	133.506	10.9452
8	934.98	131.871	12.5798
9	920.521	129.993	14.4585
10	903.904	127.833	16.6178

Mortgage of $1000.00 for 25 Years at 14.50 Percent
Monthly Payment: $12.4216

End of Year	Balance Due	Interest	Mtge. Reduct.
1	995.659	144.719	4.34058
2	990.646	144.046	5.01355
3	984.855	143.269	5.79077
4	978.166	142.371	6.68872
5	970.441	141.334	7.72559
6	961.518	140.136	8.92322
7	951.211	138.753	10.3068
8	939.306	137.155	11.9048
9	925.556	135.31	13.7501
10	909.674	133.178	15.882

Mortgage of $1000.00 for 25 Years at 15.00 Percent
Monthly Payment: $12.8083

End of Year	Balance Due	Interest	Mtge. Reduct.
1	996.035	149.735	3.96497
2	991.433	149.097	4.60229
3	986.091	148.358	5.34204
4	979.89	147.499	6.20081
5	972.692	146.502	7.19763
6	964.337	145.345	8.35486
7	954.639	144.002	9.698
8	943.382	142.443	11.257
9	930.316	140.633	13.0663
10	915.149	138.533	15.1667

Mortgage of $1000.00 for 25 Years at 15.50 Percent
Monthly Payment: $13.1975

End of Year	Balance Due	Interest	Mtge. Reduct.
1	996.381	154.75	3.61938
2	992.158	154.147	4.22217
3	987.233	153.444	4.92505
4	981.489	152.625	5.74487
5	974.787	151.668	6.70154
6	966.97	150.552	7.81714
7	957.851	149.25	9.11902
8	947.213	147.732	10.6373
9	934.805	145.961	12.4083
10	920.331	143.895	14.4742

Mortgage of $1000.00 for 25 Years at 16.00 Percent
Monthly Payment: $13.5889

End of Year	Balance Due	Interest	Mtge. Reduct.
1	996.698	159.765	3.30164
2	992.828	159.196	3.87061
3	988.291	158.529	4.53711
4	982.972	157.748	5.3186
5	976.737	156.832	6.23486
6	969.428	155.757	7.30933
7	960.859	154.498	8.5686
8	950.814	153.022	10.0448
9	939.04	151.292	11.7748
10	925.236	149.263	13.8035

Mortgage of $1000.00 for 30 Years at 8.00 Percent
Monthly Payment: $7.33766

End of Year	Balance Due	Interest	Mtge. Reduct.
1	991.646	79.6983	8.35352
2	982.599	79.0047	9.04712
3	972.801	78.2539	9.79797
4	962.19	77.4405	10.6113
5	950.698	76.5599	11.4919
6	938.252	75.6062	12.4457
7	924.774	74.573	13.4789
8	910.176	73.4545	14.5974
9	894.367	72.2429	15.809
10	877.246	70.9305	17.1213

Mortgage of $1000.00 for 30 Years at 8.50 Percent
Monthly Payment: $7.68913

End of Year	Balance Due	Interest	Mtge. Reduct.
1	992.44	84.71	7.55957
2	984.213	84.0419	8.22766
3	975.258	83.3146	8.95496
4	965.511	82.5232	9.74634
5	954.904	81.6616	10.6079
6	943.358	80.7239	11.5457
7	930.792	79.7034	12.5662
8	917.115	78.5928	13.6768
9	902.229	77.3839	14.8856
10	886.028	76.0677	16.2018

Mortgage of $1000.00 for 30 Years at 9.00 Percent
Monthly Payment: $8.04623

End of Year	Balance Due	Interest	Mtge. Reduct.
1	993.168	89.7229	6.83191
2	985.695	89.082	7.47278
3	977.521	88.381	8.17383
4	968.581	87.6141	8.94067
5	958.801	86.7754	9.77942
6	948.104	85.8579	10.6969
7	936.404	84.8544	11.7004
8	923.607	83.7573	12.7975
9	909.608	82.5565	13.9983
10	894.297	81.2435	15.3113

Mortgage of $1000.00 for 30 Years at 9.50 Percent
Monthly Payment: $8.40853

End of Year	Balance Due	Interest	Mtge. Reduct.
1	993.834	94.7362	6.16614
2	987.056	94.1241	6.77832
3	979.605	93.4514	7.45093
4	971.414	92.7119	8.19043
5	962.411	91.8991	9.0033
6	952.514	91.0056	9.89673
7	941.635	90.0233	10.879
8	929.676	88.9434	11.959
9	916.53	87.7566	13.1458
10	902.08	86.4519	14.4504

Mortgage of $1000.00 for 30 Years at 10.00 Percent
Monthly Payment: $8.7757

End of Year	Balance Due	Interest	Mtge. Reduct.
1	994.441	99.7498	5.55859
2	988.301	99.1678	6.14062
3	981.517	98.5247	6.78369
4	974.023	97.8143	7.49414
5	965.744	97.0297	8.27869
6	956.599	96.1628	9.14563
7	946.495	95.2049	10.1035
8	935.334	94.1471	11.1613
9	923.004	92.9784	12.33
10	909.383	91.6872	13.6212

Mortgage of $1000.00 for 30 Years at 10.50 Percent
Monthly Payment: $9.14739

End of Year	Balance Due	Interest	Mtge. Reduct.
1	994.995	104.764	5.005
2	989.438	104.212	5.55652
3	983.269	103.6	6.16919
4	976.42	102.92	6.849
5	968.816	102.165	7.60388
6	960.375	101.327	8.44165
7	951.003	100.397	9.37195
8	940.598	99.3637	10.405
9	929.047	98.2175	11.5513
10	916.222	96.9445	12.8242

Mortgage of $1000.00 for 30 Years at 11.00 Percent
Monthly Payment: $9.52323

End of Year	Balance Due	Interest	Mtge. Reduct
1	995.499	109.778	4.50122
2	990.477	109.257	5.02197
3	984.874	108.676	5.60303
4	978.622	108.027	6.25146
5	971.647	107.304	6.97522
6	963.865	106.497	7.7821
7	955.182	105.596	8.68262
8	945.495	104.591	9.68738
9	934.686	103.47	10.8086
10	922.627	102.219	12.0593

Mortgage of $1000.00 for 30 Years at 11.50 Percent
Monthly Payment: $9.90292

End of Year	Balance Due	Interest	Mtge. Reduct.
1	995.956	114.791	4.04395
2	991.422	114.301	4.53418
3	986.338	113.751	5.08423
4	980.637	113.135	5.70044
5	974.246	112.443	6.3916
6	967.079	111.668	7.16663
7	959.043	110.799	8.03589
8	950.033	109.825	9.01001
9	939.93	108.732	10.1027
10	928.603	107.507	11.3276

Mortgage of $1000.00 for 30 Years at 12.00 Percent
Monthly Payment: $10.2861

End of Year	Balance Due	Interest	Mtge. Reduct.
1	996.371	119.805	3.62878
2	992.282	119.344	4.08911
3	987.675	118.826	4.60754
4	982.482	118.241	5.19226
5	976.632	117.583	5.85059
6	970.039	116.841	6.59241
7	962.611	116.005	7.42847
8	954.24	115.063	8.37085
9	944.808	114.001	9.43213
10	934.179	112.805	10.6284

Mortgage of $1000.00 for 30 Years at 12.50 Percent
Monthly Payment: $10.6726

End of Year	Balance Due	Interest	Mtge. Reduct.
1	996.747	124.818	3.25293
2	993.063	124.387	3.68384
3	988.892	123.899	4.17163
4	984.168	123.347	4.72388
5	978.818	122.721	5.34949
6	972.76	122.013	6.05798
7	965.9	121.211	6.85999
8	958.132	120.303	7.76831
9	949.335	119.274	8.79712
10	939.373	118.109	9.96216

Mortgage of $1000.00 for 30 Years at 13.00 Percent
Monthly Payment: $11.062

End of Year	Balance Due	Interest	Mtge. Reduct.
1	997.086	129.83	2.91357
2	993.771	129.428	3.3158
3	989.997	128.971	3.77332
4	985.703	128.45	4.29431
5	980.816	127.857	4.88696
6	975.254	127.182	5.56189
7	968.925	126.415	6.32922
8	961.722	125.541	7.20288
9	953.525	124.547	8.1969
10	944.196	123.415	9.32886

Mortgage of $1000.00 for 30 Years at 13.50 Percent
Monthly Payment: $11.4541

End of Year	Balance Due	Interest	Mtge. Reduct.
1	997.393	134.843	2.60669
2	994.412	134.468	2.98132
3	991.002	134.04	3.40979
4	987.103	133.55	3.89954
5	982.643	132.99	4.45972
6	977.542	132.349	5.10046
7	971.709	131.616	5.8335
8	965.037	130.778	6.67151
9	957.408	129.819	7.62988
10	948.682	128.724	8.72583

Mortgage of $1000.00 for 30 Years at 14.00 Percent
Monthly Payment: $11.8487

End of Year	Balance Due	Interest	Mtge. Reduct.
1	997.67	139.854	2.33008
2	994.992	139.506	2.67834
3	991.913	139.106	3.07849
4	988.375	138.647	3.53784
5	984.309	138.118	4.06616
6	979.635	137.511	4.67383
7	974.264	136.813	5.37146
8	968.09	136.011	6.17395
9	960.994	135.089	7.09595
10	952.838	134.029	8.15564

Mortgage of $1000.00 for 30 Years at 14.50 Percent
Monthly Payment: $12.2456

End of Year	Balance Due	Interest	Mtge. Reduct.
1	997.918	144.865	2.08154
2	995.514	144.542	2.4043
3	992.737	144.17	2.77686
4	989.53	143.739	3.20764
5	985.825	143.242	3.70459
6	981.546	142.668	4.27917
7	976.604	142.004	4.94226
8	970.895	141.238	5.70898
9	964.301	140.353	6.59387
10	956.685	139.331	7.61609

Mortgage of $1000.00 for 30 Years at 15.00 Percent
Monthly Payment: $12.6444

End of Year	Balance Due	Interest	Mtge. Reduct.
1	998.142	149.876	1.85767
2	995.986	149.577	2.15613
3	993.484	149.231	2.50269
4	990.578	148.828	2.90527
5	987.206	148.361	3.37207
6	983.292	147.819	3.91394
7	978.749	147.19	4.54346
8	973.475	146.459	5.2738
9	967.354	145.612	6.12134
10	960.248	144.628	7.10547

Mortgage of $1000.00 for 30 Years at 15.50 Percent
Monthly Payment: $13.0452

End of Year	Balance Due	Interest	Mtge. Reduct.
1	998.343	154.886	1.65649
2	996.411	154.61	1.93213
3	994.157	154.288	2.25403
4	991.528	153.913	2.62952
5	988.461	153.475	3.06702
6	984.883	152.964	3.57776
7	980.71	152.369	4.17346
8	975.841	151.674	4.86841
9	970.162	150.863	5.67883
10	963.538	149.918	6.62427

Mortgage of $1000.00 for 30 Years at 16.00 Percent
Monthly Payment: $13.4476

End of Year	Balance Due	Interest	Mtge. Reduct.
1	998.524	159.895	1.47595
2	996.794	159.641	1.73022
3	994.765	159.342	2.02832
4	992.388	158.993	2.37781
5	989.6	158.584	2.78723
6	986.333	158.103	3.26746
7	982.502	157.54	3.83057
8	978.012	156.881	4.49011
9	972.749	156.107	5.26367
10	966.578	155.2	6.17041

TABLE 2   LOAN CONSTANTS Monthly payment necessary to amortize a $1,000 loan at various interest rates

Rate of Interest	*Years*						
	5	10	15	20	25	30	35
7½	20.04	11.88	9.28	8.06	7.39	7.00	6.75
7¾	20.16	12.01	9.42	8.21	7.56	7.17	6.93
7.8	20.19	12.03	9.45	8.25	7.59	7.20	6.96
8	20.28	12.14	9.56	8.37	7.72	7.34	7.11
8.4	20.47	12.35	9.79	8.62	7.99	7.62	7.40
8½	20.52	12.40	9.85	8.68	8.06	7.69	7.47
9	20.76	12.67	10.15	9.00	8.40	8.05	7.84
9½	21.01	12.94	10.45	9.33	8.74	8.41	8.22
10	21.25	13.22	10.75	9.66	9.09	8.78	8.60
10½	21.49	13.49	11.05	9.98	9.44	9.15	8.98
10¾	21.62	13.63	11.21	10.15	9.62	9.33	9.18
11	21.74	13.78	11.37	10.32	9.80	9.52	9.37
11¼	21.87	13.92	11.52	10.49	9.98	9.71	9.56
11½	21.99	14.06	11.68	10.66	10.16	9.90	9.76
11¾	22.12	14.20	11.84	10.84	10.35	10.09	9.96
12	22.25	14.35	12.00	11.01	10.53	10.29	10.16
12¼	22.37	14.49	12.16	11.19	10.72	10.48	10.35
12½	22.50	14.64	12.33	11.36	10.90	10.67	10.55
12¾	22.63	14.78	12.49	11.54	11.09	10.87	10.75
13	22.75	14.93	12.65	11.72	11.28	11.06	10.95
13¼	22.88	15.08	12.82	11.89	11.47	11.26	11.15
13½	23.01	15.23	12.98	12.07	11.66	11.45	11.35
13¾	23.14	15.38	13.15	12.25	11.85	11.65	11.55
14	23.27	15.53	13.32	12.44	12.04	11.85	11.76
14½	23.53	15.83	13.66	12.80	12.42	12.25	12.16
15	23.79	16.13	14.00	13.17	12.81	12.64	12.57

TABLE 3   CAPITAL APPRECIATION FACTORS

Appreciation of $1 at 5.00 Percent Compounded Annually

End of Year	Amount
1	1.05
2	1.1025
3	1.15762
4	1.21551
5	1.27628
6	1.3401
7	1.4071
8	1.47746
9	1.55133
10	1.62889

Appreciation of $1 at 7.50 Percent Compounded Annually

End of Year	Amount
1	1.075
2	1.15563
3	1.2423
4	1.33547
5	1.43563
6	1.5433
7	1.65905
8	1.78348
9	1.91724
10	2.06103

Appreciation of $1 at 10.00 Percent Compounded Annually

End of Year	Amount
1	1.1
2	1.21
3	1.331
4	1.4641
5	1.61051
6	1.77156
7	1.94872
8	2.14359
9	2.35795
10	2.59374

Appreciation of $1 at 12.50 Percent Compounded Annually

End of Year	Amount
1	1.125
2	1.26562
3	1.42383
4	1.60181
5	1.80203
6	2.02729
7	2.2807
8	2.56578
9	2.88651
10	3.24732

Appreciation of $1 at 15.00 Percent Compounded Annually

End of Year	Amount
1	1.15
2	1.3225
3	1.52088
4	1.74901
5	2.01136
6	2.31306
7	2.66002
8	3.05902
9	3.51788
10	4.04556

Appreciation of $1 at 17.50 Percent Compounded Annually

End of Year	Amount
1	1.175
2	1.38062
3	1.62223
4	1.90612
5	2.2397
6	2.63164
7	3.09218
8	3.63331
9	4.26914
10	5.01624

Appreciation of $1 at 20.00 Percent Compounded Annually

End of Year	Amount
1	1.2
2	1.44
3	1.728
4	2.0736
5	2.48832
6	2.98598
7	3.58318
8	4.29982
9	5.15978
10	6.19174

Note: It is recommended that you retype the forms as presented on standard 8½″ x 11″ paper. Then photocopy as many as you need to complete your investment analysis of properties in which you are interested.

In making an investment analysis notebook this way, please be aware that these forms are covered by the copyright of this book. While permission for the reader's personal use is granted, they are not released for commercial business use without further appropriate permission.

—D. M. Temple

PROPERTY ANALYSIS FACT SHEET

Date _____

Property address _____

Owner or contact _____ Phone _____

Description/use _____

_____

Investment features _____

_____

Location/neighborhood factors _____

_____

Physical condition overall _____ Age _____

Foundation/cellars _____

Heating system _____

Plumbing/water supply _____

Sewer/septic tank _____

Exterior paint _____

Interior paint/maintenance _____

Roof _____

Garaging/storage _____

Laundry _____

Furnishings/equipment _____

_____

Lot Lines/easements _____

Special title aspects _____

Need appraisal? _____ Need pest control report? _____

Special features (remodeling, rehabilitation, subdividing) _____

_____

Comments _____

_____

FINANCING

ASKING PRICE $\text{\textcircled{\$}}$_____

Data for Mortgage Loans

Source or Lender	Interest Rate	Term in Years	Monthly* Payment	Loan Fees or Points	Loan Amount
_____	_____	_____	_____	_____	$_____
_____	_____	_____	_____	_____	$_____
_____	_____	_____	_____	_____	$_____

TOTAL BORROWING $_____

Comments re prepayment penalty, etc._____

_____ CASH DOWN PAYMENT $_____

_____

*Monthly payment computation:

$$\$\underset{\text{Loan in \$1,000s}}{_____} \times \underset{\text{Factor}}{_____} = \$\underset{\text{Payment}}{_____}$$

Settlement Costs

	Expense	Capitalize	
Title Insurance	$_____	$_____	
Escrow Fees	$_____	$_____	
Legal Fees	$_____	$_____	
Appraisal/Inspection	$_____	$_____	
Prorations	$_____	$_____	
Mortgage Points/Loan Fees	$_____	$_____	
Miscellaneous	$_____	$_____	$_____
TOTAL COSTS	$_____	$_____	$_____

TOTAL CASH INVESTED $_____

Notes re damage/advance rent deposits_____

_____

OPERATING INCOME AND EXPENSES*

Annual Income

Rents $ _____

Services $ _____

Gross Annual Income $ _____

Less Vacancy At _____% $ _____

NET ANNUAL CASH INCOME $ _____

Annual Operating Expenses

Property Taxes $ _____

Insurance $ _____

Utilities $ _____

Gardening $ _____

Maintenance $ _____

Management $ _____

Miscellaneous $ _____

TOTAL CASH OPERATING EXPENSES $ _____

Annual Financing Expenses

Monthly Payment

First loan $ _____

Second loan $ _____

Third loan $ _____

Total $ _____ × 12

TOTAL MORTGAGE PAYMENTS $ _____

First Year Mortgage Interest Expense

Loan in $1,000's		Factor		Interest
_____	×	_____	=	$ _____
_____	×	_____	=	$ _____
_____	×	_____	=	$ _____

TOTAL ANNUAL INTEREST EXPENSE $ _____

*Assume purchase at beginning of the year; use annual figures.

VALUATION

Tax Assessments

	Assessed Value	Fair Market Value
Land	$_____	$_____
Structures/Improvements	$_____	$_____
Equipment/Personal Property	$_____	$_____
TOTALS	$_____	$_____

Construction Costs

Building Location or Type	Area	Current Cost per square foot	Current Construction Cost
_____	_____	× $_____	= $_____
_____	_____	× $_____	= $_____
_____	_____	× $_____	= $_____

TOTAL REPLACEMENT COST—BUILDINGS $_____

Less past depreciation at _____% per year for _____ years = $_____

DEPRECIATED COST OF BUILDINGS $_____

Add: Depreciated value of equipment $_____

Market value of land $_____

Value of landscaping $_____

TOTAL ADDITIONS $_____

TOTAL REPRODUCTION COST OF PROPERTY $_____

FUTURE DEPRECIATION COMPUTATION

Buildings

$_____ ÷ _____ = $_____

Amount to be depreciated   Years remaining   Straight Line Annual Charge

Method to be used: *Type*   *Factor*

(Circle one)   Straight Line   1.00

125% Declining Balance   1.25

Double-Declining Balance   2.00

$_____ × _____ = ANNUAL DEPRECIATION $_____

Annual Charge   Factor

Equipment

Value to be depreciated is $_____ over_____ years.

Method and computation of annual charge

_____ ANNUAL DEPRECIATION $_____

INDICATED ECONOMIC VALUE

A. *Cost Approach*

   TOTAL REPRODUCTION COST OF PROPERTY $_____

B. *Market Approach*

   $_____ ÷ $_____ = _____
     Asking Price   Gross Annual Income   Gross Rent Multiplier

   _____ × $_____ = MAXIMUM PRICE $_____
     Your Multiplier   Gross Annual Income

C. *Capitalization of Income*

   Net Annual Cash Income $_____

   Less Annual Cash Operating Expense $_____

   Net Cash Operating Income $_____

   $_____ ÷ _____ = MAXIMUM PRICE = $_____
     Net Cash Op. Inc.   Cap Rate

   $_____ ÷ $_____ × 100% = CAP RATE = _____ %
     Net Cash Op. Inc.   Asking Price

CASH FLOW FORECAST

Before-Tax Cash Flow

   Net Annual Cash Income $_____

   Less: Total Cash Operating Expenses $_____

       Total Mortgage Payments $_____

       Total Cash Expenditures $_____

       NET ANNUAL BEFORE-TAX CASH FLOW $_____

TAXABLE INCOME COMPUTATION
FIRST YEAR

Net Annual Cash Income $_____

Less: Total Cash Operating Expenses $_____

         Total Annual Interest Expense $_____

         Depreciation—Buildings $_____

              —Equipment $_____

         Total Deductible Expenses $_____

         TOTAL ANNUAL TAXABLE INCOME FIRST YEAR $_____

TAX LIABILITY OR TAX SHELTER BENEFIT

If the taxable income is positive, you will have a tax liability. ☐

If the taxable income is negative, you will have a tax shelter benefit. ☐

$_____ × _____ = $_____
   Taxable Income   Tax Rate

NET SPENDABLE

Net Annual Before-Tax Cash Flow $_____

Less: Tax Liability or add Tax Shelter Benefit $_____

         NET SPENDABLE FIRST YEAR $_____

REALIZATION ON SALE

Holding Period _____ Years. Estimated Annual Appreciation Rate _____%

Expected Selling Price: _____ × _____ = $⟨_____⟩
                         Appreciation Factor   Asking Price

Less: Sales Expense at _____% commission $_____

      Fix-up Expense $_____

      Prepayment Penalty $_____

      Total Expenses $_____

            GROSS CASH PROCEEDS $⟨_____⟩

Less: 1st loan $_____ × _____ = $_____
               Original Amount   Factor

      2nd loan $_____ × _____ = $_____
               Original Amount   Factor

      Total Amount paid off $_____

         NET CASH PROCEEDS FROM SALE $⟨_____⟩

Computation of Long-Term Taxable Gain

   Beginning Book Value: Original Cost $_____

                             Capitalized Costs $_____ $_____

   Less Accrued Depreciation—Buildings $_____

                             —Equipment $_____ $_____

            ENDING BOOK VALUE $⟨_____⟩

   Taxable Gain: Gross Cash Proceeds $_____

                  Less Ending Book Value $_____

            GAIN/LOSS ON SALE $⟨_____⟩

Income Tax Liability

Federal—

$_____ × _____ = FEDERAL TAX LIABILITY $_____
   Gain/Loss   Tax Rate

Tax Rate: Use full rate if short term; 40% of rate if long term.
           Gain/loss is long term if property has been held
           for more than one year.

State—

$_____ × _____ = STATE TAX LIABILITY $_____
   Gain/Loss   Tax Rate

                        TOTAL TAX LIABILITY $⟨_____⟩

TOTAL RETURN

Net Cash Proceeds from Sale $_____

Less: Total Cash Invested $_____

    Less Prorations $_____ $_____

    Tax Liability $_____

    Additional Investment While Owned $_____

    Total Recoveries $_____

        NET GAIN AFTER-TAX AND RETURN OF FUNDS INVESTED $_____

Add Annual Returns

$_____ × 90% = $_____ × _____ = $_____
Net Spendable   Years
First Year*   Held

      TOTAL AFTER-TAX GAIN FROM THIS INVESTMENT $_____

YIELDS

A. Annual After-Tax

                                  CASH ON CASH

$_____ ÷ $_____ × 100% =   RETURN (_____%)
Net Spendable   Total Cash
First Year*   Invested

B. Average Annual Total Return

$_____ ÷ _____ = AVERAGE ANNUAL RETURN ($_____)
Total After-Tax Gain   Years Held

                            AVERAGE ANNUAL

$_____ ÷ _____ × 100% = YIELD AFTER-TAX (_____%)
Average Annual Return   Total Cash
                        Invested

*If funds are borrowed, multiply by 90% to reflect reduction in mortgage interest as loan is paid down and income tax is increased as a result.

ANALYSIS SUMMARY

| Property Location | Asking Price | Cash Required | Indicated Economic Values | | | | Yields | |
			Cost	Market	Income	Net Spendable	Cash on Cash	Average Annual
	$	$	$	$	$	$	%	%

MONTHLY RECORD OF INCOME/EXPENSE

Location: _____ Year Ending _____

Income	Jan	Feb	Mar	Apr	May	June	July	Aug	Sep	Oct	Nov	Dec	Totals
Rents													
Deposits													
Total													
Expenses Property Taxes													
Utils.													
Insur.													
Maint.													
Mgmt.													
1st. Mtge. Pmt.													
2nd. Mtge. Pmt.													
Interest													
Total													
To Bank													
Beg. Bal													
End. Bal													

ANNUAL OPERATING STATEMENT

For Property at _____ For Year Ended _____

A. Cash Flow before Income Tax

Total Rental Income Received $ _____ _____

Other Income   _____ $ _____

Less: Property Taxes $ _____

Utilities   _____

Insurance   _____

Maintenance   _____

_____

_____

_____

Total Operating Expenses $ _____

Mortgage Payments—First   _____

—Second   _____

—Third   _____

Total Cash Outlay   _____ $ _____

Net Cash Income $ _____

B. Income Tax Computation

Total Income $ _____

Less: Total Operating Expenses $ _____

     Total Mortgage Int. Exp.   _____

     Depreciation—Building   _____

     —Equipment   _____

     Total Deductible Expense $ _____

Net Taxable Income $ _____

Income Tax Liability: $\dfrac{}{\text{Rate}} \times$ Net Tax. Inc. $ _____

(If net taxable inc. is negative, the tax liab. is your tax shelter benefit.)

C. Mortgage Reduction

Total of Mortgage Balances at Beginning of Year

Less Ending Balances, All Mortgages, End of Year

Total Mortgage Reduction $ _____

D. Reconciliation of Cash Gain

Net Cash Income $ _____

Less Inc. Tax Liab. or Plus Tax Shelter Benefit   _____

Total Spendable Cash after Income Tax $ _____

DEPRECIATION SCHEDULES

ENTER HERE THE FIGURES TO BE USED IN PREPARING INCOME TAX RETURNS

Building: Date Acquired _____ Total Purchase Price $_____

Rem. Useful Life _____ Costs Not Expensed $_____

Total $_____

Depreciation Method

_____ Less Land Value $_____

Basis For Dep'n $_____

End of Year	Beginning Bk. Val.	Depreciation	Ending Bk. Val.	Total Dep'n
19				
19				
19				
19				
19				
19				
19				
19				
19				
19				

Equipment: Description _____ Date Acquired _____

Cost $_____ Estimated Useful Life _____

Salvage $_____

Amount to Be Depreciated $_____ Method _____

End of Year	Beginning Bk. Val.	Depreciation	Ending Bk. Val.	Total Dep'n
19				
19				
19				
19				
19				
19				
19				

SUMMARY OF INVESTMENT RESULTS

Property at _____ Purchased on _____ for $ _____

Costs: Mortgage Points/Fees $ _____   Cash Down Payment $ _____

Title Ins./Escrow Fees   _____   Total Costs   _____

Other One-Time Fees   _____

Total Costs $ [   ]   Total Cash Invested $ [   ]

Year	Rental Income	Net Cash Income	Tax or Shelter Benefit	Total Cash Gain	% of Cash Invested	Cumul. Cash Recovery	Mort'ge. Redct'n.	Total Gain	% of Cash Invested	Addt'l. Capital Invested
19										
19										
19										
19										
19										
19										
19										
19										
19										
19										

NOTES: Enter data from the annual operating statement. Prepare a summary form for each separate property. This provides a year-by-year summary of investment returns and performance. The cumulative cash recovery column enables you to see when your total cash investment has been recovered.

Total gain includes the reduction in the mortgages. This will be realized only if the property is ultimately sold for at least its original cost plus resale expense. Gain on resale may be subject to income tax.

Do not include the prorations part of the closing costs when computing the amount of cash invested.

Index